# Getting a Grip

# Getting a Grip

On my game,
my body,
my mind...
myself

## MONICA SELES

JR
BOOKS

First published in Great Britain in 2009 by
JR Books, 10 Greenland Street, London NW1 0ND
www.jrbooks.com
Copyright © 2009 Monica Seles

A catalogue record for this book is available from the British Library.

ISBN 978-1-906779-43-6

1 3 5 7 9 10 8 6 4 2

Printed by MPG Books, Bodmin, Cornwall

*For those who aren't willing to settle for a life*

*less than they are capable of living.*

# Acknowledgments

Many, many thanks to John Steele and Dana Beck, for seeing this book through from an idea bouncing around in my head to the bound version; to Megan Newman, for her keen eye and endless enthusiasm; and to Miriam Rich and the rest of the crew at Avery—you are a team I am proud to be a part of.

To the great tennis fans who have stood by me through thick and thin and who never stopped cheering. Thank you for inspiring me to reach heights I never thought possible, both on and off the court.

And heartfelt gratitude to the women who have shared their own weight-loss stories with me. Your honesty and determination continue to motivate me every single day.

# Contents

# Introduction

Albert Einstein said that insanity is doing the same thing over and over again and expecting a different result. I wish I'd paid better attention to those words. When I was nineteen years old, my life was turned upside down and for the next ten years I was caught in the grip of that kind of madness. Bouncing back and forth between the two extremes of excess and deprivation, I was searching for the key to getting my old life back. But I was in a no-man's-land of severe imbalance, and by living in an all-or-nothing prison, I wasn't really living at all. The harder I tried to be the old me, the farther away from her I found myself. I searched for answers in the same places and I put myself through agonizing patterns of behavior in a futile attempt to reclaim who and what I once was. I knew I was a tennis player, I knew I used to dominate that sport, and I knew I used to be a happy person, but for ten years those identities eluded me.

Before my reality was ripped away in 1993, I'd been on top of the world, ranked number one in professional women's tennis. My whole life was in front of me. A dream future was mine for the taking. I was jet-setting around the world, signing autographs for fans, meeting fascinating people, eating in the best restaurants, staying in the swankiest hotels, and earning a phenomenal living by playing a game I loved with all of my heart. Life couldn't have been any better. And then in an instant it was all taken away. A deranged knife-wielding fan stabbed me in the back during a match and my life changed forever. Although the physical scars healed, the emotional damage cut much deeper and I was plunged into a fog of darkness and depression that I couldn't see my way out of. I retreated into my own head and numbed myself with self-sabotaging behavior. Food became my comfort and my poison. The rational side of my mind knew what I had to do to reclaim my life but the emotional side wouldn't allow it. I felt paralyzed. Taking any sort of positive action seemed like an impossible feat, so I remained stuck in the same place for a decade, spinning like a neurotic hamster on the wheel of quick fixes and extreme diets and devastated that I couldn't be the person I wanted to be. I plunged myself headfirst into Einstein's definition of insanity, and it took a long time to get back out.

During those years, January 1 was a magical date for me. A day that shone a little brighter than all the others. A fresh start. Another opportunity to get myself together, to be the person I wanted to be. To be better and happier. Every New Year's morning I'd wake up with a buzzing in my body and mind as I once again convinced myself that this time it would be different. This time it would be my year. This time I was going to turn my life around. This time I'd be the person I longed to be. What resolution did I make over and over again? To win another Grand Slam? To reclaim my position at the top of the tennis world? To work on my conditioning and strength? To get a mental edge on the game? No. My insanity was firmly entrenched in one goal: to be thin. I was 100 percent convinced that it was the key to solving all of my problems. If I could just be thin, then everything would be okay. It became an obsession. The first few days of every year were recorded in detail in my food journal:

*January 1, 1999*
*A Binding, Unbreakable, Must-Do Resolution: Lose Thirty Pounds.*
*This number is <u>NON-NEGOTIABLE</u>. So far, off to a good start:*
    *Ran on the treadmill at 7.0 mph pace for an hour and did three hundred*

*sit-ups before a two-hour hitting session. Ate one piece of wheat toast (dry) and water with lemon for breakfast.*

*One apple and one-half baked potato (dry) for lunch. Will have one piece of grilled chicken breast and small salad with no dressing for dinner. I will lose thirty pounds in six weeks.*

*I will do it.*

The first page of every journal from every year was almost identical. Blinded with the optimism that putting a new calendar on the wall brings, I was always on my best eating and exercising behavior for the first few days. But then something would happen to stress me out, and in the time it took to open a bag of potato chips, I was thrown right back into crazy thinking. It was the same every year: not one word of tournament goals, learning a new life skill, or trying to quiet my mind. Just get skinny. I know what you're thinking: *Weren't you an athlete? Weren't you working out every day? Didn't you have the best trainers and nutritionists?* Yes, on all counts. But I was still fat and I became an expert in hiding my body under layers of clothing. It's amazing how the benefits of a six-hour workout can be destroyed during a twenty-minute eating binge. And I became very good at lying to my nutritionists and coaches about my workouts and eating habits. I couldn't be left alone for a minute. I couldn't trust myself enough to be by myself. The pounds piled on until I'd gone up four sizes and forty pounds. The bigger I got, the smaller I felt as a person. But I didn't know how to stop the madness. I didn't know how to break out of the steel box I felt trapped in. I tried every diet, every workout regimen, and consulted every top fitness expert, but nothing changed and I was convinced I was destined to be an unhappy person in a body that didn't feel like my own.

Then something happened. I took a break from tennis and took a huge leap of faith. I got rid of all of the experts and advice givers, stopped counting calories, threw out my long-standing rigidly adhered to schedule, and began to spend time alone. I stopped looking for answers on the outside and started listening to the quiet voice inside of me. A fundamen-

tal shift in my mind was taking place, and suddenly I knew that the problem wasn't what I was eating, it was what was eating me. In the blur of the
nonstop tennis tour, I'd never had enough time or enough quiet to be
alone, to listen to myself. It was like getting to know someone I'd seen
around but never really let into my life. And, to my surprise, I liked her. I
began to take baby steps out of my comfort zone and started to do things
I never would have considered before. The more I lived little snippets of
real life, the more I wanted to keep doing it. As my days filled up with
quality, my stomach stopped feeling empty. Somewhere along the way my
body and my mind formed a truce. Once I stopped looking for the elusive
one-and-only answer to my problems, my life finally began to fall into
place.

I know what it feels like to be depressed and frustrated. I know what
it feels like to stay fully clothed on a hot day at the beach. I know what it
feels like to be miserable in your own skin. I know what it feels like to raid
the kitchen cupboards late at night and to wake up filled with angry regret
the next morning. I know what it feels like to think you just can't catch a
break, that an ominous cloud is following your every move. I know what
it feels like to want to give up. I have something to tell you: *It doesn't have
to be that way. You can change your life if you want to.*

This is the story of my road toward happiness. It has been a long, twist-
ing, exhilarating, and sometimes backtracking journey, but it's all been
worth it. I'm finally in the place I wanted to reach for all those years.

# – 1 –

# *Blasting Through the Comfort Zone*

For twenty-eight years, I was known as a tennis player. It had been a long time since I played a professional match, but the thought of giving up the security of that label had terrified me. *Tennis player*. A short, easy description that everyone is familiar with. It's who I was to the outside world and it's what I'd been calling myself for as long as I could remember. But it was time to move forward. I was ready to leave the past behind.

On February 14, 2008, I announced my official retirement from tennis. I'd been playing in exhibitions here and there, but I was tired of waking up every morning wondering if today was the day my foot was going to self-destruct again. When it felt good, I could play the way I had when I was at the top of my game, but when it felt bad, I couldn't walk on it. I spent years debating back and forth in my head whether I had it in me to make another run for the top. I didn't want to do it anymore. I was tired of the debate. I waited so long to make it official because I wanted to be absolutely sure it was the right decision. I wanted it to be on my timetable and I wanted to claim complete ownership over the choice to close that chapter of my life. All the what-ifs about whether I could regain my former glory and win another Grand Slam began to fade away. My life was filling up with things other than tennis; I was feeling more content than ever before and the fear had left me. It took a long time to get to this point, but I knew that I didn't need tennis to define who I was anymore.

At the time of the announcement, I didn't think twice about the date. It just happened to be when my agent, Tony Godsick, released the statement. But it's funny that on a day reserved for lovers, I declared my relationship with professional tennis to be over.

Somebody once told me that tennis is your husband, your boyfriend, your fiancé, and your best friend all rolled into one. It takes up every second of your time, every ounce of your energy, and every thought in your head. It had also been my adolescence, my education, my entry into adulthood, and my ticket to see the world. It had been my entire life and had tested me on every possible level. Somehow I'd come out the other side in one piece. Even better than one piece: I'd come out whole and healthy and strong. While staying out of the public eye, I'd been able to rebuild and fortify my core and I decided to put it to the ultimate test: ballroom dancing in front of millions of people. If I was going to test my newfound inner strength, what better way to do it than by risking total and complete public humiliation on reality television? *Dancing with the Stars* was my mom's favorite program, so when the opportunity arose to be on it, I gave it some serious thought. I had several strikes against me: two left feet, the inability to wear heels, stage fright, and absolutely zero dance experience. My mission to embrace my fears would be taken to a whole other level. My friends thought I was crazy when I decided to do it: "Monica, you know that you have to actually dance on that show, right?" they asked. "Are you sure you want to do it?" No, I wasn't completely sure, but what did I have to lose? I gave my new favorite answer to every opportunity that life threw my way: "Why not?"

I was paired with Jonathan Roberts, a show veteran who looked as dashing in person as he did when he partnered Marie Osmond, Heather Mills, and Rachel Hunter on television. One of the most patient people I've ever met, Jonathan wasn't fazed by my hips' complete inability to shake. Over and over he painstakingly went through the steps for our first two dances together, the fox-trot and the mambo. I had some prior work obligations, so we couldn't hunker down in the L.A.-based dance studios like the other contestants. Jonathan gamely met up with me all over the place: we practiced in any empty rooms we could find in Tokyo, Florida, and New York, eight hours a day for four weeks. With one week to go before the show, we headed to L.A., where the filming took place, for last-minute dance step cramming. My inner perfectionist kicked in when, with five days to go, I scheduled our dance sessions for seven in the morning.

"Seven?" Jonathan asked in disbelief. "I'm not even awake until nine."

"But I don't know the steps yet!" I was starting to panic. We'd just shared practice time with Christian de la Fuente and Cheryl Burke and they looked unbelievable gliding across the floor. I knew I was in trouble, and Jonathan—who had seen some of the other practices—wasn't pulling any punches. "Monica, I'm going to be honest. We've got an uphill battle." The whole *I'm doing the show for fun* mantra was being replaced with *I'm terrified of making a fool out of myself.*

"Okay, how about we compromise and make it eight o'clock?" he offered.

"All right, but not a minute after." I was having flashbacks to being thirteen years old and, having just moved to Florida from the former Yugoslavia, showing up at the Academy's courts at 6:40 a.m. for a 7:00 a.m. session. I was so used to the tiny windows of time that were given to me on the adult courts in my hometown of Novi Sad that I didn't want to waste a second. By the time a coach arrived, I'd already be warmed up and ready to launch straight into hitting. I'd mellowed a lot since then, but that Type A, gotta-get-it-right girl was still lurking inside me. We practiced our routines a hundred times and I videotaped Jonathan executing the more intricate footwork that I couldn't get down during our rehearsals. At night I'd go to my hotel room and watch the footage over and over again, pausing it to practice in front of the mirror. I was relieved that the first episode of the show would feature the guys. All I'd have to do is sit in the front row and smile. But I became even more panicked when I saw how good they looked. They looked like naturals. Even the guys who weren't as coordinated could pull off a decent performance by standing in one place while their professional pixie partners twirled and sashayed all around them.

The next day, as I was psyching myself up for my big dancing debut, I was in for another shock: the preparations were like a prom, a wedding, and a beauty pageant rolled into one. Spray tans, hair extensions, fake lashes, manicures, and endless layers of makeup. All in all, the process took six hours. Sitting in a chair for that long was tedious, but I did learn how to make the nose I inherited from my dad appear smaller. The tricks of shading can work wonders. When it was all over, I hardly recognized my lacquered-up new self and I was exhausted before I even set foot on the dance floor. My outfit was a long, frilly pink ensemble that looked like Cinderella swathed in cotton candy. My eight-year-old self would've died for that dress, but the thirty-four-year-old me had very different taste.

I looked around at my competition—Shannon Elizabeth (actress with never-ending legs), Marlee Matlin (actress with spunky spirit), Priscilla Presley (actress with confident grace), Marissa Jaret Winokur (Broadway star with energy to burn), and Kristi Yamaguchi (Olympic figure skater who looked like she was born to dance)—all decked out in sparkles, spangles, and heels. There was a hum of nervous energy in the air, and with a jolt I realized that I was out of my league. These women all had backgrounds in performing and playing to an audience, while I'd spent my career tuning the crowd out so I could focus on the ball. Without a doubt they'd know how to work the camera, and I didn't have the slightest idea where it was. *Was it too late to back out?*

"Ten minutes until curtain!" the stage manager yelled. Yep, it was way too late. We each took our place for the cast introduction and I was lined up at the top of the stage's stairs next to Jason Taylor, the stud NFL player who had performed beautifully the night before. I must have looked like I was about to face a firing squad because he took one look at me and said, "What have we gotten ourselves into?"

"I have no idea," I managed to squeak out.

"At least on the football field I know what I'm doing," he said as we began the dramatic descent toward the audience. I felt so much better knowing I wasn't the only one who was feeling way out of the comfort zone. If a tough football player was nervous, then my legs had every right to be shaking like a skittish colt's.

After the opening sequence, I went backstage to wait for my cue. Jonathan kept telling me to just have fun. He sounded like my dad before huge matches. There was no way I was going to have fun out there. I'd do it, but it wasn't going to be fun. I was too busy mentally replaying the sequence of steps in my head to remember something as silly as having a good time. Convinced I wouldn't hear the beat of the music, I told Jonathan to wink at me when it was my cue to start our dance. We took our places on the stage, and before I knew it, he was winking at me.

Showtime. He twirled me around the floor and I tried to keep up with his flawless fox-trot as best I could. My turns weren't as tight or controlled as they could have been, but I didn't miss a step and I didn't fall flat on my face—a success in my book. Unfortunately, not messing up wasn't a strong enough showing for the judges. I got the lowest score of the night and was told that I looked "uncomfortable" and "awkward" and that my "core wasn't strong enough." How ironic. After years of working to build up my inner core and working out with my trainer, Gyll, to strengthen my physical one, the biggest criticism was that my core wasn't up to par. Yikes. Thirty seconds of negative feedback wiped out the hesitant confidence I'd built up over the past several weeks of practice. Thirty seconds was all it took to shake me off kilter. After the show, all of the contestants moved through the press line, doing short interviews with the media outlets. To my total shock, halfway through the line, tears started flowing down my face. I finished the rest of the interviews as quickly as I could and rushed backstage to get myself together. The harder I tried not to cry, the more the tears kept coming. Jonathan immediately found me and told me there was no reason to be upset. I'd done everything I was supposed to: our goal had been to get all our steps into the routine, so who cared that we got the lowest score? Big deal. Easy for him to say. He hadn't been torn apart for being awkward, uncoordinated, and cursed with bad posture in front of millions of households in America. The thing was, I truly thought I'd done well. If I had thought I'd performed horribly, then I would have been fine with the criticism. But my definition of "well" and the judges' definition of it were not even close. I had never danced before, so my frame of reference was quite different. I was going to have to accept it. I went to my hotel that night upset and rattled. I took a look at my puffy eyes in the mirror and went into reality check mode.

*Why are you being so hard on yourself? This is a dance show. It's supposed to be fun. So what if you got a little criticism? Nobody's perfect. Shake it off and do better the next time. Your core, the inner one, the one that's the most important, is strong. It's going to take more than some dance judges to throw you off balance. Just get right back out there and try again.* I turned on the video camera and watched Jonathan perform our moves from the mambo, our next dance. I had a few days to get it together and come back with a vengeance. I showed up at our rehearsal in the morning bright-eyed and on a mission. But I was momentarily thrown off course by the Hungarian bakery downstairs from the studio. The aroma of fresh baked goodies wafted through the air and tempted me like crazy. It appealed to all of my childhood cravings. After some especially disheartening practices the previous week, I had slipped into an old bad habit and indulged in some key sugary purchases. They hadn't done me any good. *No, not this time,* I told myself as I walked right past the open door. *Pastries will not make me a better dancer.*

I mamboed myself to the point of exhaustion for the next three days and, taking the advice of the costume designer, decided to make my appearance a little more *va-va-voom*. My dress for the second dance was a gold-spangled number that barely covered my rear. I'd seen how hot Shannon Elizabeth's outfit had been and I knew I had to sex it up a little more, but there was only so much *va-va-voom* I felt comfortable with. The designer and I compromised on the hem length and I loved the finished product. I showed up for the second show ready to shake my stuff. Jonathan gave me one piece of advice: Smile.

"No matter what you do, just smile. If you miss a step, trip over your own feet, mess up a spin, just smile. If you smile enough nobody will ever know."

"Okay, got it: Smile," I repeated back to him.

"And especially on the split. Look right into the camera and smile as if your life depended on it," he added.

The music started, Jonathan winked at me, and we were off. I channeled my inner vixen and strutted all over the dance floor with as much conviction as my heels would allow. I smiled until my face hurt, and when it came time for the split, I searched for the camera. Damn. There were six of them. Which one was I supposed to grin seductively into? I took a wild guess and did my best. I finished the number without any of my bracelets flying off and hitting Jonathan in the face—again, a success in my book, but I knew it was unlikely to impress the judges. I was right. I got the lowest score again and I knew I was destined to be booted off first. Luckily for me, Penn Jillette was kicked off at the same time, so I didn't have to brave the rejection solo. Misery loves company. And I was pretty miserable for the first few days. People recognized me all over the place—at the grocery store, the gas station, the airport—and they were incredibly kind to me. The only thing I'd wanted to do was stay on the show for at least a week, and I was mortified that I hadn't been able to do it. But nobody seemed to remember just how dismal my performance was. They told me how great I looked and how gutsy I'd been to try something new. I was disappointed in my performance and crushed that it had been in front of millions of people, but those lovely dance-show-watching strangers were right—I had been brave to give it a go and my legs had looked pretty good in that gold dress.

If I'd done the same thing five years earlier, I wouldn't have come back for the second dance. I would have returned home to Florida, cried, eaten, cried some more, eaten even more, and hidden from everyone for weeks. I would have carried the sting of those comments around with me like a scarlet letter. I would have avoided social situations and spoken to few of my friends. The humiliation would have been too much. But I was a different person now, and it took only a few days of moping around before I realized that I was fine. I'd faced my greatest fear, performed despite a case of nerves that was worse than any I'd had before my Grand Slam finals, subjected myself to the judgment of total strangers, and taken criticism without falling apart in front of millions of people. In the end, it wasn't nearly as bad as I'd feared it would be. If you don't take risks in life, you won't get anything out of it. If my core could take that and still be in one piece, there wasn't anything I couldn't take on.

# − 2 −

# *Girls Don't Play Tennis*

Most professional athletes can remember the exact moment they were introduced to the sport that would be their destiny. For me, that day started with the smell of salt water tickling my nose. As we did every summer, my family was spending our vacation by the Adriatic Sea, and in the mornings a breeze would blow through the bedroom window and gently wake me up. Hanging at the beach for a precious two weeks a year was practically mandatory for European families, and we were no exception. Every August, we'd pack up the car and head to the coast. Two weeks of sun, sand, and surf. It was heaven. The summer I remember the best from those lazy seaside days was when I was five years old. I was a little pipsqueak of a girl who never stopped moving. Buzz, buzz, buzzing around all day long. It used to drive my family crazy. One morning I got up, threw on my swimsuit, quickly ate breakfast at my mother's insistence, and was dashing out the door as fast as my legs could carry me. As always, I'd planned on spending the day on the beach building intricate sand castles with moats to protect the princesses I imagined resided inside and the handful of crabs I recruited to act as their guards. But something grabbed my attention before I could make a run for the beach. It was my dad packing up a bag with cool-looking toys.

"Where are you going?" I asked.

"To play tennis," my brother, Zoltan, answered. He had a bag too.

"Can I come?" I'd already forgotten about the castles waiting to be built outside. All I heard was the word "play" and I didn't want to be left out of any fun.

"Of course you can come," my dad said, smiling. "Go put on your shoes and we'll meet you outside." I tore into my bedroom frantically searching for my sneakers. My mom found them for me and helped tie the laces nice and tight.

"Have fun," she told me, kissing my forehead and whisking me out the door, happy to have a little peace and quiet for herself. It didn't happen often. My mother, Ester, worked long hours in an accounting firm and whipped up three homemade meals a day for our family, and those two weeks were the only time she had to relax. As a five-year-old, I didn't understand what it meant to need a vacation, but I'm sure my mom did. I ran outside and caught up to my brother and dad. We walked down three different streets until we got to the local court. Jumping around like my shoes were on fire, I couldn't wait to get started. Started at what, I had no idea, but I knew something fun was about to happen. My dad and Zoltan unsheathed their rackets and started hitting a ball back and forth. It seemed to go on forever. I was getting bored sitting there; I had thought this was going to be a lot more fun. When my brother put down his racket to get a drink of water, I took advantage of my chance. I ran over, picked it up, and started imitating what I'd seen him do.

"Good, Monica!" my dad called to me from the other side of the net. He hit a ball my way. I'd like to say that I fired a two-handed crosscourt backhand from the baseline. I'd like to say that in that split second a star was born. But I can't. I missed the first ball. And the second, and the third. Zoltan, showing an amount of restraint and patience that is unusual in thirteen-year-old brothers, let me go on like that, swinging his racket wildly as I ran back and forth across the court not making contact with anything. But my dad noticed something right away. The racket was nearly as big as I was but I was handling it as though it weighed nothing. My swing wasn't sending any balls over the net, but the form wasn't half bad. We played all afternoon, Zoltan and I taking turns with the racket, and I never got tired. Some sports prodigies are born with superb hand-eye coordination, abnormally flexible shoulder joints, or extremely efficient red blood cells. Me? I just had freakishly strong wrists. Years later, my dad would insist it was because, as a toddler, I walked around our apartment carrying his four-kilogram dumbbells everywhere I went. I don't remember for sure, so I'll have to take his word for it. The three of us spent the rest of our vacation at the tennis court together.

When we got home from the Adriatic, I begged my dad to keep playing tennis with me. While Zoltan was an active player in European junior tournaments, my dad had only hit around a couple of times in his life. He played more during that vacation than he ever had before. But he had a hard time saying no to me, so he figured out a way to make it happen. Our hometown of Novi Sad—a medium-size city nestled on the banks of the river Danube—had only four courts, and kids weren't allowed on them until they were twelve years old. The tennis club had an elitist attitude that could have rivaled Wimbledon's Centre Court. There was a mandatory dress code of all white, and it was difficult to secure a court time, nearly impossible to find the financial means to pay for it. It was a far cry from the everyman sport of soccer, the most popular sport in my country, where all you needed was a ball, a patch of grass, and the will to run.

"No problem," my dad told me after the club would not let a five-year-old play on its courts. He took a ball of string down to the parking lot in front of our apartment building, cut a long piece off, and tied the ends to cars placed about ten feet apart. Voilà! We had our own private, free, always available court where dress whites were optional. I devoted every afternoon to playing in that parking lot. After a month my dad saw I was serious about it—and that Zoltan's patience with loaning out his rackets was growing thin—so one weekend he got in the car and drove seven hours until he crossed the Italian border, where the closest equipment store with child-size rackets could be found. He'd done the exact same thing for Zoltan seven years earlier, so he knew the drill. He picked out the best one he could find, had it wrapped up, jumped in the car, and drove straight back home the same day. I was thrilled with my new racket and carried it with me everywhere. My dad and I continued to play every single evening, staying outside until my mom called us in for dinner. Even then we'd stay outside a little longer until she'd call us a second time. Then we knew she was serious. We didn't dare test her a third. Over dinner Zoltan would tell us about his upcoming tournaments and I'd hang on his every word. I loved tennis with every bit of my heart.

Until winter rolled around. I decided I'd had enough tennis and what I was really meant to do was ice-skate. I retired from my illustrious parking-lot career and asked my parents to sign me up for ice-skating lessons. You'd think my dad might have been a little annoyed, after jumping across country borders to support my tennis obsession, but he was just as happy to take me to the rink at five in the morning as he'd been to drive to Italy. He didn't care what I did, as long as I was doing something that made me happy. Ice-skating was great, until I fell on my butt the first time. Waking up before sunrise in an attempt to beat the hockey players to the rink (I had to claim my little area of ice before their pucks went flying all over the place) got really old, really fast. And falling on my bony backside was not easy. Ice hurts. A lot. I was spending more time skidding on the ground than standing upright, and I had the bruises to prove it. The dresses in ice-skating were gorgeous—that had been my original motivation in deciding to be a skater—but they just weren't worth those kinds of sacrifices. After two weeks I hung up my skates, and by the summer I'd come out of retirement and started playing tennis again.

Every morning was the same. My mom left early for work but she always made time to get our breakfast ready. I'd eat it in front of the television while watching my beloved *Tom and Jerry* cartoons, then hurry down several flights of stairs in our apartment building with my racket in hand. I'd practice hitting against the brick wall of our building over and over again. Ice, rain, snow, wind—no matter what the weather was like, I was out there. I owe an enormous debt of gratitude to the people who lived on the first floor. Never once in all my years of using that wall as a hitting partner did they ever complain. They were either extremely kind or extremely hard of hearing. Either way, I owe them a huge thank-you. Every now and then my dad would lean out over our balcony railing with a cup of coffee in one hand and a newspaper in the other. A political cartoonist, he had to be up to date on everything going on in the world and was rarely seen without his nose in a book or an international paper of some kind. If he leaned over just so he could catch a glimpse of my scrawny arms swinging my racket over and over. Both hands on my backhand, both hands on my forehand. When I first started going to tournaments, coaches pulled my dad aside.

"Karolj, you aren't going to let her keep playing like that, are you?" they'd ask.

"Yes. Why not?" my dad answered.

"Because it isn't right. It isn't how she is supposed to play tennis. She will never be a great player with both hands on the racket." The list of reasons for me not to play with two hands could go on and on. Less mobility, less time to get in position, less reach. Nobody did it. My dad usually interrupted before they got too carried away.

"That is how she picked up the racket. That is what feels natural for her. So for Monica, that is the way she is supposed to play." He'd then thank them for the advice with a warm handshake and quietly walk away. One of the best things about having my artist/tennis-novice dad as my coach was that he didn't know what I was supposed to do. He approached the world of tennis with a completely fresh mind. Open to anything that might work, he didn't let how things used to be done color the way things might possibly be done. To him, hitting a forehand with two hands was just as good as hitting it with one. The fact that nobody else was doing it didn't mean anything. It just meant we had to make it up as we went along. So we did.

The number one rule was easy: Have fun. If I wasn't having a good time on the court, then there was no point in being there. If I was going to sulk or be stubborn or mad, I was wasting my time. Just put the racket down and go home. But my dad made our practices so much fun, I never once stormed off the court in a huff. I was still a kid, so if it had been boring or too difficult, I would have walked away without a second thought. When you're young, the choice is so easy. If it's fun, do it; if it's not, don't. Wouldn't it be great if life could always be that simple? Going to Hawaii and drinking Mai Tais on the beach? Fun. Do it. Cleaning the house and paying bills? Not fun. Skip it.

My dad took his cartooning skills to our makeshift tennis court. Knowing that I couldn't get going in the morning without my usual dose of *Tom and Jerry*, he drew the brown mouse's face on every ball. He then told me that I was Tom and my job was to go after Jerry with all of my ferocious predatory might. That's how he taught me to hit the ball on the rise. Thanks to his university background in biomechanics, he figured out that hitting the ball as it was rising up would translate into more power when it rebounded off my strings than it would if I waited for it to come to me. Cutting down the reaction time of your opponent—this was an extremely aggressive approach that few players were using. I had no idea that I was learning an entirely new way to hit the ball. I just thought I had a mouse to catch, and I went after that furry little guy with everything I had. When I wasn't pretending I was a cat, I was aiming to take out my dolls on the other side of the court. My dad would collect a bunch from my room, carry them with him to the parking lot—not caring in the slightest who saw him loaded down with baby dolls and teddy bears—and set them all up just inside our makeshift baseline. I'd take my position on the other side of the court and, one by one, take them down. I was a one-girl firing squad. If I hit them all, I got a new stuffed animal. Nothing like bribery to get a kid to work hard! (I have to admit that there were more than a few times when I missed the mark completely. I'd get the new toy anyway.) It worked: by the time I was eight, I was the number one junior player in

Yugoslavia. I was beating girls twice my size but I still didn't know how to keep score. I just hit away until I heard applause, then I'd look at my dad to make sure I'd won. It took me a long time to get the whole scoring thing down.

When I began winning matches all over Europe, our local courts finally gave in and let me play during off-peak hours. I also got my first dose of media attention and a peek into being a celebrity. One time I was shopping at the market with my mom when I heard someone gasp.

"Is she that tennis player? Look at her! She's so skinny! Look at those little stick legs!" My ears started burning and my cheeks prickled with fire. These days I'd love to hear people going on and on about my lithe frame, but back then it was horrifying. I couldn't believe they were talking about me. And apparently they thought they were in an invisible, soundproof bubble, because they were standing only a few feet away from me but were going on and on about how my parents should start giving me food. My mom quickly ushered me out of the store and then let me eat spoonfuls of Nutella when we got home. Ah, Nutella. Just talking about my dear childhood friend brings back the sweetest memories. I put it on everything: fruit, toast, pastries—anything that could be covered in that brown goo, I tried it. But the best way was straight up, right out of the jar.

With my tenth birthday, the intensity of the media attention cranked up. One morning I woke up to see a picture of me on the cover of a national newspaper with the headline "Sportswoman of the Year" hovering above my smiling face like a crown of hype. Can you imagine? Sports-*woman*? At ten years old? I wasn't even wearing a training bra yet. I was painfully shy and didn't want any attention drawn to me; this was not going to help matters. There was a big presentation downtown with a lot of important-looking people in business suits. I felt tiny and lost and very aware that I looked out of place. The next week there was a ceremony at my school honoring the achievement. I'd tried very hard to keep my tennis life and school life separate, but this blew my cover. When I felt people's eyes on me, I became very self-conscious. Why on earth I picked tennis—the most solo sport around—I still don't know. You can't be much more in the spotlight than serving match point at Wimbledon. People might be watching you. But back then I wasn't thinking about any of that. When I first started playing, I thought it would just be my dad, Zoltan, and me playing together forever. I never thought about further down the road. I had no idea what life had in store for me.

# — 3 —

# The Land of Plenty

*Welcome to the Happiest Place on Earth!*

It was the first thing I saw when we pulled into Disney World. I was convinced I was dreaming, and I had to pinch myself on the leg a few times when I got my first glimpse of Mickey Mouse's headquarters. I was nine years old and I'd qualified for the Sport Goofy Tournament in Orlando. Life didn't get much better than that.

I loved the United States before I'd ever set foot in it. I'd heard about Disney World—a place with rides, candy, and cartoon characters walking around like real people—but I didn't think I'd ever be able to see it. If you had told me that the streets were paved with gold and the trees were made of chocolate, I'd have believed you. It was a far-off magical land, and when I went to bed at night I'd think about it, trying to picture myself there, celebrating my match victories with Goofy and Donald. As soon as we found out I had made the tournament, I got on the phone, made my family's airline and hotel reservations, and counted down the minutes until our departure.

The first shock was how warm it was when we got off the plane. It was the dead of winter in Yugoslavia, but people in Florida were walking around in tank tops and shorts. It took a while for my nine-year-old mind to process that this place had existed the entire time I'd been alive. These people had been walking around in tank tops and shorts in the winter *all this time* and I was just finding out about it now? How could I have not known? How could it have taken me nine whole years to get here?

My family stayed in a hotel while I stayed in a dorm with all the other kids. It was a mini United Nations at a bunk-bed slumber party. Exchanging country pins, hometown chocolates (I was an expert at that), and little stuffed animals, our multiethnic enclave was a live incarnation of the "It's a Small World" ride. As only preteen girls can do, I became best friends with Angelica by the end of our first day there. She was from Mexico and became my official partner in adventure. The day before our match against each other, we ran all over the park and rode ride after ride—for free! The tournament gave us all-access passes, one of the best perks tennis ever gave me. Fun friends, amusement parks, good matches—I thought tennis was the greatest thing in the world. It was a dream come true.

That year I placed in the top sixteen and the next year I made the jump to twelve-and-under singles champion. I also got to umpire a fourteen-and-under match starring an up-and-comer named Michael Chang. Five years later he would go on to win the French Open. There is some serious talent at those junior tournaments. My trophy was in the shape of Mickey Mouse and I got a huge Mickey Mouse stuffed animal that I toted on the plane back to Novi Sad. Proudly displayed in my room when we got home, they were the only sign of sports in an otherwise pink and frilly bedroom with Barbies and teddy bears spilling out of every corner. (I'd won an awful lot of those firing-squad games, and I had the loot to prove it.)

When I qualified for the Orange Bowl, the most prestigious world junior championship, I felt like a veteran waiting to be reunited with all of my old buddies. The top junior players around the world get to know one another quickly when they are thrown together at these tournaments. Without the pressure of money on the line, kids make tons of friends and keep in contact with each other via postcards until the next tournament. Junior tennis spurred a whole international pen-pal system and I couldn't wait to go to Miami for a couple weeks of sunshine, giggling with friends, and chocolate exchanges. I had no idea that my life was about to change dramatically.

I glided through my matches, and right after I accepted the trophy for winning the twelve-and-under championship, my dad was approached by Tony Cacic, a fellow Yugoslavian. He said that a famous coach wanted to meet me. My dad was hesitant at first, since dozens of agents and coaches had approached him since I was eight years old, but Tony assured him this was the real deal. His daughter, Sandra, was my age and played at this coach's academy. "Okay," my dad said as he took my hand. "Let's meet him." We were led over to an incredibly fit middle-aged man sporting wraparound sunglasses and the darkest tan I'd ever seen. He was charming and funny and had more energy than all of us combined. He was Nick Bollettieri, the legendary coach who had founded the world's first tennis boarding academy in Bradenton, Florida, and he offered me a scholarship on the spot. While the offer was tempting, I'd only just turned twelve, and packing up and moving to Florida sounded too scary. I loved my family and my bedroom and my friends at home. "Why don't you just come for a couple of weeks? See if you like it," Nick offered. That I could certainly do.

In the spring of 1986, my dad and I took Nick up on his invitation and spent two weeks playing in the sunshine on the academy's courts. At home I had never practiced with more than ten balls. At Nick's there were endless carts filled to the brim with brand-new balls waiting to be smacked around. I had unlimited access to the courts: clay, indoor, hard court, you name it. It was the polar opposite of tennis at home. After Disney World, it was the best experience of my life. I felt as if I'd stumbled into another dimension where everything was newer, bigger, and better. One day, one of the coaches took us on a drive around town. I stuck my head out the window to see the tops of the palm trees. Like everything else, they dwarfed what I was used to seeing in Europe. Cars whizzed by, each one larger and shinier than the last. "People really love their cars here, don't they?" I asked my dad. "Yes," he agreed. "It is much easier to have a nice one when it doesn't have to survive the winter." I thought about how brutal winters were back home. I missed a lot of things in Novi

Sad, but bracingly frigid mornings were not among them. For five months of the year I could see my breath while I was practicing outside. My hands often grew numb from gripping the racket in the cold and my lips would chap and crack from the wind chill. It wasn't Antarctica, but it was far from a hospitable climate for tennis.

When I got back home, I was so thrilled to see my mom and my friends that I didn't think about the academy much. I got right back into my usual routine of getting up before the sun to squeeze in time at the local court before the adults came to play. Summer was just around the corner, so I wasn't freezing during my hitting drills and I was spending more time playing my second-favorite sport: soccer. There was a park about a mile from my house. It was where all the neighborhood kids gathered to play pickup games. In Europe soccer is a religion, and I could have easily worshipped at its altar. Riding my bike to the park and checking out the latest game was how I spent almost every day when the weather warmed up. When I could convince the boys to let me play—which was more often than not—the afternoon got even better. I adored being part of a team. I loved the camaraderie, the energy, the magical feeling that always goes with being part of something bigger than you are. It's strange that I ended up devoting my life to a sport in which the socialization is limited to a quick nod of the head to your opponent before the start of a match and a cold demeanor is celebrated as a sign of being "focused."

The summer reprieve from my school's demanding course load of twelve subjects and a short break from the private English lessons all the kids took at home gave me more time to focus on tennis. My dad used his engineering talents to rig up contraptions to improve my balance and coordination long before I ever went to a gym. Balancing on a narrow wooden beam, I'd practice my volleys until they were ingrained into my muscle memory. I'd go on runs through my neighborhood, trying to beat my time from the day before. After placing two of my dolls ten feet apart, my dad would time me to see how quickly I could pick them up and put them down five times in a row. The more physical I was, the more I wanted to do. The faster my clocked times, the faster I wanted to go the next day.

Something was lit inside of me, and it was starting to grow hotter. I wanted to be the best I could be, so working out wasn't a burden. I loved it. And I spent time with my dad, so I was never bored. By the end of the summer I'd grown stronger and faster, and when we could snag court time, I could see the results in my game.

I had a decision to make. At twelve, I still had no idea that I could make a living playing tennis. Do it as a job? Like a teacher or a lawyer? No way. The only matches broadcast on our television were the men's and women's finals at Wimbledon and the French Open. For all I knew, those were the only four matches played every year, and Martina and Chrissie were the only professional female players in the world. But what I did know, with absolute certainty, was that I wanted to play as much tennis as I could. And I wouldn't be able to do that in Novi Sad. The opportunity to play at the academy was huge, and as the weather grew colder in Novi Sad, I couldn't stop thinking about the warm courts in Florida.

These days I hear about parents dropping off six-year-olds to be groomed into multimillion-dollar champions. These parents show up at the doorsteps of top sports academies to offer up kids who can't even read yet. It wasn't like that for me. Choosing to move to another country was a decision that my family took very seriously. We debated the pros and cons for hours over dinner, but when it came down to it, my mom and dad made it clear that it had to be my decision. They didn't want to pressure me either way. I decided to go. My parents would stay behind; Zoltan, who had just finished his obligatory one-year service in the military, would come with me. That took a lot of my anxiety away. Having a big brother look out for you is the best security blanket in the world. I made one-way airline reservations, filled two suitcases, carefully packed up my Walkman, and left our family's home. I had just turned thirteen.

If I had a daughter, I don't know whether I would let her do what I did, even if she had her older brother to protect her. Leaving the comfort and safety of home and family at such a young age, especially for a girl, can be disastrous. If you aren't 100 percent focused on your goal, you can easily lose yourself—becoming boy crazy, developing an eating disorder, being surrounded by money-hungry people looking to exploit young talent. There are so many pitfalls along the way, and if you are by yourself, it is very difficult to avoid them. The odds of everything falling into place, of making it into the top echelon of professional tennis, are minuscule and far outweighed by the risk of something going wrong. It worked out for me, but it is a gamble that can have tragic consequences.

# – 4 –

## Academy 101

Arriving at the Academy (I soon learned that the serious nature of training there necessitated a capital letter) was a crash course in tennis, international style. Kids came from all over—Hungary, Germany, Argentina, Venezuela, and, of course, America. It was a melting pot like the Sport Goofy tournaments, but without the lighthearted fun. Everyone was bronzed and beautiful, walking around the Academy grounds' forty acres with a single purpose: to become the best they could be. It was like a factory farm of sun-kissed mini tennis peacocks, strutting and posturing, checking out the competition.

In order to subsidize the kids on scholarship, the Academy had a large number of tuition-paying students. It wasn't cheap, so there was a chasm between the rich tuition-paying kids and the kids who had been plucked from junior tournaments around the world and dropped off in this champion-making headquarters. The scholarship kids were there because they showed unusual talent and promise, and to be that good they had to be hungry for it. They usually came from modest to meager backgrounds and used tennis as a way out of their town. The tuition-paying kids were there because they loved tennis and their families had the money to give them every opportunity to pursue it. They could buy whatever they wanted in the clubroom—it was the place to be every evening if you didn't feel like eating chicken for the five hundredth time in the cafeteria—and I saved my spending money to splurge on a small carton of chocolate chocolate chip Häagen-Dazs ice cream. I could afford this luxury once every other week and I looked in disbelief at the kids who could buy hamburgers, hot dogs, and chips at the clubroom grill every night and make unlimited trips to the vending machines. Their free access to the pricey snacks that didn't fit into my budget seemed just as impressive as when they flew home on private planes for the holidays. They had the best tennis gear on the courts, the trendy Guess clothes off the courts (I desperately wanted zippered jeans with matching jean jackets in every color), the best hair, and the best tans. They just looked cool. Like *90210* before *90210* even existed.

During my second month at the Academy, the difference in our backgrounds smacked me right in the face. I was walking to the courts for an afternoon hitting session with Raul Ordoñez, a Colombian pro with unbelievable hands, when I heard a commotion in the parking lot. A shiny red BMW convertible pulled up to the front of the Academy and one of the cool girls with perfect hair was behind the wheel. It was her sixteenth birthday and the car was a gift from her parents. I stood there staring at her in shock. A brand-new car? For a birthday present? My beloved *bajadera* chocolate paled in comparison. I wasn't jealous so much as dumbfounded. I couldn't understand how someone could just be given something like that. Maybe it was the Eastern European work ethic that had been instilled in me, but it just seemed strange to be handed something so valuable just for existing. I left the parking lot thinking how lucky it would be to have that kind of life. But I didn't, so it was time to get back to practicing my forehand. At that moment I realized I was going to have to make my own luck. There was no other way.

Although some kids were rich and some were far from it, everyone was there because they wanted to sleep, eat, and breathe tennis. Some had the goal of making a collegiate tennis team while others wanted to be number one in the world. The talent varied as much as the wardrobes. The kids from Eastern Europe had a style that looked as though it was a few years behind the Americans, while those from South America wore everything tighter and shorter than the others. Most kids went to school at Bradenton Preparatory Academy and fit several hours of playing into every day. It was unlike anything I'd ever seen before. In Novi Sad, none of my friends played tennis, so I could keep that part of my life compartmentalized. On the weekends I'd traveled around Europe, playing in tournaments, but during the week I was a regular kid who loved listening to a-ha on my Walkman and going to my friends' apartments to play Barbies. The Nick Bollettieri Tennis Academy was a shock to the system. There was no delineation among tennis, school, and home life.

My brother and I shared a room in the dormitory. While my new school's course load was far lighter than at my school in Novi Sad, adjusting to hearing English all day long was a struggle. The teachers spoke too quickly and I labored over my homework every night, frustrated that I couldn't whip through it as I had back home. Straight As were going to be much harder to get in Florida. Zoltan, whose English was better than mine, would spend time every evening going over new vocabulary words with me. During our first month in the dorm, I got up from my desk and walked to the window.

"Where are you going?" he asked. "You aren't finished with this chapter yet." He was helping me study for a history quiz the next morning, but there was something else that had grabbed my attention. A hundred yards away I could see a cluster of tennis courts. They were lit up for playing at night. I'd never seen that back home. We were so aware of using electricity that out of habit I always turned the lights off when I left a room. Lighting up an entire court was unheard of. If you wanted to play tennis, you went during daylight hours during the small window of court time you'd been able to wrangle.

"Zoltan, look at this!" Reluctantly, he walked over to the window.

"Yeah, I know. They light up their courts here." At twenty-one, he wasn't as easily impressed as I was. Or at least he didn't show it. For the rest of the night I spent every ten minutes jumping up from my desk to see if the lights were still on. There wasn't anything that could have impressed me more than those glowing courts. They didn't shut them off until after ten o'clock. It seemed like a magical tennis kingdom. People could play year-round and all day and night if they wanted to. Maybe Bradenton was even better than Disney World.

At first, I thrived in the military culture that the Academy was built around. I was expected to work out like a world-class soldier training for the battle of her life.

A typical day in the Bollettieri Way:

6 a.m.: Wake up, eat breakfast
7 to 8 a.m.: Special practice focusing on technique
8 to 11 a.m.: Hitting session
11 a.m. to noon: Lunch
Noon to 4 p.m.: School
4 to 7 p.m.: Hitting session
8 p.m.: Dinner
8:30 to 10 p.m.: Homework
10 p.m. sharp: Lights out

RULES:
No television during the week.
No phone calls during the week.
No late arrivals to practice.
No whining.

Nick had been an army paratrooper, and he brought the same regimented discipline to the Academy. It was boot camp, and you had to give 100 percent of yourself to survive and succeed. Every now and then we were treated to a weekend field trip to the mall or the beach, but other than that it was tennis twenty-four hours a day. It was a very insular existence. It was a crash course in tennis as a life instead of tennis as a game. I wasn't sure if I liked it, but I was so nervous about messing up and losing my scholarship that I did everything I was told. Plus, my English was far from fluent, so I spent the first few months just nodding my head up and down whenever someone said something to me. More than once Nick would spew off a list of things for me to keep in mind, and the only word I'd catch was "dear" (he called every girl "dear"). I'd nod my head up and down, but I wouldn't say a word. Zoltan would quickly come over and ask me if I'd understood anything. No, I'd answer. Then he'd rattle off the translation as fast as he could before the ball machine started pelting its missiles my way. Nick had a commanding presence on the court and I didn't want to disappoint him, so it was crucial that I understood his directions.

The daily regimen at the Academy was grueling for kids, but Nick led by example. Every morning he woke up before five and would have his first workout finished before anyone else was out of bed. No matter what, he was the first one on the court and the last one off. He practiced what he preached and wouldn't put up with anyone who whined, so I never did.

In that kind of pressure cooker environment, things become very intense. Making friends proved to be difficult, because everyone was competing against one another. When I first arrived, I hit around with girls who were six years older than I was. It didn't go well and they usually left the court fuming. I had too much power and I needed to hit against someone who was stronger than I was if I was going to improve. Soon I was hitting exclusively with my brother or the pros who worked at the Academy, so that immediately set me apart from the other girls. I ate lunch with my brother or with my friend Sandra, whose dad, Tony, had approached my dad at the Orange Bowl. One day my brother was busy hitting with the older guys and Sandra was nowhere in sight. As I walked into the cafeteria, I had a minor panic attack because I'd have to sit by myself. I felt like all eyes were on me, although in reality I doubt that anyone was paying attention to me. But try telling that to a late-blooming thirteen-year-old girl who has to walk into a bustling cafeteria alone. I was frantically searching for an open spot to claim as my own when I saw a blond girl smiling and gesturing to the open spot at her table.

"Hey, I'm Lisa," she said as she threw her hair into a ponytail with the scrunchie that had been on her wrist.

"I'm Monica," I answered.

"Yeah," she laughed. "I know." I didn't know what that meant. Maybe I stood out because I practiced on the backcourts with the boys and not with the girls. Or maybe because my clothes were different, or because I spoke mediocre English with an accent. I didn't dwell on it for very long, because Lisa made me feel welcome right away. She was two years older and I loved hanging out with her. Unlike most of the other kids, Lisa was laid-back and easygoing. In all of our meals together in the cafeteria, we never once talked about tennis: she liked it but it wasn't her life, and I found it a relief to have someone at the Academy who talked about something other than grip technique and upcoming tournaments. A lifelong friendship was formed at that cafeteria table.

It wasn't until I'd been practicing for several weeks that I realized there was something different about me. I thought the other girls didn't like me just because I wasn't cool enough, not because I could beat them. I'd been beating kids since I was six years old and it had never prevented me from having friends. But this was different. At the Academy, tennis was a business and the players didn't accept losing gracefully. It didn't take long before I was practicing on the backcourts by myself, hitting with my brother or a pro while the older guys practiced on the court next to me. Today they are household names, but back then I knew them as Andre, Jim, and David—the popular, cocky, and cool group of top male players at the Academy. Andre Agassi looked like he was in a rock band, and since it was the eighties, that meant spiky long hair and fluorescent clothing. Girls loved him. He had the rebellious flair of James Dean. He could practice a quarter as much as everyone else and still be the best out there. That's what being born with natural talent does for you. Jim Courier was a workhorse and lived to play matches. When he wasn't practicing, he was playing the drums. Everyone was surprised when he won a Grand Slam before Andre, but that's what a nonstop, hard-driving work ethic will do for you—something that Andre developed later in his career when he mounted one of sports' all-time greatest comebacks. David Wheaton, the number one junior player in the country, would practice the same drill over and over until it was perfect. His obsession to get it just right was almost as crazy as mine. Zoltan—the guys nicknamed him "Z-man"—practiced and hung out with them, but I barely opened my mouth when they were in the vicinity. What could I say to them? They were popular older boys, and I was an awkward, self-conscious girl who'd just entered teenage-dom and was still all skinny arms and legs. They were three years older than I was, but it was like dog years. They seemed so tall, confident, and old to me.

One blazingly hot afternoon, Nick asked Jim to hit with me. I was so excited. I'd never said more than hi to the guys, and we'd never set foot on the same court, although we practiced in adjacent courts every day. I saw how seriously they took their hitting sessions: they always wanted to obliterate each other. I wanted to make a good impression. I wanted to prove that I could keep up with them. I guess I tried a little too hard, because our hitting session only lasted ten minutes before Jim stormed off.

"Don't ever ask me to hit with her again!" he yelled at Nick as he grabbed his bag and left the court without looking back. Uh-oh. I thought it had gone fine, but Jim hadn't appreciated being run all over the court by a girl half his size. He teases me about it now, but back then I didn't understand what I'd done wrong. Most people will hit back and forth to each other, but that's not how I operated. Right from the start, I was hitting it from side to side at crazy angles; I wasn't making anything easy for him. I figured, *Hey, if I'm going to be out here hitting, I might as well hit them like I mean it.* Understandably, Jim didn't appreciate it, and that was the end of my court time with the boys.

# — 5 —

# She's Not All That

I kept up the appearance of doing okay for the first few months. My introduction to a more-is-better culture (finding out I could get seconds and thirds in the cafeteria was mind-rattling), a confusing language (American slang was a bizarre, unintelligible dialect: it took me a long time to figure out that "Yo" wasn't a common name in the States, it was just how kids addressed each other), a new intensity of tennis (I was constantly tired: I'd never known that kind of exhaustion before), and the scorching heat (by noon I felt I might melt into a puddle on the court) had been a whirlwind and I was doing my best to keep my head above water. But without my parents around, my foundation was quickly crumbling, and the stress of all the recent upheavals in my life was starting to catch up with me. Then, one afternoon in the cafeteria when I was getting seconds for lunch, I met peanut butter. After my first piece of toast slathered with it, Nutella was forgotten and I had a new best friend. The more I missed my parents, the more I went to the cafeteria. The more homesick I felt, the more peanut butter sandwiches I ate. If I could jump into a time machine and go back to that place I would have taken that young girl aside and said, "*No! Stop!* This is not the way to deal with what is going on in your life. This is not the pattern you want to set. Believe me, you'll be sorry one day."

My peanut butter consumption went into overdrive when the two-handed forehand that my game had been built around for eight years was taken away. The coaches at the Academy were convinced that I had to transition to the more orthodox one-handed position. Top players didn't use two hands, so why should I? It was a mistake. It's very hard to change something like that after you turn twelve. Pete Sampras was able to turn his two-handed backhand into a one-handed beauty when he was thirteen, but he's *Pete Sampras*. His case was highly unusual. My fundamentals were strong, but I just couldn't get used to the strange feeling of a one-handed swing. I felt totally awkward and not connected to my body; I wasn't used to being out of sorts like that. The new swing wasn't working for me and it was destroying my confidence. After losing by a horrendous margin (6–1, 6–0) to Carrie Cunningham, a player I'd easily beaten in the days of the Sport Goofy tournaments, serious self-doubt set in. Could I really be a top player? Did I have it in me or had I already hit my peak? Agents who'd been circling upon my arrival stopped coming by to check out my practices. I heard the sentence "Maybe she won't pan out after all" over and over. I went into a total panic. Terrified my scholarship would be taken away, I tried harder to master my new game, but the harder I tried, the tenser I got. Nick told me not to stress about it, to regroup and just focus on my short-term goals, but I couldn't. I was no longer experiencing pure fun, the reason I'd fallen in love with tennis that day by the Adriatic Sea. I couldn't remember the last time I'd broken into uncontrollable giggles. Thirteen-year-old girls should spend most of their time amid laughing fits. I missed my friends, I missed my parents, I missed knowing where and how I fit in. My English was getting better, but this new life was foreign in every way and I was struggling to find fluency in it. I knew something had to give.

Homesickness had buried itself deeply within me, and the seven hours of daily practice weren't enough to combat my peanut butter sandwich therapy. Ten extra pounds appeared on my body in the blink of an eye. I was a slow-maturing waif who could stand to put a little meat on my bones, but the rapid gain on my frame completely changed my body shape, and with my new chubby cheeks I started to resemble a chipmunk. The whispering about what had "gone wrong" with me was turning into loud gossip everywhere I went. After overhearing a group of cool girls with perfect ponytails talking about me in the cafeteria at lunch, I hit my breaking point. I ran to my room, collected all the quarters I'd been saving for the monthly phone call to my parents (e-mail, international calling through your computer, Web cams, and instant messaging have revolutionized being away from home; my frantic call was back in the digital Stone Age), and dialed my home number as fast as I could. After nine months of keeping a stiff upper lip at the Academy, I gave in. Each ring seemed interminable. I bit my fingernails as I waited for one of my parents to pick up. The second I heard my mom's voice, I broke down in tears.

# – 6 –

## *Back to Basics*

There have been several times in my life when I've been overwhelmed with the extraneous. Pressure mounts to the point that I can't see straight, I feel pulled in a million different directions, and I have a hard time figuring out how to make things better. After many, many years and lots of trial and error—more error than I'd like to remember—I've come up with a three-point plan for surviving these tempests in life:

1. **Clean house.** This means getting rid of everything that isn't essential in your life right at that moment.
2. **Don't be afraid to say the magic word.** It isn't "please." It's "no." People won't be as upset as you think they will be.
3. **Embrace the power of being you, without apology.** It's a power that is too often overlooked and squashed by others and by you.

I didn't know any of this when I was standing outside with the phone in my hand, sobbing to my parents an ocean away, but I had an idea that whatever I was doing wasn't working. My life had become too complicated and I needed it to revert back to the simplicity I'd thrived on when I was home. Cartoons in the morning, practices with my dad, and dinner with my family. That's all I needed. Nine months of built-up emotion burst out and my parents were caught off guard. Every call they'd received up to that point had been a fake. It was expensive to call Europe, so we spoke every three to four weeks. It had been easy to put on a happy face during our few phone calls. I'd told them over and over that things were going well, that I was adjusting without any problems, that my tennis was great. Finally, in one big gush, the truth came out. I'm sure they wanted to get on the next plane to the States but they had their jobs and their lives to think about. They couldn't just pick up and go, could they?

Most tennis parents get lumped into one group: overbearing, money-hungry publicity hounds who are living vicariously through their kids. But not all tennis parents are the same. There are a lot who stay far away from the game, letting their kids handle everything on their own. Others sacrifice everything to help their kids succeed—not because it is the parents' dream, but because it is their kids'. Mine fell somewhere in the middle of the last two. It didn't matter what I chose—it could have been rock climbing, drama, or oil painting—they would have supported me completely. Without them, I simply would not have had the career I did. Grand Slams would have remained a far-off dream, and I never would have set foot in Roland Garros Stadium. But, together as a parental team, they never pushed me too hard or put pressure on me. They were like yin and yang: if one got too wrapped up in the pressure of the tennis life, the other would step in and put it into perspective. When I was on the tour, at least one of them would travel with me—which, as a teenager, is an invaluable emotional support to have. They protected me without coddling me, and when my fame grew exponentially and I was doing magazine shoots and filming television ads, they kept my ego in check. My dad lost his own father at a young age, and my mother left her family at the age of twelve to get a better education, so they personally knew the power of being self-reliant. From the beginning, whether it was going to a junior European tournament instead of a friend's birthday party or leaving home for Florida, they made it clear that whatever I chose they'd support me, but it had to be my choice. I forged my own path, but they gave me unbelievable backup.

The only argument over tennis that I can remember was when I was seven and my morning hitting sessions were growing in frequency and intensity. I'd fallen head over heels for tennis, and nothing—not even my beloved Barbies—could tear me away from it. My mom—with the vocal and wholehearted support of my dad's mom, who had been horrified to see my tiny calloused hands during an afternoon of baking in her kitchen—had suggested that I stop playing.

"But what can I do?" my dad asked as he piled my dolls into his tennis bag. "She loves it. I can't forbid her from playing."

"Shouldn't she be playing with dolls instead of knocking the stuffing out of them? Sports aren't for little girls." My mom came from an era when the thought of girls playing as hard as the boys was ludicrous. When it came to athletics, she was the polar opposite of my dad. He had been a triple jumper and he did it barefoot, as was the norm in those days, taking athletic devotion to a whole other level. She scoffed at moving any faster than a walking pace. He spent years coaching track-and-field athletes in preparation for the Olympics and excelled at every sport he tried: soccer, basketball, running. She had zero athletic ability and zero desire to develop any. I got my love for sports from my dad and my intense dislike of gyms from my mom. She didn't want to exert herself unless there was a point to it.

My mom's complete lack of interest in tennis gave me a good balance. I never once felt the pressure to win her love by winning on the court. She would have preferred reading magazines and trying out new recipes with me to going to a tennis match any day of the week. That's why, when I told my parents how miserable I was in Florida, I didn't think they'd actually move there to be with me. I just assumed they'd say, "Okay, honey, come home." I told them I couldn't do it on my own and that I wanted to get on the next plane out of Florida. I was thirteen—one of the worst ages to be for a girl—I didn't have many friends, and I didn't feel comfortable in my own skin. Though puberty hadn't yet hit me, I was walking around in a body that felt like it didn't fit. Those extra ten pounds were a symptom of my deeper emotional state, and they took their toll on me.

"Just hang in there another week and we'll figure something out," they assured me.

"Okay," I said through my sniffles. I hung up the phone and with some relief started to mentally pack my bags. It was too bad. I'd worked so hard all year and gritted my teeth through unbearable homesickness for tennis, but I didn't want to spend another moment being miserable. Nothing was worth feeling like that. Not even tennis. I guessed I just didn't have what it took, but that was okay. I'd go back home, back to my friends, back to my school, and play tennis when the local courts would allow it. Of course, in a perfect world, I'd transport Bradenton's climate and unparalleled tennis facilities to Novi Sad or I'd magically whisk my parents to Florida. I knew that both options were impossible. My mom had worked at the same accounting firm for twenty-eight years and was just two years away from getting her pension. My dad had been having a lot of success working for a local newspaper and getting his cartoons published around the world. He'd also been awarded a Palme d'Or for his work on a documentary that covered the relationship between politics and sports. Although the economic situation in Yugoslavia was starting to look bleak, they'd created a good life. They had a home, jobs, and relatives there. And they were already in their fifties; they couldn't start a whole new life in a new country.

I knew that in Novi Sad my tennis would never get to the level I'd achieve in Florida, but I knew that my parents just couldn't uproot their lives and move across an ocean to be with me. Could they? The more I thought about how much I'd be missing by leaving this sun-drenched capital of tennis, the more I let myself daydream. What if my parents decided to come? My dad had liked Florida during our tournament trips. Who doesn't love an eighty-degree day in December? Would they be up for an adventure? No, no, I told myself. Don't get your hopes up. It was too good to be true, and I didn't dare speak my hopes aloud to Zoltan. I was holding them like precious cargo in the back of my mind, careful not to bring them out for inspection too often. I knew the chances were almost zero, so I focused on what I assumed was going to happen: I'd be moving back home. When the week was finally up, I called my parents to give them an update on how I was doing. I didn't even get to say the words "I'm still miserable, I want to come home" before they told me the news: they were moving to Florida. I thought I'd misheard them. I asked my mom to repeat what she'd just said.

"It's true," she said excitedly, as though she could barely believe it herself. "We've decided to come out there."

Relief flooded my entire body. "But how? Why? What about your jobs? What about Grandma and Grandpa?" The questions came out in a tumble as my shock dissolved into relief. Things were going to be okay. I'd have my family and I'd have tennis too.

"Slow down, Monica." I heard my dad's voice on the line. My mom had passed the phone to him. "Everything will be fine. Don't worry about us. Just focus on being happy. We'll be there soon."

"But how?" I asked again. I still didn't understand. I was scared that this was all a joke. I needed to know the details.

"It's simple. We love you and Zoltan, we want you both to be happy and we want our family to be together again. It isn't a sacrifice, it's what you do for family."

"But what about your jobs?" I asked.

"Your mom and I are taking six-month sabbaticals and I can publish my work from anywhere in the world. The Academy is going to help us get settled. After that, we'll see how it goes. This is a great opportunity for you, Monica. You have a gift and you shouldn't waste it. And don't worry about your grandparents: they'll be fine. We can call them and write to them all the time."

Six months. So it wasn't permanent. It was like a test run for the Seles family in Florida. Cool. I liked the idea of that. I started counting down the minutes until their arrival.

✳

My dad almost didn't recognize me at the airport terminal. "You've grown so much!" he said as he engulfed me in a huge bear hug. I knew he wasn't talking about my height, but I didn't care. My family was reunited and I knew I'd be back to my old tennis self in no time. He never made another comment about my weight again, not even when, ten years later, I ate myself forty pounds up the scale during the dark days of my depression. At that point he didn't care about my weight, he just wanted me to get better.

The first night in our new apartment was just as I'd been dreaming about. Mom had a sauce simmering on the stove while she was whipping up my favorite salad loaded with feta cheese and olives; Zoltan and my dad were sitting at the dining room table talking about the latest soccer scores from Europe; and I was sitting right in the middle of it all, pretending to do my homework but really just soaking it all in. We didn't speak a word about tennis all night. I couldn't stop smiling and I was overwhelmed with the warm, incomparable sense of being home again.

First things first: My dad and Nick had a long talk, and they both decided that my two-handed forehand should be reinstated immediately. The one-handed was just not going to work, no matter how much I practiced the awkward swing. I was thrilled. It was like being reunited with my best friend. My practice schedule eased up considerably and I started enjoying two days off a week, one more than I'd been having. The number one reason promising players don't make it past junior tennis is burnout. My dad was very worried about it and he didn't want to push my still-growing body beyond its limit, so he made those two days off a mandatory rule. But a tired body wasn't the only way to burn out. It could happen just as easily to your mind. Overdosing on tennis can cause paralysis through analysis, and I'd been eating, drinking, sleeping, and breathing the sport all year. Maybe that's why the one-handed forehand never worked for me. I thought it to death, so it never really had a chance.

My dad couldn't believe how serious I'd become since I left home, so he took out his notebook and started firing off cartoons like an assembly line. I got the fun back into my game. Having a parent as a coach may sound strange and too high pressure, but it is a common thing in tennis, especially for girls. Martina Hingis, Anna Kournikova, the Williams sisters, and Maria Sharapova were, or still are, coached by a parent. There is a protective aspect there as well as a financial one. Having a private coach twenty-four hours a day is a luxury that even the top players on tour don't have. Good coaches are in high demand, and scoring one for your exclusive use is nearly impossible. When you are still a young teenager who hasn't even turned pro yet, you won't have much luck finding a coach who can devote all of his time to you, so it becomes a natural evolution to depend on a parent more and more for coaching support and advice. Sometimes those relationships work, and sometimes they fall apart in a catastrophic manner.

From the get-go, my dad kept our coaching relationship separate from our father-daughter relationship. Most people were skeptical, and I don't blame them. If I hadn't lived it, I wouldn't have believed it was possible either. Surely, something would have to give, or my tennis or my family life (or both) would be damaged in the end. Many families have been destroyed while attempting the same thing. Somehow it worked. We could clash like cats and dogs on the court over some technical issue ("Approach the ball with your foot like this, not like that! Bend your knees more. More!"), but the second we got off the court, one switch flicked on, one flicked off, and we were like two different people. And if I showed up at practice with a bad attitude, my dad was the only person who could make me laugh within seconds and turn my energy around for the rest of the day.

If my parents hadn't come to Florida, I would have been burned out by my fourteenth birthday.

# — 7 —

## The Training Wheels of Professional Tennis

Oh my God, I've got to, like, calm down," I whispered to myself as I walked into the players' locker room at the Virginia Slims tournament in Boca Raton. I was fourteen years old and fluent in American slang. I'd been practicing tennis out of the spotlight at the Academy for the past year and it had been a long time—almost a year and a half—since my last tournament. I was more than ready to get out and play someone other than a hitting partner. But this wasn't just any tournament. I was still an amateur but this was my first *real* tournament with *real* pros, and I was sick to my stomach as I sat on a bench in a locker room in Boca Raton trying to tie my shoelaces with sweaty hands. A Virginia Slims tournament—the cigarette company was the sponsor of the WTA (Women's Tennis Association) in the seventies and eighties—was a world away from Sport Goofy.

My first match was against Helen "The Hurricane" Kelesi. She was a retriever with fierce ability from the baseline. Right before the match, my dad told me to just have fun. *Ha! Easy for you to say*, I thought as I walked to my side of the court on less-than-steady stick legs. The second I hit my first shot, my nerves disappeared. I battled to take the first set 7–6 and then closed the match by winning the second set 6–3. It wasn't that different from the practice matches I played at the Academy, but it was still surreal. First of all, I was playing a woman instead of Zoltan or Raoul; and second, she was a professional and she was good. Three months after our match, she'd go on to reach the quarterfinals of the French Open. Players were playing for money here, something I'd never done before. Technically I was still an amateur, so I wasn't playing for cash, but everyone else was. I'd survived my first professional match. I felt relieved until I remembered who I'd be playing in the second round: Chris Evert. As in *Chris Evert*, one of the greatest players in the history of the game, former number one and now number three in the world, not to mention the best-dressed tennis player I'd ever seen. When I was seven years old, I sat with my nose inches from the television screen watching her win her third Wimbledon title. With adorable color-coordinated ribbons flowing from her hair, she had been my style icon since I was a little girl. I wanted to look just like her: a girlie girl who could really whack a ball. A perfect combination. I didn't know what I wanted to do more: play against one of the greatest legends of the game or get tips on how to make the perfect ponytail. I didn't sleep much that night.

Before the match my dad and Nick told me to just have fun—again that advice! My dad would keep saying it to me for the next ten years; he probably thought it would eventually sink in through sheer repetition. It never did. I love tennis, but I can honestly say that I never once had fun during a match. I had loads of fun preparing for matches, but playing under pressure? Beating someone else? It just wasn't for me. I was born with an unshakable people-pleasing personality, and I never loved winning at someone else's expense. I loved winning points, but I hated seeing the other person upset at the end of the match. Focus, motivation, drive—I had all those things. But the desire to wipe up the court with my opponent was never part of my game. Worried about buckling under pressure but not wanting to make the person across the net angry, I never had much fun out there. So when I got that advice, I just nodded and promised them I'd try. I didn't have to try for very long. Chrissie took the match in two sets, 6–2, 6–1. I was thrilled I hadn't been shut out. My only goal at that point was not to throw up on the court from nerves, so I'd say that I exceeded my expectations that night. I mean, she was Chris Evert and I was a fourteen-year-old girl who was so paralyzed by self-consciousness and nervousness in the locker room that when a player tried to talk to me, the only words I could squeak out of my mouth were "Hi" and "Uh-huh" before I cranked Duran Duran up on my Walkman as loud as Simon Le Bon could go. I played in two more tournaments that year, making it to the second round in one and the semis of the other, but other than that I kept a very low profile, honing my game in the backcourts at the Academy and avoiding talking to any of the older guys. They'd all joined the pro tour by then but still came back to practice at the Academy in between tournaments, so they seemed even older, stronger, and cooler than ever.

When I think back to those days, I don't think of myself as a teenager who was about to turn professional. I was an athletic phenom, but mentally and physically I was still a little girl, at least two years behind my biological age. Flat-chested and gawky, I was a long way off from growing into my looks. I felt much closer to childhood than adolescence, much less womanhood. At fourteen, my favorite thing to do when I wasn't playing tennis was to watch cartoons. Nobody else my age did that. When I left home right after turning thirteen, I think I stayed stuck in the same place emotionally. Trying to catch up with everything I had to learn in a new country, compounded with the pressure of performing, stunted my growth into the next phase of being a teen. My time was so consumed with tennis and my life was so insular. I was still a kid with very few social skills and not much confidence off the court. All I wanted to do was play tennis, listen to my Walkman, and watch cartoons in the morning. My life had changed dramatically since I left Novi Sad, but in some ways it was exactly the same.

# – 8 –

# The Big Time

I t is a decision every promising player has to make: to turn professional or to go to college. In some sports you can do both, but in tennis, especially on the women's tour, your best years fly by before you hit the legal drinking age. If you're going to make a run for the top, you can't spend four years in college. It's a sad truth about tennis. On February 13, 1989, it was official: I was going to give the pro world a shot. The crazy traveling circus of the WTA tour was about to sweep me up in all of its frenetic energy and not put me down for several years. Turning pro when you're barely fifteen turns your life upside down, and if your feet aren't planted firmly in reality, they'll get kicked right out from under you. You have to have the steadiest of support systems and an honest team who will tell you what is what. There is a danger in professional sports of being surrounded by too many yes-men, too many people who just tell you what they think you want to hear. That doesn't help anybody and it can make you lose all touch with reality. I didn't have that problem. Even after I won my first title at the Virginia Slims tournament in Houston, the first thing my mom told me to do when I got back home was to clean my room.

The title was a big deal not only because it was my first but also because I had to beat Chris Evert. I'd gotten through the first four rounds, including a redemptive victory over Carrie Cunningham (6–0, 6–1), almost the same score she'd beaten me with at the Academy, but my confidence vanished the evening before the final. Worrying about how badly Chrissie had beaten me in our last match the year before, I was convinced I'd be jettisoned off the court in two sets. I didn't think I'd be able to win, but I at least wanted to look cute. It was, after all, my first appearance in a final, and it was against the player who always looked as if she'd just stepped out of the pages of a glamorous sports magazine. Clothing sponsors had yet to come knocking at my door, and I didn't have anything in my suitcase that was special enough, so I begged my dad to let me buy a new outfit from a vendor at the tournament site. He agreed without too much reluctance.

A red shirt was hanging up in one of the clothing booths, and I knew it would be perfect. It was adorable. I took it back to our hotel and laid it out on my bed as though I were getting ready for the first day of school. I had a white skirt and white barrettes that would look great with it. Unlike all of the other players, my outfit wouldn't be covered with logos. In the morning, when we got to the tournament site, I told my dad how nervous I was—more than I'd ever been before. The possibility of doing better than I had in our previous match-up seemed small.

"Monica," he said with great calm, "please do not look at the finish line. Right now, the finish line does not exist. Just play each point and don't think past the next one. That is your only goal today." He gave me a big hug and I ventured toward the locker room. I wouldn't be able to talk to him again until the match was over.

*Just play every point. That's all I have to do.* I saw Chrissie in the locker room and she gave me a quick nod of recognition. She was all business, so I followed her lead. I put on my headphones, sat down cross-legged on the floor, and zoned out to "Hungry Like the Wolf" until an official called us out. Even though I tried not to let my nerves show, they were on display in front of the whole crowd. I was playing tight and not getting into the flow of the game. I was reacting to her shots instead of taking the lead through sheer force of power. *I'm in the final, I'm in the final!* raced through my head, and I couldn't shake those words out no matter how hard I tried.

It was like a dream and the real me was hovering above the court, watching the pretend me suffering another loss at the hands of Chrissie. She took the first set 6–3, but instead of feeling more pressure, I felt less. I had nothing to lose in the second, so it was time to just go for it. *So you're in the finals: big deal. Just focus on every point*, I reminded myself. I found my rhythm, and with each point I won, the next one came a little easier. Before I knew it, I'd won the second set 6–1—my first victorious set against one of the greatest tennis players in the world. But I didn't start patting myself on the back. There was still another set to play.

In the third I tightened up again, this time because the thought of actually winning—something I'd been too hesitant to consider—kept popping into my head. It was distracting, so I repeated my dad's advice out loud. Every point. Every point. I loosened up and went for broke. I won the third set 6–4 and looked straight at my dad for confirmation that what I thought had happened really had, indeed, happened. He was on his feet clapping and nodding his head up and down as if to say, *Yes, you won. You aren't dreaming*. I walked to the net and, for the second time, shook the hand of my idol. The thing about being fifteen and achieving something extraordinary is that it isn't fraught with the same drama that it would be when achieving it as an adult. I was fifteen, what did I know? If I'd been older, I might have psyched myself out. I might have thought I didn't deserve to win and let negative thinking sabotage my success. But at fifteen I didn't know any better. If I played the best that I could, why shouldn't I be able to beat her? Teenagers are fueled by a naïve invincibility that can lead to tremendous achievements—it just goes to show how much power the mind has. Before you've been knocked down by life and seen your share of disappointments, you think anything is possible.

Chrissie was gracious in defeat, and when we got back to the locker room she gave me some valuable advice: "Enjoy every day you have on tour now. Before you know it, a new generation just like you will be rising up, but they'll be faster and stronger. You'll have everything to lose and they'll have everything to gain." I just nodded my head and offered my usual self-conscious "Uh-huh." Her speech was kind of a downer but it wasn't out of bitterness: she was genuinely trying to be helpful. And she'd just been beaten by a player less than half her age, so maybe it was a way to vent her frustration. But I was fifteen at the time and, like most fifteen-year-olds, the thought of ever being thirty was something I couldn't wrap my head around. *Thirty?* It sounded old. By then I'd be married with kids and I'd be shuttling around in a little space car in the sky. It was a long way off. Too far off to think about now. Why would I worry about getting old? I'd be young forever. I had no idea that Chrissie's advice would turn out to be dead-on.

For winning the tournament, I received a check for $50,000. They presented it to me in a jumbo-size form for publicity photos. I'd never seen so many zeros before and I thought that, because it was a lot of money, it had to be written on a really big check. I was convinced that I had to take it to the bank to cash it, so after the awards ceremony I kept walking around with it even though it was nearly as big as I was. The tournament director explained that they'd give me another check, one that I could put in my pocket, but I was so thrilled with my victory that I wanted to hold on to that big piece of cardboard for as long as I could. My dad carried my bags for me and I struggled to hold on to the check as we walked through the parking lot. I wasn't represented by an agency yet, and during the short walk to our rental car we were besieged by well-dressed executive types giving us their business cards. During my quiet practice time at the Academy over the past year I'd been shielded from the business side of tennis, but beating Chrissie had catapulted me onto the radar of every sports agency in the world. Things were going to change. After squeezing my check into the backseat, we headed to the airport, where I claimed it as my carry-on luggage. For the next twenty-four hours it went everywhere with me. I'd never been so proud of myself.

I spent early spring preparing for the French Open, a Grand Slam I'd been fantasizing about for years. Clay is hands-down my favorite surface, and that year my love affair began with Roland Garros Stadium. After I unpacked my bags in the hotel, my dad came into my room.

"How are you doing? Are you tired?" He looked concerned. It was my first Grand Slam and my first trip overseas for a professional tournament. I could tell he was worried it would be too much for me to take in.

"I feel great!" I was so pumped on adrenaline that a long flight and a six-hour time change weren't having an effect on me.

"Want to get some fresh air?" he asked. "It will help with the jet lag."

"Yes, of course!" I couldn't wait to hit the streets of Paris, but we didn't have time to set off on a whirlwind sightseeing day. Versailles and the Louvre would have to wait awhile. As it turned out, they'd have to wait sixteen years until I was able to see Paris the right way.

Our walk took us down the sidewalks of the 16th Arrondissement, the ritziest neighborhood in the city, with grand apartment buildings. I was amazed by the women who whisked by on the sidewalk with hair as silky as their Hermès scarves. It was an effortless chic, and I was hooked on the glamour that seemed to be their birthright. I wanted to look like that. We made our way through the leafy and gigantic Bois de Boulogne until we ended at Roland Garros Stadium. It was *the* Roland Garros, the stadium I'd been dreaming about since seeing it on our TV in Yugoslavia.

"You want to go in?" my dad asked, although he knew the answer. Without waiting for my reply, he was already through the front gate. I went half running, half skipping after him. Up and up we climbed until we reached the top row of the stands. You know how sometimes when you see a famous person, they look smaller than you'd imagined? Or you see a movie or television show being filmed and the set looks way smaller than it does on the screen? That's not how the stadium was for me. Seeing it with my own eyes was startling. It was twice as big, twice as grand, and twice as intimidating as I'd thought it would be. All those spring days spent in front of the television watching the players duke it out on Court Central had been abysmal preparation. I felt small and young. I felt like a kid pretending to be a tennis player. I let out a big sigh.

"What is it?" my dad asked.

"It just looks so huge." The butterflies in my stomach were getting an early start on making me a nervous wreck. My dad took off his sunglasses and pointed down to the court.

"Monica, look down there." There were rows and rows of seats between me and the court. It looked so far away.

"That court is not huge," he continued. "That court is the same size you've been playing on your whole life." He waved his arms around the stadium. "All of this, it doesn't mean anything. Just look at the court." He was right. There wasn't anything different or special about this red clay court. It may have been housed in one of the most famous and legendary stadiums in the world, but it didn't make the actual court any harder to play on. On our walk home, my butterflies grew tired and went to sleep.

My first Grand Slam was won in Paris, but it wasn't destined to be that year. Instead, I inadvertently offended an opponent. On my way out to the court to play a third-round match against Olympic doubles gold medalist Zina Garrison, two little girls handed me a bouquet of red roses. I didn't know what to do with the flowers, so I threw some to the spectators and offered the rest to Zina at the net. Oops! Kids are much more media savvy now. Sports academies have media training classes for players before they hit their teens. But back then I was a young girl who thought flowers were pretty and wanted to do something nice for the fans. I took a lot of heat for it in the postmatch conference. Nobody asked me about the match; they just wanted to know why I threw flowers to the crowd. What statement was I trying to make? I didn't have an answer for them. I just wanted to focus on my next match. I got through the next two rounds in two sets each and reached the semifinal. It was the first match in what was to become a rivalry with Steffi Graf, the epitome of on-court athleticism and eye-popping agility. She was four years older than I was, but I remembered seeing her at junior tournaments in Europe. Even as a kid she could bound around the court as if she had springs in her long legs. She was the type of athlete who probably would have excelled at any sport she chose. I lost the semifinal to her 3–6, 6–3, 3–6, but I wasn't distraught. The stadium in France might have been bigger than anything I'd ever played in before, but I belonged there just as much as anyone else.

# The Grand Dame of Grand Slams

There is an energy at Wimbledon that is different from the other Grand Slams. It may be the formalities, the presence of the royal family, the perfectly polished silver, the high tea, the well-dressed and serious crowd that rarely claps even on amazing points, the all-white dress code, or just the fact that it's been around the longest that gives it such a special aura. While the French is a gut-wrenching war of attrition played out through long, grinding points on clay, Wimbledon is a fast-paced clash of high-flying egos and beautiful serve-and-volley skills, an integral part of the game that I never mastered. The media works itself into a frenzy leading up to the action on the court, so by the time the players get there, the energy is already pumping before the first-round matches have been played. Players get the same number of points in every Grand Slam, but there is an undeniable cachet that goes along with adding your name to the plaques on the wall of the All England Club.

There are three different locker rooms at Wimbledon. The top sixteen seeds get one locker room, the next thirty-two get another locker room, and the rest get a third locker room. It is the only tournament that divides the players and it sets a very formal tone right away. Normally we're all crowded into the same place, and as the days go by the room begins to slowly empty out until just the last two players are left. It's hard not to talk to your competition, but you can't be too friendly, otherwise you won't be able to harness the do-or-die instinct you may need later on the court. If you're not emotionally invested, you can remain coolheaded when it counts. My philosophy was always "Get to know people as little as possible; that way nobody gets hurt." It won't give you the happiest life, but it will improve your tennis game a lot.

When I walked into the locker room at Wimbledon for the first time, I thought I'd taken a wrong turn. It looked more like Buckingham Palace than a tournament site. Silver trays and china were laid out in perfect alignment on tables, and a stunning display of food was right in the middle of the room. It was the fanciest thing I'd ever seen. It was like I'd stumbled back in time to a tea party in Victorian England. Plates were filled with finger sandwiches of every kind and there were tins upon tins of shortbread cookies waiting to be feasted on. When it comes to my willpower, shortbread cookies are almost as bad as peanut butter. Before each match I'd treat myself to two of them, but I made sure to stop because I didn't want to feel sick on the court.

I made it through the first three rounds but was halted in the fourth when I came up against Steffi. I didn't fare as well as I had three weeks earlier in Paris. Before our match there were rumblings that Princess Di would be there. I wasn't an easily starstruck kid, but Princess Di was special. She transcended celebrity status. A tournament official pulled me aside as I was walking out to Centre Court. What was going on? Was the match canceled? Did we have one of those rain delays that Wimbledon was notorious for? No, just a quick lesson in how to curtsy to royalty.

My lesson lasted ten seconds before the official was pushing me toward the court. The sun was shining brightly on the green grass, and I hadn't the slightest idea of where to look for the princess. I did a weird sort of sweeping curtsy move covering as much room as I could, hoping that somehow I'd aimed in her general direction. During the match I finally spotted her. Her grace, elegance, and poise made her stand out in the crowd of thousands—though not enough to let me spot her when it had counted. She was a beautiful princess. The All England Club was straight out of a fairy tale. Unfortunately, my score against Steffi was not a happy ending: I lost 6–0, 6–1. But I'd made it to the final sixteen and I got to see the best locker room on the grounds. It could have been a worse run. My long, rocky relationship with Wimbledon had just begun.

# – 10 –

## Hitting My Stride

Bursting into the top ten rankings is a baptism by fire into the business side of tennis. I was sixteen when it happened. I had to grow up fast. The strong showing I'd put on during the '89 season carried me right up the rankings to a solid number six. Suddenly the phone started ringing. The sports management firm IMG was representing me, and there were equipment, clothing, and advertising sponsors sending them boxes and boxes of free merchandise to give to me. It's funny how when you really need things, nobody will give you anything, but when you are finally able to afford what you need, you're given far more than you could ever use. My parents, who despite having two good jobs when I was growing up still had to run our household on a tight budget, taught me that money means very little. It comes and it goes but it doesn't define you and it certainly isn't something to base your self-worth on. I don't remember playing in tournaments for the money. I played in them because I loved playing tennis. The money part just allowed me to keep at it.

Deciding to play tennis is like cutting a hole in your wallet. The money just disappears. It takes a team to build a successful player: a coach and hitting partner travel with you everywhere. They are paid whether you win or lose, and often there are bonuses for them when you score a title.

You are responsible for more than just your own livelihood, so it puts that much extra pressure on you to win. People are depending on you. Logistics can be a nightmare. You are responsible for making plane and hotel reservations, which can change at the drop of a hat, depending on how you perform at each week's new tournament. I never knew any of this when I was a teenager. I took care of the travel details but I had no concept of how much everything was costing. My dad was my coach and Zoltan, who handled the finances, was my hitting partner. We were a closely knit, efficiently run family business. It wasn't until I was in my twenties and out on the tour alone that I saw the challenging cost-benefit nature of being a professional tennis player. If you hit it big, you will never have to work again in your life. But if you're struggling and ranked in the mid-twenties to -thirties, which is still a really impressive worldwide ranking, it can be very difficult to make it work financially.

❋

"You look like a tipsy jackrabbit out there," Zoltan said to me over dinner one night.

"What?" I had no idea what he was talking about. I'd just lost a disappointing third-round match in Boca Raton, but the press didn't care too much because it was where Jennifer Capriati, the thirteen-year-old American phenom, had just made her professional debut. All eyes were on her. I wasn't the youngest on the tour anymore—not even close.

"You know, jumping all over the place, like this . . ." He got up from the table and performed a perfect imitation of me. From the time I was little, I'd had a silly superstition of not stepping on lines. I have no idea where it came from. I knew I looked ridiculous hopping and walking awkwardly around the lines between points, but I had convinced myself that if I didn't do it I wouldn't win. It was a bad habit. I didn't want it to affect my game or, worse, my head. Zoltan had pointed out the obvious: I did look crazy out there. I asked myself a simple question: Was my superstition adding something positive to my game? Was it really the reason I was winning matches? During the beginning of 1990 my performance had been far from fulfilling, so it was clear that avoiding the lines wasn't adding anything to my winning percentage. If I was serious about being in the top ten (I'd started that year's season at number six but was rapidly losing ground), I had to leave my childhood security blanket behind. In the next tournament in Key Biscayne, I stepped on the lines. I won my first title of the year.

Things happened really fast after that. Labeling me as the "most mentally strong and tenacious player on tour," the media projected that I'd break into the top three by the end of the year. I didn't want to hear about that. I didn't want to think about the numbers. It gave me a headache. I just wanted to play the best tennis possible. A short while after I vowed to break my line superstition, I took another giant step: I left the Academy. You know when you have an uneasy intuition that something is about to go wrong but you don't know how to stop it? My dad and Nick both had big egos, and they were bound to clash. I was too young to grasp exactly what was going wrong—I hated anything involving the business side of tennis—so I just ignored the whole thing, hoping it would go away. It didn't. Shortly before the Italian Open in the spring, we left the Academy. At the end, there was miscommunication, misunderstanding, and a lot of hurt feelings. We'd all reached a breaking point in our relationship and it didn't make sense to stay there anymore.

My time at the Academy was intense. My memories of those years are filled with a lot of tears, a lot of laughs, and a ton of hard work. Nick and his staff had been very supportive, and it had been an incredible place for me to hone my skills in preparation for the tour. After eighteen years I can look back on those times with a big smile on my face. I still see Nick and his wife, Cindi, at tennis events throughout the year. In 2004, they founded Camp Kaizen, a nonprofit fitness and weight-loss camp for teenage girls. They are doing such good work, and I love catching up with them. At seventy-seven, Nick looks as tan and as fit as ever. He still gets up before the sun and works harder than anyone else at the Academy. His intense work ethic has paid off: his record in producing top players is unmatched. A lot has happened since our departure from the Academy, and I will always love Nick and be grateful for the opportunity he gave me.

Our family left Bradenton and found a new place in Sarasota. It was time to get back to basics again. I didn't want to hear about money, endorsements, or how rankings translated into dollars. I was sixteen and I just wanted to play tennis.

Most kids my age were taking driving tests and getting ready for the spring formal. I didn't have time to go joy-riding around town with friends, and dating wasn't even on my radar. Traveling for eleven months of the year ruined any chance that I'd go through the trials and tribulations of puppy love. I was too busy packing up to go on the European swing of the tour: Rome, Berlin, Paris, and then London, with no time to breathe between each city. I'd had a taste of the Grand Slams the year before and I couldn't wait to go back. With my mom and dad as my support team, we flew into Rome, where I had a breakthrough victory in the final against Martina Navratilova. We'd played twice before and I'd fallen to her superb game both times. In Rome it was my turn. I beat her 6–1, 6–1 and felt infused with the confidence it takes to win a Grand Slam. I belonged there just as much as every other player. With that win, Rome made a deep imprint on my heart. My dad and I worked out every day near the Tiber River, and I was primed for Paris. This time I was ready.

I beat Jennifer Capriati in the semifinal 6–2, 6–2, and faced Steffi in the final. Winning my first Grand Slam came down to what was going on between my ears. If I believed I could beat her, I would. Rome had made me feel invincible, and I walked into Roland Garros a far different person than I'd been the year before. And the climate in the locker room was changing. A new generation was taking over. Chris Evert had retired and was commentating for NBC; Martina had skipped Paris to prepare for Wimbledon; and Arantxa Sánchez-Vicario, Jennifer, and I, all still teenagers, were proving to be the forces to be reckoned with. In two years tennis had become a whole new game. Riding the energy of the new guard, I thought I had a chance in the final.

First things first: To feel good, I thought, you have to look good. I was feeling mighty cute in my pink and purple Fila outfit. Remember when no ensemble was complete without color-coordinated scrunchies? Of course, one wasn't enough for me, so I layered a purple one on top of a pink one in my ponytail. I shudder when I look at those pictures now, but back then I thought I looked great. I went out ready for battle. After I lunged forward with a 3–0 lead in the first set, a rain delay was called. Rain delays are dreaded when you are winning, and hoped for when you are losing. When we returned to the court, Steffi came back to tie it up. She had taken advantage of the delay and completely regrouped. We went back and forth until it was tiebreaker time. I was still unproven on the Grand Slam scale, so it was important that I close out the first set. I had to assert my power early. If I blew this one, I'd have little chance of beating her two sets in a row. Seven is a lucky number when it comes to tiebreakers, and I had to beat Steffi to it. I focused all of my attention on placing the ball in the farthest angles of the court, keeping her running from side to side—and I did it. I owned the first set and the momentum was in my corner. I didn't want to lose it. I won the next set 6–4 and, with the cloudy sky turning more ominous by the second, hoisted my first Grand Slam trophy above my head.

That night we went out to celebrate, Parisian style. My family and a few friends indulged in a decadent meal at the Ritz Paris. Mark McCormack, the head of IMG, was there to join in the celebration. In fact, our whole group was made up of adults, with me being the youngest by far. Living in the vacuum of being a tennis prodigy had a strange effect on me. While I was still emotionally a few years behind my peers, I had no problem relating to adults. It was like I skipped over adolescence and never learned how to relate to people my own age. I was a kid caught up in an adult world, but I never had a smooth transition between the two. Constantly jumping back and forth between them, I had little time to digest what my life had become and who I was becoming as a person. I was making a lot of money, giving interviews, hanging out with high-powered people much older than I was, and going to fancy restaurants; but I still lived at home with my parents, still had to do chores, and still liked to watch cartoons in the morning. It was a strange universe I was living in.

Mark's wife, Betsy, also a player on the tour, couldn't make the dinner because she had already left London for another tournament in Birmingham: the engine that drives the professional tour never lets up. My agent from IMG, Stephanie Tolleson, was there. I'd first met her when I was ten years old, and scouts were coming to tournaments in Europe to check me out. The business side of tennis starts early. James La Vea, a close family friend, joined us, as did Virginia Ruzici, another family friend and former tennis player who had won the French Open in 1978. The night could not have gotten any better. Well, maybe a little. Johnny Carson and his wife, Alexis, good friends of the McCormacks', celebrated with us too. It was a dream dinner. Mr. Carson, who loved tennis even more than I did, was charming and funny. He kept the table in stitches all night long. At the end of the night he asked me to be on his show. I couldn't believe it. I was a huge fan! My life was definitely changing. Two months later, a few weeks before the U.S. Open, I flew to Los Angeles to tape the show. My blond hair was bigger than ever, and my nervous giggling took up most of the segment. It was so much fun. Mr. Carson was a true entertainer and a true gentleman.

There were many celebratory toasts that night at the Ritz, and we were all a bit punch-drunk from the stress of the previous two weeks. I was decked out in a hot-pink vintage designer dress with silver trim. I'd found it in a little boutique in New Orleans and I added long dangly earrings to complete the look. It's one of the only outfits from my early playing days that I don't look back at and wonder what the heck I was thinking. On the outside, surrounded by such accomplished and sophisticated adults, I felt older and more experienced than my sixteen years, but on the inside I was jumping up and down and giggling my head off with glee. I'd just accomplished one of my dreams and I was ravenous from the effort. I cleaned every plate that was brought out to me over the five mouthwatering courses and couldn't make up my mind when it came time for dessert:

everything looked so good, and choosing just one was nearly impossible. I chose two, the crème brûlée and apple tarte tatin with crème fraîche. They even brought out a specially made cake with *Congratulations, Monica!* beautifully written across the top. A mini tennis racket poked out of the icing, and I held on to it for the rest of the night. Nearly two decades later I can't remember the scores of my Grand Slam matches, but I remember the meals in Europe in vivid detail. After I inhaled both of my desserts, someone said, "You really eat like a horse, don't you?" I just smiled, nodded my head, and reached over for a bite of my dad's warm chocolate cake. My size two dress was roomy, and the thought of ever not being able to eat anything I wanted was laughable. Of course I ate like a horse: I was an athlete! When I think about that dinner, it's hard for me to go back to being in that mind-set: to not worry about calories, to not give what I was eating a second thought, to not feel guilty after devouring two desserts, to not care what people thought about my eating habits. It's like I was a different person.

# – 11 –

## Reaching the Top

Being sixteen was sweeter than I ever could have expected. My first Grand Slam win and a record-breaking four-hour, five-set match against Gabriela Sabatini at the season-ending championships in New York City capped off my year. It's the only tournament that uses the five-set format for the women, and the sport hadn't seen a match that long in ninety years. I was mentally and physically destroyed at the end, but I won the title and our duel was named one of the greatest matches of the Open era. With that end-of-the-year title, my new name seemed to be "Monica Seles, the youngest player ever to win (fill in the blank)." The French Open, a Grand Slam, the Virginia Slims championship—I'd won every single one at a record-setting age. I don't know if that was a good thing. When you accomplish so much before you can legally vote, where is there to go? At sixteen, I still had a whole career ahead of me, but I'd already accomplished something that players spend decades trying to achieve. I didn't have time to think about the greater picture of my early success, because a few weeks after the championships in Madison Square Garden it was time to pack up again.

It had been just under two years since I'd turned pro, and I had packing down to a science. One suitcase was filled with my tennis gear and the other was filled with my clothes. I divided the clothing bag up into sections. At the start of the trip, three quarters was filled with tennis and workout clothes and one quarter was filled with cute clothes. By the end of the trip it would turn into a mountain of chaos: clothes that needed washing, souvenirs I'd bought in new cities, stuffed animals and trinkets from fans; I'd have to sit on my suitcase and fight with the zipper to force it to close. Every tournament has cocktail parties and sponsor dinners that players are obligated to attend, so the trick was to find clothes that would stand up under the pressure of international travel and several rounds of unpacking and repacking. I rolled everything—shirts, jeans, dresses, shorts, underwear, skirts—to maximize space and keep everything unwrinkled; I crammed all of my socks and a few pieces of cheap jewelry into my shoes; I picked dark colors that would survive a few wearings (hotel laundry service is shockingly expensive, and finding a local laundromat in a new city when you are desperate for one is nearly impossible). The best tip I picked up along the way was to pack my pajamas and toothbrush at the top of my bag, so if we checked into a hotel late at night, I didn't have to go rooting around my luggage in search of them. I didn't start wearing makeup until I was eighteen, so my toiletry kit was light: just a few bottles of anti-frizz shampoo, conditioner, gel, and hairspray to keep my fluffy hair under control.

Right after the five-setter against Gaby, I turned seventeen. I spent my precious two weeks off at our condo in Florida and my whole family sat down to collect itself. The year had been filled with nonstop travel, press coverage, and sponsor demands. We had started the year in Chicago, then went to Washington, Boca Raton, Key Biscayne, San Antonio, and Tampa. We got home, packed some more bags, and flew over the Atlantic for the European swing: Rome, Berlin, Paris, and London. As soon as I arrived back in the States, I was off to the other side of the country to play in Los Angeles, then boomeranged back to New York for the U.S. Open. That was followed by a long plane ride to Tokyo, a stop in Oakland on my way back, and a final stop in New York for the season-ending championships. I'd become a frequent flyer whose miles could rival any international diplomat's. I also shot a few of my first magazine layouts. At the first one, Sonia Kashuk, the legendary makeup artist, worked on me. I didn't wear makeup in my regular life yet, but I knew she was a master so I paid careful attention for future reference. The stylists and makeup artists did a great job, but I was so young: trying to make me look older had the opposite effect. When I look back at those photos, I don't look like a glamorous woman; I look like a child playing dress-up. I was not a mature teenager and I didn't have the first clue about how to handle myself in the cyclone of fame and success that was swirling around me. I just hung on and went along for the ride. "Yes . . . yes . . . yes," I said to everything that was asked of me. If my family hadn't been with me, that first full year on the tour could have been a disaster.

The middle of December is the only time during the year that players have two weeks in a row off. It is just enough time to empty your suitcases, do your laundry, and catch up on paying your bills. As soon as you start to catch your breath, it's time to start packing again. We spent Christmas Day on a plane heading for Australia. It was the best time of the year to fly, and since we had always celebrated the holiday on January 1 in Yugoslavia, I didn't feel as though I was missing out on anything. I love Christmastime— the decorations, lights, and trees are fanciful and fun—but I don't have a sentimental attachment to it. At that point in my life, a half-empty plane was the best gift I could have wished for. It was my first trip Down Under and I was just as excited to see a koala bear as I was to play in the Australian Open.

Within the first hour of landing in Melbourne I knew it would be my home away from home. Fantastic people, beautiful weather, and the laid-back energy of the culture calmed my nerves. I lost only twelve games in the first five rounds and faced a tough battle against Mary Joe Fernandez in the semi. The last two times we'd met on the court I'd beaten her in two sets, but she wasn't going down easily this time. In the second set my game fell apart and she took it 6–0. Our third set went back and forth like a seesaw and we played until 9–7. I was exhausted but I was on my way to the final. Years later Mary Joe would become one of my best friends and

I'd dread playing against her. If we'd been friends back then, I don't know whether I would have been able to summon the gritty focus it takes to win a set that close. Jana Novotna, a gifted doubles player from the Czech Republic, was waiting to play me in the final. She was five years older and had beaten me in two sets at an indoor tournament during my first year as a pro, but I had an advantage now. This was her first Grand Slam singles final and I'd already won in Paris. In a monumental event like a Grand Slam final, if you don't have confidence, you don't have anything. I'd already been on the court in a final and prevailed. I knew I could do it.

I was furious with myself when she took the first set 7–5. My mind started to slide down the canyon of negative thoughts, but I stopped it before it was too late. *Just play each point*—my dad's words came back to me at full volume. I won the next set 6–3 and, with the momentum on my side, took control of the rhythm and didn't let up until I won the third set 6–1. I'd done it. I won my second Grand Slam title under the unforgiving Australian sun. In front of the boisterously supportive local fans and playing on 130-degree hard courts, I proved that I was more than just a clay specialist. I was more than a one-hit wonder, and with that win I was within striking distance of being number one, a position Steffi Graf had held for the past three and a half years. Two months after Australia the points were tallied and I became the top-ranked female player in the world.

Tennis is different from other sports in the way the number one spot is determined. The ranking system is based on an intricate mathematical equation that gives varying points to players for their performances in tournaments. The harder the tournament, the more points it is worth. Tier I events and Grand Slams are worth the most and the points decrease down to Tier IV events. Having a good showing in one Grand Slam can be worth more than winning a handful of tournaments with fewer points. All season long the rankings are changing and your schedule has to be carefully planned out in order to maximize your potential for points.

By the beginning of March it was just a matter of time before I moved into the number one spot. I was at a tournament in Palm Springs and, according to the ranking calculation, if I beat a top-five player in the finals, I'd net enough new points to move up to the top of the tennis world. If I didn't pull off a strong finish, I'd have to wait until the new calculations came in the following week. Steffi had lost to Gaby at a tournament in Boca Raton, but her points hadn't been affected yet.

I headed to Palm Springs with my parents and Astro, my loyal sidekick, who went with me everywhere. He was a tiny Yorkshire terrier who had joined our family the year before. Ever since I was a little girl I had begged my dad to get me a dog. "No, Monica, absolutely not" was his usual response. I even tried to bargain: "If I play well in the twelve-and-under tournament, can I get a dog?" The answer was always the same. No. Our apartment in Novi Sad was just big enough for our family, and my dad was intractable on the pet front. My whole family knew about my mission to get a dog, and every year for my birthday my grandmother fueled my obsession by baking me a delectable sugar-filled pastry in the shape of a dog. Sugar and dogs, my two favorite things in the whole world. It was a special treat that was made only on birthdays, and I couldn't wait for the next 364 days to go by so I could get another one. After my parents moved to Florida to be with me, the begging resumed at its usual intensity. Finally my dad relented: "Okay, you can get a dog," he said, "but if you get it, you must promise to take care of it by yourself."

"Absolutely," I agreed.

"And another thing," he added. "Under no circumstances is the dog allowed into any of the bedrooms."

"Got it," I promised, already jumping up and down.

The next day I ran to the corner store to pick up a copy of the *Bradenton Herald*, our local weekly paper. I tore it open to the classifieds, where I found a listing for the dog that I knew had to be mine. I named him after the big, goofy mutt from my second-favorite cartoon, *The Jetsons*. Back in Yugoslavia we only got *Tom and Jerry*, so moving to Florida was like cartoon nirvana for me. I got to know the Jetson and Flintstone families as if they were my own. Even though my Astro never perfected barking "Ruh-roh!" like his namesake, it only took a week before my dad fell under his cuteness spell. A few days later I saw Astro curled up at the foot of my parents' bed. My dad didn't say a word. The no-dogs-in-the-bedroom rule was quickly forgotten, and Astro started coming to all the tournaments with us. The little ball of fluff sat in the player's box with my parents and never once made a peep. I was excited to take him to Palm Springs: I'd never been there before, but I was sure my four-legged best friend was going to love it.

On the day before my first match, Astro was attacked by another dog. My mom had taken him on a walk and a big dog came out of nowhere, charged him, and threw his little body up into the air. He was huddled in a ball and I could barely feel him breathing. I started frantically petting him and calling his name, trying to get him to respond. Nothing. We found a local vet who did the best that he could, but over the next two days Astro got worse. Stitches and painkillers weren't enough. I was cuddling him in the middle of the night when he started shaking. I knew something was horribly wrong, so I woke my parents up and we drove to an all-night clinic. The vet confirmed my fear: an infection was ravaging his tiny body and there was a chance he would die. I hated leaving him there alone, but there was nothing I could do. I had a tournament to play and I didn't have a veterinary degree, so I gave him a kiss on his silky head and reluctantly left the examining room. Rain delays had forced the tournament organizers to cram the entire event into two days. I needed all of my concentration to get through four matches that quickly, but my mind was still with Astro at the vet clinic. Through force of will I got through the first three matches, but the final wouldn't be as easy: I was pitted against Martina Navratilova. We'd played each other six times before and our record was tied at 3–3. There wasn't a doubt in my mind that she wanted to tilt that stat in her direction.

I practically handed the first set over to her: I only won two games. Midway through the second set I woke up and my competitive side kicked in, but it was too late. She beat me 7–6 and I knew that becoming number one wasn't going to happen that day. When the match was over, we went straight to the vet to check on Astro. As we stood in the waiting room I shoved my hands into my pockets and tightly crossed my fingers. When the veterinarian came out, I crossed them even tighter as I held my breath, waiting for the news.

"He had a nasty infection but he's going to be fine," he said. "That's one tough little fighter you've got there." I let out a squeal of relieved joy. An assistant came out holding Astro. I ran over and gently scooped him into my arms. I held on to him for the whole ride back to the hotel, kept him by my side as I packed up my suitcase, cuddled him on the way to the airport, and snuck him up onto my lap during the flight home. Having to wait an extra week to be number one was the furthest thing from my mind.

# – 12 –

## Ego Check

A week later it happened. The latest tournament points were calculated and I was officially number one. Within an hour of the announcement, the interview requests increased tenfold. At seventeen years
and three months, I was the youngest number one in the history of tennis
and every reporter wanted to know the same thing: What did it feel like?
I never knew how to answer that question without disappointing them.
The truth was it felt the same as it did when I was ranked sixth, third, and
second. Nothing tangible had changed, and when I looked in the mirror I
looked exactly the same. It was like when, on your birthday, people ask
you if you feel different. No, not at all. Just the same old me. Reaching
number one was something on paper. It didn't change my tennis, but it
changed how busy my agent was. Stephanie was fielding calls from sponsors who hadn't given me the time of day when I was climbing my way up
to the top ten. When I hit number one, I landed my first big endorsement
contract with Matrix, the hair company.

In the early nineties it was unusual for an athlete to be featured in a
beauty campaign. Male athletes were in shaving commercials, but female
athletes were never on TV or in magazines selling makeup or hair products. The era of female athletes being viewed as sexy was still a long way

off, so it was a coup for me to land that contract. There was a catch: I had to cut my hair. I'd cut my hair once when we lived in Novi Sad and I'd hated it. I remember sitting in my bathroom in our apartment, grabbing two-inch-long sections of hair and pulling on them, hoping to speed up the growing-out process. It hurt a lot, and it didn't help.

But business was business and I had to live up to my side of the bargain. Arriving in Europe with a fresh new look would be great publicity for Matrix, so I flew to Manhattan to meet with the company representatives and they took me to a chic salon on Madison Avenue for the big chop. My hair was in a ponytail, and as I took a deep breath the stylist took a pair of supersize scissors and chopped it all off. She spent the next hour shaping and styling it, but when I looked in the mirror, only one thought raced through my mind: *What did I just do?* My hair looked like a yellow mushroom sprouting out of my head. It wasn't the stylist's fault: My hair was thick and curly with a mind of its own. It refuses to be tamed and is even more unruly when short. It was going to take a long time and a lot of hair products to get through the growing-out process.

I went back to Florida, loaded up on hats and headbands, packed my bags for Europe, and got on a plane. Interview requests came flooding in every day, and there was a lot of hype surrounding my arrival. I'd be arriving in Paris as the reigning number one, with the enormous expectations that entails. I'd reached the pinnacle of the tennis world, but I was afraid to look around to enjoy it. It had been much easier working my way up from the sixth spot. When you're playing opponents ranked higher, you've got nothing to lose. Now, playing as the number one, I had something to lose in every single match. "Don't think about the number, just think about the game" became another of my dad's favorite refrains and a nonstop mantra in my own head. I warmed up in Hamburg and Rome and I arrived in Paris primed to defend my French Open title. I sailed through to the semifinal against Gaby Sabatini, who had just beaten me in front of an ecstatic crowd in Rome. I didn't want to lose to her a second time on European soil. I won the match 6–4, 6–1 and next faced Arantxa, who had just taken out Steffi, in the final. After two sets of pounding the ball as hard as I could, I emerged the champion. I didn't think anything could top the feeling I had the first time I lifted that trophy above my head at Roland Garros, but I was wrong: it felt even better the second time. I'd proved I was there to stay.

Or not. Excruciating shin splints destroyed my chance of going to Wimbledon. I had to pull out of the tournament at the last second. The London tabloids went crazy with that one. Rumors were flying around that I was pregnant: a particularly clever headline screamed *Wimblemum!* Putting any pressure on my foot sent excruciating pain up my leg, so I needed help from the best to get me back into playing shape. Once the media hurricane died down, I was able to rehab without dodging paparazzi. I took refuge in Vail at the Steadman Hawkins Clinic, the best place to go for treating orthopedic injuries. Dr. Steadman and Dr. Hawkins are the best in the world. I spent three weeks focusing on getting my shin splints under control—they posed a danger of leading to leg fractures, and if that happened I wouldn't be back in the game for months. After tons of therapy, the pain began to lessen and I was ready to go home.

I'd healed my legs in Vail, but there was another ailment that had been plaguing me all year. In between fashion magazine shoots, high-paying endorsement deals (I'd recently switched my racket from Prince to Yonex), and shooting commercials, I'd developed a nasty case of rapidly swelling ego. Fame and fortune in a seventeen-year-old's life can easily result in unbearably obnoxious behavior and a grandiose belief in her own importance. My case was no exception. Although my parents had done a phenomenal job of keeping my feet on the ground, their down-to-earth approach to life couldn't compete with the glitz and glamour I was sur-. rounded with every day. It was impossible to keep my tennis blinders on forever: I went from being a kid to being a celebrity in the world of adults. In the early nineties the WTA and the ATP (Association of Tennis Professionals) were making a big push to add Hollywood flair to tennis. Charity tournaments loaded with top players and famous people were popping up all over the world. When I jetted to Monte Carlo earlier in the year, I met Prince Albert and played with Pierce Brosnan and Regis Philbin, two hard-core tennis fans. Regis passed me at the net once—just once—and to this day he's never let me forget it. "I got you!" he still yells every time we see each other. He also gave himself the nickname "Net Man." I think he may be even more competitive than I am.

I loved meeting people from Hollywood, but I was never starstruck. The time I beat Chris Evert, I had the blessing of being young and naïve. Why couldn't I beat her? I hadn't yet built up a lifetime of insecurities and self-doubt. I was nervous, but I didn't question the possibility that I just might have a chance. It doesn't seem fair that the older we get, the more we become used to disappointment. Through tennis I met a slew of celebrities, and they always seemed like normal people. Because of tennis, I wasn't able to spend hours watching stars on television or on a movie screen, so they didn't seem bigger than life when I met them in person. Except for their whiter teeth and better clothes, they were like everyone else (except for Princess Di at Wimbledon: I really was starstruck by her).

But living in a world where everyone was successful and everyone had a lot of money bred some bad habits in me. I started becoming used to getting what I wanted when I wanted it. After my rehab in Vail, I went to New Jersey to play in an exhibition. Before the match I heard one of the promoters saying that Guns N' Roses was playing at the Meadowlands. *Appetite for Destruction* was on heavy rotation in my Walkman, and I was counting down the days until the *Use Your Illusion* double album was released. I didn't have tickets, but there was no way I was going to miss the show.

Stephanie couldn't come to New Jersey, so she'd sent Tony Godsick, her intern, to take care of me. Now he's one of the top agents in tennis, with Roger Federer, Tommy Haas, Anna Kournikova, and Lindsay Davenport on his list of clients, but back then he was a football player from Dartmouth who was brand new to the tennis scene. Right before my match I called him over.

"Hey, Tony, Guns N' Roses is playing tonight and I really want to go. Get a few tickets and we'll take off after my match."

"Tickets? Concert tickets?" he asked. He looked like a deer taken by surprise on a busy highway.

"Yeah, I'm dying to see them! I'll be ready by nine tonight."

The thought that I couldn't get those tickets hadn't even crossed my mind. I worked my butt off in tennis and I'd just been featured on the cover of *Forbes* magazine for being one of the top-earning athletes in the world. Why shouldn't I be able to do whatever I wanted in the little free time I had? I deserved it, didn't I? I had developed a raging case of entitlement and I was becoming more spoiled by the second. My parents weren't with me, so there was nobody to stop me. I don't know how he did it, but Tony got us front-row tickets and backstage passes. After the exhibition, my brother, Tony, and I jumped in a rental car and cruised half an hour south, blasting Guns N' Roses on the cassette player. I was seventeen and on my way to see the biggest band in the world. Life was good.

From the opening strains of "Welcome to the Jungle" to the last notes of "Paradise City," I was on my feet dancing and bopping my short bleached-blond hair up and down. I felt very rock 'n' roll cool. After the show we hung out backstage with the band, and it was not a disappointment—it was just as crazy as I'd thought it would be. Stephanie Seymour was dating Axl Rose, so she was there with her crew of knockout supermodel friends, including Elle Macpherson. They looked just as stunning as they did in the pages of *Vogue*. Gorgeous girls in tiny spandex dresses filled the room, bottles of Jack Daniel's were being passed around like water, and people were jumping up on tables to dance and knocking over anything in their way. It was wild by any standards, but especially compared to my usual nights at home with Astro. I'd been kept in a bubble for most of my life, but I was suddenly filled with a sense of urgency that I had to make up for lost time. It was like I was regressing. I'd gone from a child to an adult with my first Grand Slam win, and now I was searching for my lost adolescence.

The scene was a little intimidating, but I tried to come across as a backstage veteran. Axl couldn't have been nicer to me. He was a major tennis fan, which surprised me. I've learned over the years that you can never, ever predict who is a tennis addict. He loved the game and he wanted to talk strategy all night long. Stunning leggy girls kept prancing around him like lost baby giraffes, but he was completely focused on our conversation. I remember thinking, *Why is he paying so much attention to me?* I couldn't understand it. Some of the world's most beautiful women were standing an arm's length away, but he wanted to talk to me?

I looked at my watch and had a mini panic attack that it was already three in the morning. If I left that second I wouldn't get back to the hotel until four o'clock, six hours past my usual bedtime. I had a one o'clock exhibition match the next day and there was no way I'd be able to play without any sleep. *Oh, who cares?* I thought. *It's just one night. I'm seventeen! I'm allowed to have fun every once in a while.* But I couldn't get over the nagging feeling that I was doing something wrong, and to be completely honest, I don't know how much of that night was actually fun and how much of it I convinced myself was fun, because, hey, I was out with the biggest rock stars in the world. Why wouldn't I be having the time of my life? I remember looking at the entourage: they were all partying without a care in the world. I wondered why I didn't feel the same.

My worker bee side kicked in and I made an executive decision: we had to leave. I said good-bye to Axl and herded Tony and my brother out. I'm sure they would have been perfectly happy to stay there. The ratio of models to mortals was better than a Victoria's Secret fashion show. I finally fell into bed and got three hours of sleep. I felt like I'd been run over by a freight train in the morning. I dragged myself through an early hitting session and, even though I ended up winning the tournament, I played far below my usual level. But I hadn't learned my lesson yet. I was determined to put some non-tennis-related fun into my life, and it was a mission I was taking seriously. Feeling awful during my match wasn't enough to prevent me from doing it again.

When Zoltan and I got back to Florida, I told my dad I wanted to start traveling alone. Without my family. He hadn't come to New Jersey because it was just an exhibition, but he and my mom had been planning on coming with me on the West Coast swing through July and August. I was convinced I didn't need a coach anymore; I knew everything there was to know about tennis. And I didn't need my family to take care of me: I was a globe-trotting seventeen-year-old who could take care of herself. The only thing I'd have to do is add a hitting partner, but I'd just pick up whatever local pro was available at the tournament site. It would be easy enough. My dad didn't object; he told me to do what I thought I needed to do. No matter what I decided, he said he'd be supporting me, even if it were by watching my matches on our television at home.

I decided to go it alone. The first stop was San Diego, where I took my new freedom out for a test drive by sleeping in and booking late-morning hitting times. It's a bad habit to get into, because that's when the courts are the busiest. It's difficult to clear your mind in preparation for that day's match when you are surrounded by other players and fans. The energy starts to build too early and it can harm your game. Tony found a local guy to be my hitting partner, and unlike when I was with my dad and brother, he let me take the lead and I had some of the slowest, laziest warm-ups of my life. I wasn't hustling, I wasn't pushing myself. I was settling for the bare minimum.

My laissez-faire preparation didn't affect me until the final, where I faced Jennifer Capriati. The first time we played each other I beat her in two sets; the second time it took three. This time she was ready for it to be her turn. I took the first set 6–4 but she came firing right back and grabbed the second 6–1. The never-say-die grit that was usually raging in me by the third set was failing me. I kept up with her, but my usual skill and stamina had disappeared. She won the third set 7–6 and I left the court angry with myself. If I'd failed to close a match like that in the past, I would've gone straight to a warm-up court and hit for at least another hour. This time, I went back to my hotel and sulked. Then I stayed up half the night watching movies and was even more beat down the next morning.

The next stop was Los Angeles, where I'd heard Prince was playing. Tony was still on the road with me and he got us tickets right away: he was a quick study. I got through my first three matches without a problem and went to the Prince concert thinking I had nothing to worry about. I could get up late, hit around when I felt like it, and still be number one.

The concert was amazing and backstage it was the polar opposite of Axl's scene. It was like walking into a yoga studio. A zen vibe filled the air and there wasn't a bottle of Jack Daniel's anywhere. It wasn't as crazy a night but I still got home late—a big mistake when you're facing Arantxa Sánchez-Vicario in the semifinal.

Arantxa was ready to fight for every point the moment the match began. We took turns claiming games and kept each other running from side to side on the baseline during the first set until she took it 7–6. I hate losing a set like that. When you are that close and you don't aggressively shut down your opponent, it's like throwing the set away. I was mad and I used my anger to rip the ball over and over until I tied up the match with a 6–4 victory in the second. *Just one more,* I thought. I was tired and I could feel my legs dragging more than usual. I knew the reason: keeping odd hours was starting to catch up with me, and now I had to beat one of the best players in the game. I gathered all of my frustration and channeled it right onto a tiny patch of green felt in the middle of the ball. *Whack! Whack!* over and over until I pulled out another 6–4 score. It took so much out of me that for a second I would have sworn it had been the final. Then I remembered I wasn't finished yet: I had one more to go.

The final was against Kimiko Date, a Japanese player with an attacking game. I didn't know much about her style except that she liked to come to the net. My game was an attacking one, too, so I was going to have to assert my power early and often to take control of the match. I got a lot of sleep the night before and my body thanked me by carrying me to an uneventful 6–3, 6–1 victory. Right there, as I was being presented with a trophy, I decided that if I was going to be a tennis player, then I was going to be a tennis player 100 percent of the time, not 50 percent tennis player, 50 percent celebrity. There was a difference between being famous and being a celebrity; I'd just never realized it before. I could be on the cover of magazines, spend hours signing merchandise for fans, and star in commercials, but I didn't have to play the rest of the fame game. For a short time I'd been caught up in what I thought I had to do in order to act the part, to be the cool celebrity who plays tennis. But that wasn't who I really was. I was a tennis player who just happened to be famous because she won matches. Being a celebrity wasn't mandatory. All of the extra fuss and glamour was a side dish, an afterthought, not the main course in my life. It was my first lesson in feeling comfortable in my own skin and learning to claim my decisions as my own. I didn't need to apologize for being the girl who went to bed early and liked to spend her free time with her dog!

After the match, I called my dad up in Florida and told him I needed him. I needed both of my parents with me. There was no way I could be the player I wanted to be if I was alone. Like when I was thirteen years old and miserable at the Academy, I knew with total conviction that the only way I'd be okay was if I had the comfort and strength of my family back in my life.

"Are you sure?" my dad asked. I think he'd known this call would be coming, but he also knew that I'd have to reach the decision on my own.

"Yes, I'm positive. Can you come to the U.S. Open?"

"I'll be there," he told me.

Three weeks later we were all in New York together. I was back on my normal eating, practicing, and sleeping schedule and I was focused on the tournament and nothing else. I didn't even look at the paper to see which bands would be playing at Madison Square Garden during our stay.

I love the U.S. Open. The New York fans can't be beat and no other Grand Slam gets as rowdy. At Wimbledon there is total silence, but at the U.S. Open fans will scream your name in the middle of a serve. I thrive on that kind of energy. The flow of tennis was back in my life and I jumped out of bed every morning with a newfound motivation. Tennis was what I wanted to do. It was the only thing I wanted to do.

I got to the semi without any problem, where I met Jennifer for another long, drawn-out three-set match. They were becoming our trademark. We were both power players and we shared the same hatred of losing. It was just a matter of who hated it more on any given match day. Back and forth we went, both of us hugging the baseline, each of us putting her entire body into pushing the ball's power to another level. Just when I thought she couldn't hit it any harder, she did. And I'd answer her right back. Some of the points seemed endless, and I could tell from the astonished gasps from the spectators that this wasn't like most matches. We were playing a new kind of tennis and the crowd loved it.

We each took a set 6–3 and each went into the third determined to come out as the victor. The fans were on the edge of their seats and yelling for Jennifer, America's tennis sweetheart, as loudly as they could. But I was in the zone. *Don't let this get away from you. Stay in control.* Jennifer served for the match two times but couldn't capitalize on it. I was ready to pounce. I won the next two games and we were tied 6–6 in the third set of a U.S. Open semifinal. The pressure was cranked up. It was time for a tiebreaker and the race to reach the lucky number seven was on. The match could have gone either way. It went mine. I held my serve and raced to reach seven points. The crowd went crazy and Jennifer looked crushed. It had been an intense battle of wills and we were both used up. I don't know that I could've played another point. It was time to go back to the hotel and rest for my final against Martina.

I chose a pink and white Fila ensemble for the big day—tame by U.S. Open standards. It is the most lenient of the Grand Slams when it comes to the players' outfits. Some of Andre Agassi's craziest getups were debuted there. My hair was growing at a torturously slow pace, so I piled on the hairspray, hoping it wouldn't double in size once I started running and sweating all over the court. Curly hair doesn't react well to moisture. I was focused on tennis, but I was still a girl and I didn't want to look ugly out there.

The first set felt like a continuation of my last set against Jennifer. We traded points back and forth until we were tied 6–6. I had to stop myself from obsessing on being the first to get to seven. Instead I played my dad's voice in my head: *Play every point as it comes.* It was just what I needed to hear: I won the tiebreaker 7–1. My quick tiebreaking victory did a number on Martina's confidence, even though we'd been tied at 6–6, and I took the second set 6–1.

Here's a quick breakdown of how you can fall apart the moment you lose one game: If you don't have games on your side, you don't have momentum. If you don't have momentum on your side, you've got to dig deep to come up with some confidence. If you can't find the confidence, fake it. If you can't fake it, it's over.

My victory in New York gave me my fourth Grand Slam, my third that year. I was so thrilled after the last point that I forgot about looking cool and I pranced around the court like a pony.

# – 13 –

## *In the Zone*

My Grand Slam triplet in 1991 had given me the confidence to walk into the players' locker room with my head held high and it forced the other players to respect that I was going to stay a while. At the beginning of the year, I made my annual trek to the National Tennis Center in Melbourne. My family rented a house near the stadium and I rode my bike to the tournament every day.

At most tournaments, almost all players stay in a designated hotel. But I've always preferred staying somewhere else, away from the commotion of the players' headquarters. It helps me get centered and stay focused on the task ahead of me. If I run into an opponent in the elevator and get caught up in tour gossip in the lobby, my mind starts to drift away from the singular purpose of playing solid tennis. I loved staying in our rented house and I stayed calm throughout the entire tournament. I cruised to the semi, where I beat Arantxa 6–2, 6–2 and then won my second Australian Open title after beating Mary Joe 6–2, 6–3 in the final. The crowd's applause was overwhelming, and I was smiling so widely my cheeks began to feel numb. The year was off to a great start and I was still solidly in the number one slot.

In the spring I made a stop on the beautiful northeastern coast of

Spain, where I learned that beating a Spaniard (Arantxa) in her home-town (Barcelona) a few months before that city is hosting the Olympics is a tough feat to pull off. The crowd was losing its collective mind and vocal cords trying to pull her to victory. The clay was slow and every point seemed interminable. I had to go deep into my head for this one. *Block them out. You aren't hearing thousands of people against you: that's just the roar of the ocean nearby.* I managed to pull off a victory in three very hard-fought sets. It was my twenty-fifth title, which set off a whole new round of "youngest-to-ever-win" chatter. I'd had a break from that pressure after Jennifer Capriati, who was three years my junior, made a big impression at Wimbledon and the U.S. Open the year before. I loved not having the "youngest" label hanging over me.

On that trip to Barcelona I also ate my weight in seafood—it's impossi-ble not to—and realized that I had a love of architecture that had been lying dormant deep inside me. The first time I laid eyes on a building de-signed by Antoni Gaudí, I thought I was hallucinating—it was the most gorgeous, surreal, bizarrely beautiful thing I'd ever seen. I couldn't believe something like that existed. It was as if the elaborate drip sand castles I used to make during our family vacations by the sea had come to life. That day I found an English bookstore, bought a book on Gaudi, and devoured every word of it by the time I arrived in Paris.

I was going for my third straight title within the storied Roland Garros Stadium. I'd figured out how to balance my playing duties (win) with my sponsor responsibilities (be available and grateful) with my media obliga-tions (be punctual and straightforward). I was doing everything exactly as I was told, when I was supposed to do it and to the best of my ability. Every day. I was bound to have a little freakout. It came in the form of a bottle of hair dye. Before setting foot on the court for my first match, I embraced my rebellious, bad-girl side and dyed my hair jet-black. Just when my short haircut was finally starting to look presentable, I had to sabotage its progress. In the grand scheme of the drunk-driving arrests, drug rehabs, bar fights, and scandalous videos that define the celeb land-scape today, I know that dyeing my hair wasn't a big deal. But the sponsors and media went ballistic because of all of the interviews and promotional work I'd done pre-bad-girl hair. My sponsors were not fans of the new look, that's for sure. I felt awful and reshot all of the ads and interviews out of guilt. My little attempt at marking my individuality failed miserably. I wasn't such a badass after all. No matter: I'd leave a lasting impression in Paris by winning a third straight title.

On my way to the fourth round, I dropped only six games. Expecting to reach the semis without too much trouble, I was caught off guard in the fourth round when Akiko Kijimuta, a player I'd beaten 6–2, 6–0 in the first round of the Australian Open, pushed our match to three sets. I'd taken control of the match early and wasn't surprised when I beat her 6–1. But she charged ahead, took the second 6–3, and was up three games in the third. I didn't understand what had just happened. Maybe I'd been too cocky. Maybe I'd taken it for granted that I'd make it to the semis. I had no time to lose. Paris was my turf and I wasn't going home yet. I won the next five games in a row and advanced to the quarterfinal against Jennifer.

Our match was a straightforward two-setter and I won it 6–2, 6–2. Jennifer wasn't her usual self, and I was happy I didn't have to engage in one of our marathon hitting battles. I'd need all my energy to beat Gaby Sabatini in the semi.

The match with Gaby was played under brutal weather conditions. We slugged it out through bone-chilling cold and pelting raindrops on slower-than-usual clay conditions. It was like trying to high-jump in quicksand: each step was more difficult than the last, and no matter how hard I tried, my legs just wouldn't move across the clay like they normally did. We split the first two sets and I'd had enough. I didn't want to be out in the cold anymore. My legs were tired. I was ready for the match to end but I wasn't ready to pack up my bags. I found another gear and closed out the match 6–4. I took an hour-long steaming-hot bath as soon as I got back to the hotel. The cold had reached my bones and I couldn't get rid of it. I was positioned for a center court throw-down against Steffi Graf, so I needed my legs back. The bath did the trick and I felt like my old self by the next morning. The hype around my match against Steffi mounted quickly: we looked to be the prime replacement for the longtime rivalry that Chrissie and Martina had endured for years. And it had been fifty-five years since a woman had won three French Open titles in a row, a statistic I tried to push out of my mind.

I tuned out all the superfluous and zeroed in on the clay surface and what I was about to do on it. In front of sixteen thousand fans and on a turf that over the past three years had gone from being overwhelmingly intimidating to feeling like my home, Steffi and I pushed each other to the limit. In the third set I missed four match points when I was up 5–3, but I refused to let it rattle me into defeat. After nearly three hours, I took the set 10–8. It was named the WTA's Greatest Match of the Open Era. Winning my sixth Grand Slam was beyond anything I had imagined when my dad and I were sitting in the top row of that empty stadium three years earlier. The icing on the cake was being treated to a visit to Chanel's atelier to pick out a dress. I'd been named the Player of the Year for the previous season, and this was a huge perk. All my girlhood fantasies of making outfits for my Barbies and meticulously picking out tennis dress patterns for my aunt to whip up for me were realized as soon as I walked into the shop.

I picked out an elegant black dress and the tailors flitted around me like helpful birds in a Disney film. It fit me perfectly. It's not often that you realize your life is good in the moment it is good. Usually it's months or years later that you are sitting around thinking about the good old days when suddenly you think, *Back then was when life was good. I wish I'd known it so I could have appreciated it*. That spring in Paris was one of the best times of my life. And I was lucky because I knew it.

Wimbledon swiftly took care of that. Perhaps in retribution for not showing up the year before, the media were on hand to flag down the feel-good train I'd been riding throughout the European swing. Critics can kill your spirit if you let them. When I think about it now, it seems obvious that a backlash was bound to happen. I'd shot to the top of tennis at a young age and I'd gone through a brief though high-profile sowing of my wild oats. I wasn't afraid to try new fashions—some were smart, some weren't—and the rumblings about my grunting were getting louder. *People* magazine named me to their "Worst Dressed List," and my grunting provided loads of material for *Saturday Night Live* sketches. I laughed most of it off, but I really needed a tough skin that year.

My harshest critics had an SW-19 postal code (London), came armed with pens and notebooks, and had midnight deadlines. "A face screwed up like a rodent" was among the more flattering descriptions of how I looked when I played. The "Grunt-o-Meter" recorded the decibels of my vocal exertions: apparently I was quite loud. It's hard to believe, but I had no idea I was that loud when I played. None. The first time I saw a tape of myself grunting, I thought it was a joke. That's how in the zone I was. It made a lot of people uncomfortable. Tennis officials, fans, even other players made it an issue, but I didn't know how to stop it. In the quarter-final, Nathalie Tauziat, a player I'd faced several times before, tried to interrupt the rhythm of our game by complaining to the umpire about the noise I was making. I was up one set, we were tied 3–3 in the second, and she'd never mentioned my grunting before, so her complaint was questionable. I finished her off 6–3 with my grunts toned down a few decibels.

The next day nearly every British newspaper had a headline that worked the word "grunt" into it. When I passed the newsstands on my way through Wimbledon Village I tried not to look. When I played Martina in the semi, the grunting drama intensified. We'd played each other a dozen times before and our record was nearly split down the middle. I'd never heard a peep of a complaint from her about the way I played the game or what I sounded like during it. After I won the first set and we were playing a tiebreaker in the second, it all changed. Martina complained to the umpire about the noise and I was asked to quiet down. I did as instructed and she won the tiebreaker 7–3. I didn't want everyone to be angry with me, but I didn't know what to do. It was like trying to change my two-handed forehand: I simply didn't know how to play tennis without those loud exclamations accompanying every swing. In the third set I'd had enough, so I started playing the way I wanted. Martina complained again. I was asked to be quiet again. It was getting ridiculous. Was this how all of my matches were going to go from here on out? I held my breath as best I could and took the set 6–4. I'd be facing Steffi, who was becoming more of a rival every day, in the final.

Right before the postmatch conference, Martina stopped me to apologize. I was more confused than anything else. I grew up watching Jimmy Connors do the same thing, so I didn't understand why it was unacceptable. Were there different rules for the women, like the unequal prize money? Was it a strategic tactic? Did people want to win so badly that they'd pull stunts like that? The competitive side of tennis was an ugly one, and I'd never seen it that bad before. It didn't seem fair but I made the unwise decision to muffle my noise in my final against Steffi. Big mistake: it's one of the only things I've regretted in my life. Our five-and-a-half-hour match was not the result of a close score; it was thanks to the temperamental London skies that forced us to take three rain delays. Even more time to worry about my noise levels as I sat in the locker room, waiting to be called out to resume play. Obsessing over being as quiet as a mouse threw my game off and I lost 6–2, 6–1.

If there's anything positive that came out of the nightmare that unfolded in slow motion on center court that day, it's that I experienced a harsh lesson in people pleasing: Don't do it. I've always struggled with that part of my personality. I hate feeling like I've disappointed someone or done something to upset them. But the danger in being a people pleaser is that you often end up never pleasing the person who matters the most: you. It would take years before this would sink in. Nineteen ninety-two turned out to be my only appearance in a Wimbledon final, and I let it slip right out of my hands so people would like me. It wasn't worth it.

There is a shelf in my house that is devoted to every self-help, motivational, life-improving book I've ever bought. It is a big shelf. And within the pages of every single one there is at least one mention of finding balance, achieving a perfect equilibrium where your personal, professional, physical, emotional, and psychological lives are all working in perfect harmony. When this happens, you are living at your optimal level and anything is possible. In order to make the books marketable and seem full of fresh ideas, publishers give this concept different names, but the general idea of balance runs throughout all of them in some form.

With a renewed focus and a rehabbed ego, I felt like I was getting a little closer to that balance. At the end of 1992 I still didn't have a life outside of tennis, but it didn't matter: everything else was flowing well, and I told myself that as long as those things stayed perfectly positioned I'd be fine. I'd turned eighteen; long gone were the days when I'd be mortified into muteness if another player talked to me in the locker room. I no longer kept my head down, lost in Duran Duran blaring from my headphones. It would have been easy to blow my career. Money and fame were part of my life, and it would have been very tempting to give in to them. But it was hard to get a big head when I still had to do the dishes at home with my family, clean up after the dog, book my own court times, and pick up my own balls during practice. These are tiny things that sound insignificant, but they kept my ego small enough to fit through the door every time I came home from a tournament. When you are on tour, it is high-pressure and high-profile. Without someone around to keep you normal, you are in major danger of becoming a person you wouldn't even recognize. If I hadn't had my family with me, I don't know who I would've become.

My entire focus was on tennis and I was comfortably chugging along on the tour, still holding the number one position, and had just added a seventh Grand Slam to my tally with a 6–3, 6–3 win over Arantxa at the U.S. Open in September. It was the first time in my career that everything seemed okay and under control. My biological age was starting to catch up to the adult world I'd been thrown into four years earlier. My metabolism was starting to leave the hyperkinetic adolescent realm in favor of the slower-paced adult one, and my hips were incontrovertible proof: they no longer looked like a teenage boy's. I started getting curves and the press took notice.

"Monica, are you wearing a different style of dress because your body has changed?" a journalist asked me during a press conference in New York.

"Excuse me?"

"Your backside," he clarified. "It's gotten bigger over the last year." I was caught off guard and very embarrassed. I tried to laugh off the question but he was staring at me, waiting for an answer. My clothes had been feeling tighter, but I didn't know it was that obvious. I deflected the awkward moment by saying that I was getting older and I had to start paying attention to what I ate. I couldn't wait to get away from the reporters and their cameras.

For years I'd been the scrawny and gangly girl, and my image of her was still embedded in my mind. Even though my body had filled out in the last year, I still thought of myself as a skinny waif. I guess I wasn't anymore. *Fine,* I thought, *no problem. I'll just start being more careful about what I put into my body.* I was embarrassed because a stranger had asked me about my butt in public, but I didn't start crying when I got back to my hotel and I didn't feel bad about myself. It is almost impossible for me now to go back inside that head. Food and my body weren't my enemies then: I had no idea what kind of struggle lay ahead of me. At the end of the year I won the season-ending championships for the third time in a row. I knew the key to staying at the top was not to get too comfortable there. I remember telling the press, "I hope this isn't the height of my career. I still have a lot to learn." I meant every word of it.

Never—not in a million years—did I think it would end up being the pinnacle of my playing days.

# − 14 −

## Derailed

I never know how to handle this part. There isn't an easy, antiseptic way to say it. It's something that was so traumatic, shocking, and violent that when I mention it today it's like I'm referring to something that happened to someone else. It can make people uncomfortable because they don't know how to react to it; they don't know what to say to me. There isn't much to say. It's a horrible thing that happened in my life and it irrevocably changed the course of my career and inflicted serious damage to my psyche. A split second of horror fundamentally changed me as a person.

I was stabbed. On the court. In front of ten thousand people. The main thing people want to ask but usually don't is: *Did it hurt?* Yes, it hurt a lot. It was worse than any pain I could have ever imagined. Once I understood what had happened, I went into shock, which is an amazing defense your body puts up to protect you from feeling the gravity of what just happened. The physical pain and the psychological confusion would be too much to process all at once. During the ambulance ride, as I clutched my brother's hand, the shock shielded me from having to handle my world falling apart all at once. That would come later.

Things had been humming right along when the 1993 season opened.

I won my third Australian Open and had the best time hanging out with my family and reconnecting with an old friend in Melbourne. It was nothing short of a revelation: I could be happy on the road. I'd made a New Year's resolution to embrace my last year as a teenager, to try to add fun—even just tiny bits here and there—into my tour schedule. I had grasped the concept of going out for dinner without staying out all night. I was reaching the point of understanding the commitment it would take to remain number one while making enough space in my life for the non-tennis-related outlets that would keep my mind centered and keep tour burnout at bay.

After Australia, I took off for Chicago to play a Virginia Slims tournament, then flew across the Atlantic to Paris to play an indoor tournament. Then I got sick. A relentless travel schedule and too many time and climate changes finally caught up with me. My body shut down and it told my mind, which stubbornly wanted to keep going, who was boss. I couldn't get out of bed without being hit with dizzy spells. I was sleeping sixteen hours a day, and walking to the bathroom was the most physical exercise I could handle. Instead of pushing through and going to tournaments so I wouldn't disappoint the organizers, I decided to say the magic word: *No*. I just couldn't do it, not without risking my health. I needed comfort and a change of scenery, a place where time didn't matter and tournament organizers couldn't get ahold of me. Jamaica was the perfect antidote. In March, Zoltan and I left home to spend two weeks in the sun. I lay on my towel all day long listening to the ocean and feeling the sun's rays warm my skin and repair my spirit. At the end of the trip I felt like a new me.

I'd skipped several tournaments while healing myself—a risky thing to do when leading up to the European spring swing—and I wasn't about to walk into Roland Garros cold. I headed to Germany for a warm-up tournament in Hamburg.

April 30 was a sunny day with a bracing chill in the air. After seven weeks away from tennis, it was my own little comeback. When you are number one, the press watches your every move, since missing just one tournament can affect the rankings. Luckily I had enough points to stay firmly at the top. I breezed through my first few rounds and was ready for my quarterfinal against Magdalena Maleeva on Friday. The youngest of the three Maleeva sisters on tour, I'd beaten her in our only previous match-up. I was up 6–4, 4–3, and we took a break during a changeover. I remember sitting there, toweling off and thinking, *Just two more games. I can close this out quickly and go home to rest.* I leaned forward to take a sip of water; our time was almost up and my mouth was dry. *Drink this down quickly,* I thought.

It's strange how the tiniest thing can have the most tremendous impact on your life. Doctors later told me that if I hadn't bent forward at that precise second, there was a good chance I would have been paralyzed. The cup had barely touched my lips when I felt a horrible pain in my back. Reflexively, my head whipped around toward where it hurt and I saw a man wearing a baseball cap and a vicious sneer across his face. His arms were raised above his head and his hands were clutching a long knife. He started to lunge at me again. I didn't understand what was happening: for a few seconds I sat frozen in my chair as two people tackled him to the ground. He had plunged the knife one and a half inches into my upper left back, millimeters away from my spine. I tumbled out of my chair and staggered a few steps forward before collapsing into the arms of a stranger who had run onto the court to help. My parents had stayed at the hotel that day— my dad hadn't felt well—and I was desperately looking around for someone I knew. Zoltan and Madeleine van Zoelen, a trainer with the tour, were by my side in an instant. I heard people yelling for help, calling for the paramedics. It was chaos. I was in shock but I remember one thought clearly racing around in my head: *Why?*

The hospital stay was a blur of police officers and doctors. I didn't understand a word of German or how bad my injury was. The scene was total mayhem and it was becoming a publicity nightmare for the tournament. On Sunday morning, two days after the stabbing, Steffi came to visit me in the hospital. By then, everyone knew that the attacker was a deranged fan who wanted Steffi back at the top of the rankings. Our conversation lasted just a few minutes before she had to leave to play in the finals. I was confused. *The tournament was still going on as if nothing happened?* I'd been in a bubble of pain and shock for two days and I'd lost track of time, but I'd assumed that the tournament would have been canceled. The organizers thought differently. That was a harsh lesson in the business side of tennis: it really is about making money over anything else.

After Steffi left, two police officers came into my room. One of them was holding plastic bags. "We have evidence that we need you to identify," the male officer said. I didn't say anything. I was by myself—my family had run out to get some lunch—and too overwhelmed to understand what they wanted from me. I didn't want to see anything from that day on the court. I couldn't speak. I just stared at the female officer as she opened one of the bags and pulled out my white and pink Fila shirt, the one I'd been wearing on the court. It was ripped and covered in blood-stains. I felt like I was going to throw up.

"Is this yours?" the male officer asked. I nodded my head. The other officer opened a second bag. She pulled out a long, curved knife. I knew that knife: the last time I'd seen it, it was being raised above my head. My mouth filled with saliva and I had to swallow hard to keep myself from gagging.

The male officer pointed to it. "Is this the knife the attacker used?" he asked. There were streaks of dried blood down the sides of the blade. I nodded quickly and stared at a spot on the wall as they packed up my shirt and the knife and left the room. As soon as the door closed, I grabbed a plastic bowl sitting next to my bed and threw up into it. I dry-heaved until my stomach muscles ached.

My agent at the time, Stephanie, had flown to Hamburg to handle the media storm. The first order of business was to get me back to the States. I needed a safe place to decamp and collect myself. A place where I could breathe without chaos swirling around me. Where I could find out just how bad my injury was. By Sunday night, two days after the attack, I was on a plane headed for Colorado. I was going back to the Steadman Hawkins Clinic, where I'd had my shin splints treated in 1991. I needed the best treatment and I needed people I could trust. Dr. Steadman and Dr. Hawkins were the obvious choice.

I'd been stabbed with a nine-inch serrated boning knife. It had damaged the muscles and tissues surrounding my left shoulder blade, but my surgeons were cautiously optimistic that I'd make a full recovery if I followed their instructions:

- No activity for five weeks. My shoulder was to remain immobile other than massaging and gentle stretching.
- After three weeks, we'd start assessing how much rotation I had in my shoulder. From there, we'd create a rehab plan to get my shoulder as strong and agile as possible.
- If all went perfectly well, I might be able to be back in time for the U.S. Open in August, although playing in that tournament without any warm-up tournaments would not be a good idea.

I'd left as the number one and I wasn't going to accept going back to the tour if I wasn't at that level again. I wasn't going to go out in the first round. Just taking a week off of conditioning dramatically affected my game, and now I'd be missing several months of elite level training. It was going to take a toll. If I made it back in time for the U.S. Open, great; if not, at least I'd be back in serious tournament shape by the end of the year.

# – 15 –

## *Another Hit*

During that first week in Vail, I couldn't move my arm but I let myself be filled with little rushes of hope that I would make a full recovery and be back to my old self in a matter of months. I think I was running on adrenaline: the enormity of what had happened to me in Hamburg hadn't sunk in yet.

Within a week of my stabbing, a meeting of seventeen of the top twenty-five players was called in Rome. They were asked to vote on whether or not to freeze my ranking while I recuperated. Nobody knew how long it would be—two weeks, two months, two years (or more, as it turned out)—and they all voted with their business hats on. Every player except for Gaby Sabatini, who abstained, voted against freezing it. I was hurt when I heard the news, but from a business standpoint I shouldn't have been surprised. Going up one spot in the ranking system could translate to big money and new sponsorships. People were going to make a lot of money while I was away. A sponsor deal I had been close to signing before the stabbing was yanked and given to Steffi, the new number one. Like the decision not to cancel the tournament, it wasn't personal—it was business. But it was hard to take when the wound in my back was still fresh.

Then I was dealt some of the worst news of my life. There was a reason my dad hadn't felt well enough to go to my match on that fateful day in Hamburg. When he and my mom joined me in Vail the day after my arrival, he was still feeling sick. His color was bad and he looked weak. Dr. Steadman immediately knew there was something wrong. He told him to go to an internist to have blood work done as soon as possible. My dad, an old-school guy who hated going to doctors and couldn't stand having a fuss made over him, finally agreed to get checked out. It was prostate cancer. I'd just been stabbed and now my dad had been handed a grim diagnosis. I was devastated. It was like some sort of sick joke. My dad flew to the Mayo Clinic in Minnesota for top-notch care. The plan was aggressive: immediate surgery followed by radiation therapy. All of this happened in the first few weeks following the stabbing.

While I was trying to digest what was happening to my dad, more details about my attacker came out. His name was Gunther Parche, a thirty-eight-year-old unemployed German citizen who had been obsessed with Steffi Graf for years. He'd sent her disturbing fan letters and envelopes of money, instructing her to buy herself a birthday present. His letters were signed *"freunde für ewig"*—"friends forever." He had pictures of her covering the walls of his room. In 1990, I beat Steffi at the Lufthansa Cup in Berlin. My victory infuriated him and he began to follow every step of my career. When I knocked Steffi out of the number one position, his obsession cranked up and, according to a psychiatric evaluation, he was determined "to teach Monica Seles a lesson." He desperately wanted Steffi back at the top of the tennis rankings, stating that I was "not pretty. Women shouldn't be as thin as a bone." His life became devoted to finding a way to take me out of the game. In Hamburg he accomplished his goal. But I had unwavering faith that justice would be served, so I let the police department and the court system in Hamburg do their jobs without any interference from me.

The unknown can be worse than the known, and in the spring of 1993 I felt like I didn't know a thing. I was sick with anxiety over my father and over my playing career. In Vail, I did a lot of waiting by the phone to get

updates from my parents in Minnesota. My dad's surgery had gone well
and he was undergoing chemotherapy. I wanted to be with them but I had
to heal myself first. The phone would have to be our lifeline.

In between my physical therapy sessions, I killed a lot of time by watching television. I'd been at the clinic for just over a month and the French
Open was going on. As I watched Mary Joe and Steffi battle it out in the
final, I was sick with frustration that I was not there. I was supposed to be
on center court defending my title for the fourth year in a row. When
Steffi held the championship trophy above her head, I couldn't stop myself from thinking, *That should've been me*. A month later she was holding
the sterling silver Rosewater Dish above her head at Wimbledon and I
thought, *He did it. He got his wish*. She was back to being number one and
I was struggling to hold my arm above shoulder height.

For two months I'd been funneling my frustration into my physical
therapy, attacking it with the same intensity and focus I brought to all of
my matches. I was meeting with therapists for four hours a day, one session in the morning and one in the afternoon. I was being put through
painful mobility exercises and countless muscle-strengthening workouts
using Thera-Bands, those long, wide strips of soft plastic that pack a ton
of resistance. By August, I was right on track for making a comeback before the end of the year. But watching those two Grand Slams go on without me was excruciating. I hadn't heard from any player since I arrived in
Vail, and although I'd gotten a crash course in the "Tennis is a business"
lesson, it still hurt. It was like I didn't matter, like the stabbing had never
happened. I'd gone from being on the A-list to being invisible. I'd gone
from winning Grand Slams to struggling to swing a tennis racket. Instead
of staying motivated, I started to feel listless. The inner drive that had
been my constant companion since I was five years old began to disappear.

An integral part of my rehab revolved around my cardio sessions. I had
to keep up my endurance in order to make a comeback. I continued with
my therapy, but I started finding excuses for avoiding the treadmill. I'd
never made up an excuse in my entire life and now I was making them

daily. Even ten minutes of walking was torture. I just didn't want to do it. *What was wrong with me?*

There was a problem that no CAT scan or MRI readout could diagnose. Darkness had descended into my head and it was going to stay awhile. No matter how many ways I analyzed my situation, I couldn't find a bright side. I could play again? Great. Maybe I didn't even want to play again. I was still in shock, still waiting to wake up and think, *That was an awful nightmare.* Then I'd get out of bed, walk down to the kitchen, and see my perfectly healthy, strong dad sitting there reading the morning paper and sipping his coffee.

The life that I knew before had ceased to exist. I couldn't see tomorrow, let alone a four-month plan for making a comeback. I started to cry a lot. My surgeons suggested I get some psychological therapy, so at their recommendation I flew to Lake Tahoe to see Dr. Jerry May. I'd never been to that kind of therapist before and I was very nervous and self-conscious. Opening up to my friends and family is hard enough for me so it felt really strange to be talking about my problems with a total stranger. I just wasn't ready for it. So after a couple of weeks I went back to Vail and continued to avoid the treadmill. The only solace I found was going on hikes with Astro. Walking through the woods with my quiet, steadfast friend was the only thing that calmed me down. At nineteen, I was facing the frightening prospect of a life without tennis. What if I couldn't make a comeback? Tennis had consumed me from the time I was six years old, and I was scared that I didn't have an identity without a racket in my hand.

Who was I without tennis?

# – 16 –

## *Keep Running*

Home: an elusive concept for a professional tennis player. From the time I left Novi Sad with my Walkman and two suitcases, I'd lived like a nomad. For six years I'd rarely been home for more than a month straight. I'd become halfway decent at making hotel rooms feel like home. I'd unpack my things the second I walked in the door and mess up the bed so it looked more like me. And as long as I had my parents with me, I always felt a connection to home. A sanctuary to return to at the end of a bad day. But I'd longed for a real place to call home for years. Not a rental house or a hotel room: those wouldn't do anymore. It was time to put down some roots, especially because my whole family was feeling so vulnerable. We needed to sit on our own couch, put our feet up on our own coffee table, and let the storm pass over. We got lucky on this one. By the time I finished with my therapy and my dad finished with his chemo, we moved into the house we'd been building in Sarasota for the past year. It felt good to have a real home again. Finally.

My parents and I fell into this strange rhythm of "normalcy" we hadn't had since I was little. We hung out around the house, reading books, watching movies, cooking . . . normal stuff. But the reality was anything but normal. All of this togetherness was thanks to tragic circumstances and an unmistakable heaviness hung in the air. I was terrified that my dad's cancer would come back—it would take a year to know if the chemo had been successful—so it was like waiting for the bomb to drop every time I asked him how he was feeling. I'm sure I drove him crazy. And I was dealing with my own demons. Food became the only way to silence them.

I began to eat a lot. I'd walk into the kitchen, grab a bag of chips and a bowl of chocolate ice cream, then head to the couch and eat in front of the television. I'm surprised I didn't wear a deep groove in the hardwood floor between the fridge and the couch. I still don't know why my anguish found solace in food that summer. Other than my brief peanut butter phase when I was thirteen, I'd never used food as a crutch before. Maybe I was bored and I kept finding myself wandering into the kitchen, scanning the cupboards, even though I'd just eaten an hour before. Maybe I was subconsciously reacting to Parche's angry comment that "women shouldn't be as thin as a bone." If I padded myself with extra weight, I'd be protected from being hurt again. Maybe I was scared that my comeback would fail, so by eating myself out of shape I could guarantee I'd never do it. I'd never have to be on the public stage again. I may never know what started me down this dark path; it could have been all or none of those things. But that summer what would turn out to be a decade-long battle between my mind and my body began. I wish I could have stopped myself. I wish that I'd paid better attention to what I was doing, acknowledged the bad habits that were forming, and corrected them before they got out of control. But I didn't. I was too depressed to think deeply about what I was feeling and I was too lost in my own head to take a step back and see the kind of damage I was inflicting on myself.

By the middle of September I'd gained over fifteen pounds and I was briefly shocked into action. I still had just enough willpower left to say to myself, *Stop! This isn't helping.* In May my goal had been to be back in playing shape by the fall, and I was far from it. My dad and I decided to pull out all the stops. My slothlike behavior had to come to an end. We called Bob Kersee, Olympic fitness trainer extraordinaire. My dad and I flew back out to Vail to meet with him and I was hit with ten weeks of the hardest workouts of my life. My dad's inner track-and-field athlete came alive watching me sprint down the straightaways. He was in heaven watching all of Bob's innovatively grueling workouts. It was total hell, especially because I was hauling around the extra weight—a daily reminder of what had happened to me in Hamburg. I wasn't the same person I'd been on the morning of April 30.

Despite the pain, I loved working out with Bob. Jackie Joyner-Kersee, Bob's multiple gold medal–winning stud athlete of a wife, frequently joined us on the track. Watching her explosive power and indefatigable work ethic spurred me on. She was superhuman and an inspiration to me. She could take the most torturous workouts, ask for more, then do them even faster. Seeing Jackie whiz by me in a blur stoked my competitive fire. I'd never done workouts like that in my life, and I was running like a madwoman. I was running like I was trying to get away from something dangerous, and back then my mind was a very dangerous place to be. Sweating out my rage, confusion, and frustration did more for me than one hundred hours of talk therapy.

The ten weeks I spent training with Bob were the only time that my depression lifted an inch. I was too busy surviving another round of interval sprints around the track to flounder about in my own messed-up head. Who has time to delve into the abyss of *Why me?* when you're trying to churn out ten 400s in a row in under one minute and twenty seconds each?

Bob got my heart rate pumping to 210 up in the high-altitude Colorado mountains. But ultimately I was just replacing the torment in my mind with torment in my body. I was too exhausted to think about what had happened to me in Hamburg, but it was just a temporary solution—a flimsy Band-Aid that could fall off at any moment, leaving a gaping wound. I was still wildly out of whack and my life was off-kilter. The damage to my psyche was hiding behind sit-ups, push-ups, plyometrics, and supersets with twenty-pound dumbbells. Extreme nightmares were replaced with extreme exhaustion. How long could I keep that up?

As soon as the Kersees left Vail to spend the holidays at their home in Illinois, my dad and I went back to Florida and I ate for two weeks straight. Pasta, burgers, potato chips, and late-night runs to Taco Bell. My mind was no longer being quieted with workouts, so I kept it busy reading fast-food menus. In ten days I gained back all the weight that I'd lost with the Kersees. *Poof!* Ten weeks of Olympic-caliber training gone just like that. It didn't help that during my training I received some shocking news—it almost knocked the wind out of me when I heard it. The man who stabbed me had gone to trial on a charge that was ridiculously less than it should have been: "bodily injury." In front of thousands of spectators, the guy attacked me, and was trying to go back for more when he was wrestled to the ground. "Attempted murder" would have been a much more accurate description. The German court didn't agree with me, my lawyer, or the court-appointed prosecutor. He was charged with the lesser offense, to which he pled guilty. His sentence? Two years of probation.

When my brother told me the news, I was stunned. I called my lawyer and told him to urge the prosecutor to file an appeal immediately.

# – 17 –

## *Happy?*

Sometimes when life comes at you, it comes at you full throttle. It comes at you with a vengeance to see just how much you can take. After many years of being tested, I can now take misfortunes and turn them around into opportunities for growth. I can look at something bad and think, *What is this trying to teach me? How am I supposed to grow from this really awful situation?* But in the winter of 1994, all I felt was overwhelming frustration and sadness.

We didn't have to wait a year to find out the status of my dad's cancer. The wait ended up being a few months. During a routine checkup, he was told it hadn't gone into remission. Instead, it had spread to his stomach. Another operation was immediately scheduled and it left him with a crescent-moon-shaped scar running across the width of his torso. My family was camped out near the Mayo Clinic while he recovered and underwent another round of chemo. I spent a lot of time under fluorescent lights, either in the hospital or in the grocery store.

After spending the day with my dad, I'd trudge through the mid-January Minnesota snow in my brand-new snow boots and make a late-night stop at the local Hy-Vee mega grocery store. The rush of air from the heating vents and the steady roll of my shopping cart's wheels were a form of meditation for me.

Spending a month braving a harsh midwestern winter doesn't sound appealing to most people, but it was a refuge. The stress of my dad's illness had put another fifteen pounds on me. I had reached the mid-160s, a solid thirty more than I'd ever weighed before, and the freezing-cold weather meant I could hide my expanding waistline under layers of sweaters and baggy track pants. Relieved to be away from sickness and the constant thinking about the worst version of "What if . . . ?" I'd lose myself in the cookie and cracker aisle. I'd load up with Oreos, Pop-Tarts, pretzels, and barbecue potato chips.

As I filled my cart with junk food, I knew what I was doing was wrong. First, I knew it wasn't going to help get me back on the tennis court; second, I knew it wasn't going to save my dad. I knew my behavior was extreme and unhealthy, but I just couldn't stop myself. Every evening, the moment I walked out of the hospital, I'd head to the market and load my cart. When I reached the checkout line, I'd unload my purchases onto the conveyer belt with my head down, hoping nobody would get in line behind me to gawk at the junk. Not one nutritious calorie among my loot. I felt empty and damaged inside, and all I wanted to do was stuff myself with empty, damaging food.

While driving back to the hotel, I'd rip into the bag of potato chips and within a few minutes it would be empty. We had a kitchenette in our suite to make things easier during our long stay, and I'd wait anxiously by the toaster as my frosted Pop-Tarts turned a perfect golden color. The moment they were finished, I'd grab them. I burned my fingers countless times because I couldn't wait another thirty seconds for them to cool off before fishing them out of the toaster. My binges were done in secret. My mom, brother, and I took turns visiting my dad, so as soon as my shift was over I made a beeline for the nearest food store and was careful to discard the empty bags and grocery store receipts. My family had no idea how much I was eating. I started having uncontrollable crying episodes, and I did these in secret too. When I couldn't sleep at night—which was becoming more and more often—I'd get up and lose myself in another bag of cookies. My dad was sick and I couldn't make him better. My career was in tatters and I couldn't make it better. My eating was getting out of control and I couldn't stop it. By February we were back home in Sarasota and I was exhausted. Mentally and physically I didn't have anything left. My insomnia had grown worse and I felt like a shell, a big, unhealthy, hopeless shell. I was tipping the scale at 174. I'd gained forty pounds in less than a year.

March went by in a blur. After filling up every hour of every day of my life with tennis for years, I didn't have the slightest idea of how to keep myself occupied during the day. I walked around the house looking for things to do, never finding anything that held my interest, and invariably ended up on the couch watching daytime TV. Finally, one afternoon, my dad, who was determinedly getting stronger every day, reached his breaking point. While he was working on regaining his health, I was passively destroying mine. He told me I had to go back to see Dr. May in Lake Tahoe. After a week of dragging my feet and making excuses, I finally got on a plane. I underwent two weeks of intense therapy and was diagnosed with post-traumatic stress disorder, something I'd never heard of before. I didn't know what it meant or how to get rid of it. I just knew that I wasn't the same person I used to be and I didn't have the slightest idea of how to get back to my old self.

I learned that after a traumatic event it was possible to be haunted by intense anxiety that can leave you feeling emotionally numb. No amount of food or sitting on the couch was going to make it go away. Dr. May suggested techniques for cutting off my negative thought patterns and a few relaxation methods to calm me down when faced with anxiety-producing situations that freaked me out—which was pretty much everything at that point. Maybe if I'd been ready for therapy my condition would have improved, but I wasn't in that place yet.

While it was somewhat of a relief to have an official name for what I was going through, I was hoping for a quick fix and that wasn't it. What had happened to me had never happened in any sport, so there wasn't a rulebook for getting better. It was hard to get the "right" advice from anybody because the "right" advice didn't exist. I was muddling through uncharted territory. I just wanted to get better, and every day I was getting more frustrated because I wasn't feeling "normal." What I didn't yet understand was that I would never be who I used to be.

There was something that I knew for certain and I was having a hard time moving past it. There was an indisputable fact that no amount of therapy would change: the man who stabbed me was still walking around free and there was nothing I could do about it until the appeal was brought before the highest court. I'd just have to wait it out. Maybe then, maybe once justice was served, I'd be able to move on.

At the end of the year I turned twenty-one. My friends tried hard to plan something, but I refused to commit to anything. I felt horrible about myself and I wasn't in a celebratory mood. The last thing I wanted to do was stay out all night barhopping with friends and flirting with guys. I hadn't felt good about my body in almost two years. Besides, I didn't have anything in my closet that fit anymore. All of my cute going-out clothes were four sizes too small! I'd spent almost the whole year in athletic clothes: oversize T-shirts, track pants, and sweats. I rang in the big birthday sitting on the couch with a bag of peanut-butter-filled pretzels. I turned off my phone so nobody could reach me and I watched television until I fell asleep. I didn't feel sorry for myself; in fact, I didn't feel anything at all.

The next day my dad sat me down for another talk. Talk therapy in Tahoe hadn't done much good, and I could tell he was desperate to do something—anything—to bring his daughter back to life.

"What do you want to do, Monica?" he asked me. I knew where he was going with this but I didn't feel like getting into a deep conversation. I just wanted to watch my lineup of television shows.

I shrugged. "I don't know," I said. "Just hang out at home, I guess." I was flipping through the channels on the remote control. He gently took it from me.

"You know I don't mean that," he said. He knew I was in a crisis. I used to be happy. I used to bounce around the house and the tennis court with a spring in my step. All of that was gone and it was getting worse.

"I know what you mean," I replied.

"Are you happy?" he asked. Before his illness, my dad thought he was superhuman. He hadn't been sick a day in his life. My stabbing and his cancer had been a shock to our family, a devastating realization that we weren't invulnerable. While I couldn't pull myself up out of my misery, I knew that his priorities had changed. He didn't care anymore about improving my game, he just wanted me to get back into life. Happiness had become the most important thing to him.

"No, of course I'm not happy. You know that." An infomercial for a super-powered blender was on TV. My dad turned the television off.

"I know." He nodded. "What are you going to do about it?"

"I don't know."

"If you had to guess, what do you think would make you happy? College? Retiring? Starting something new?" He was really trying, but his suggestions weren't helping.

"I have no idea. I really don't."

"It's okay. There is no pressure. Do not go back to tennis unless it is for the right reasons. It's just a game, it's not your life. You don't have to decide today or tomorrow or next year."

"I know," I mumbled.

"Your only obligation is to do what makes you happy. It is that simple." He was right. Financially, I didn't have to ever set foot on a tennis court again. I could do whatever I wanted. Most people would love to be in that situation; why couldn't I appreciate it? My dad made it sound so easy—just do what makes me happy.

## − 18 −

# *Baby Steps*

A few weeks later, when New Year's resolutions were being made by optimistic people everywhere, I made my own: Find out what makes me happy. After twenty months of almost total seclusion I vowed to get out of the house more. I said yes to more invitations. I visited Betsy and Mark McCormack in Orlando and spent hours swimming in the ocean, whipping around on a Jet Ski, and doing my best to learn how to water-ski. One day, Shaquille O'Neal, a neighbor of theirs, joined us out on the water. While I was hesitantly learning to ski, Shaq got behind the wheel of the boat and took off. I did my best to hold on but I didn't have a chance. He took a corner fast and I went flying in the opposite direction. By the time I surfaced, the boat had doubled back to pick me up and everyone was cracking up. I laughed along with them even though I didn't find it quite as hilarious as they did.

Spending time with Betsy did so much for me. A paragon of health, she spent most of her day outside getting exercise. "Go, go, go" is her motto. And she did it with a smile on her face. Working out for her was never a chore; it was something she looked forward to when she woke up every morning. I joined her during the workouts, although it was hard to keep up. I hadn't done any serious exercise in over a year. As I began to feel a little better, I decided that the key to getting back in shape was to surround myself with people who were healthy. I was convinced their good habits would rub off on me.

Just as I was taking my first steps back on the fitness trail and getting my weight down into the 160s, I was hit with another blow. In April, two years after the stabbing, I found out that Gunther Parche's sentence was upheld. He'd go free and there was nothing I could do about it. I'd put off doing the hard work—delving into the deepest corners of my mind—for two years because I was counting on the court system to solve all my problems for me. I was shocked when the sentence was upheld. With a vicious jolt, I realized that I would never get the justice I'd been waiting for. It was out of my control. The only thing in my power was how I lived my life.

After months of searching to find what would make me happy, I suddenly knew what it was. Tennis had been my life's passion and I still loved it. I'd already lost two years of my life to depression and anxiety; I wasn't ready to lose tennis too. That was what my attacker had wanted and I refused to give it to him. With the support of Mark McCormack, my dad and I began to plan my return. In July I made my comeback in an exhibition against Martina Navratilova, who had been very supportive over the past two years. She'd sent me faxes from tournaments and had made it clear that if I decided to come back on tour, I'd be welcomed by everyone. It was something I needed to hear, since I'd felt completely isolated and abandoned after the players' vote on rankings.

Our match was in Atlantic City and it went smoothly. I felt like a kid again, with my nerves making my legs shake as I prepared to walk out on the court. My dad pulled me aside and told me the same thing he'd been telling me since I was little. "Just go out there and have some fun, Monica." He looked nervous, too, but he looked good. His cancer was in remission and he looked stronger and healthier than he had in two years. Maybe things were starting to turn around. The crowd welcomed me with overwhelming warmth and I felt at home right away. After the first few games I fell into a good rhythm and knew I could do it. I could be back on a tennis court in front of a crowd again. A month after that, surrounded by a team of security guards, I played in the Canadian Open, my first WTA match in two and a half years—a lifetime in women's tennis. Amid a roaring and supportive crowd and my teary-eyed family, I won the title. I was officially back.

＊

The first comment was at the 1996 Australian Open. My family and a friend were sitting in the players' box when they heard it.

"That's Monica Seles? What happened to her? She looks huge!" The guy was a stranger and he didn't know my family was sitting right there. My friend turned around and told him to lay off. If he wanted to make ignorant comments, then he could take them elsewhere. I was still packing an extra twenty pounds on my frame and it was obvious that my body was not the same as it used to be. My loose shirt couldn't hide the extra roll around my waist. I thought I could hide my body, but out on the court I still had to wear a tennis skirt! During a serve or when reaching for a ball, my thighs were on full display for everyone's judgment. I'd never played with that kind of self-consciousness, and I hated it.

That year in Melbourne, amid the media hype of my comeback, I won my ninth Grand Slam. I should have been ecstatic and filled with pride: I'd come back and won another Grand Slam, something that just eight months earlier would have seemed impossible. My mom and dad were on their feet, clapping wildly. They looked so happy. I should have been happy. But I couldn't be in the moment. I was too upset about the way my body looked. During the awards ceremony I kept thinking about getting off the court and putting on my sweats. I didn't give myself permission to enjoy a moment of that victory. Besides, I didn't have time. I was back on the nonstop express train of the tour.

Early the next morning I got on a flight for Tokyo. On the first day of the tournament, I injured my rotator cuff and had to go home to recuperate. I managed to pile on another ten pounds by the time I rejoined the tour at the French Open. As the hype over my return subsided, the rumors about why I'd stayed out of the game started to swirl around me. The most persistent one was that I'd been waiting for a big insurance payout. It wasn't true: for those two and a half years, I didn't earn a penny.

I tried to focus on the positive: I was back. But I couldn't shake the feeling that maybe I didn't belong there anymore. The self-confidence that had fueled me for so many years wasn't there. I'd wake up every morning and go to bed every night asking myself if I'd made the right decision in coming back. Was my prime behind me? Was winning the Australian Open a fluke?

I worked hard to get my rotator cuff ready for the European swing. Being in Paris that year wasn't full of the magic and excitement it had been. My mom went back to Yugoslavia to be with her dying father, and I could tell there was something wrong with my own dad: he just didn't look right, but he was adamant that he was fine and that I shouldn't waste my energy worrying about him. I was distracted and lost in the quarterfinals, my worst Roland Garros showing ever. That embarrassment was swiftly upstaged by my crashing out in the second round at Wimbledon to a player ranked fifty-ninth. The newspapers had a field day and said that I looked like a sumo wrestler. My weight was creeping into the high 160s, the self-doubt grew worse, and my dad started throwing up blood. Things were spiraling out of control again. We went back home to Florida, where my mom and I made him get more tests. My biggest fear came true: his cancer was back in full force.

# – 19 –

## A Resolution

Two tablespoons of lemon juice
Two tablespoons of maple syrup
Ten ounces of filtered water
A dash of cayenne pepper
Stir, drink, and get skinny.

By the fall I was in a panic to lose the weight. After my dad's diagnosis, I again resorted to the unsteady crutch of food. Not even the ultimate test of athletic ability—the Olympics—could force me to get into shape. I made the U.S. team and headed to Atlanta in July for my first Olympics. Lindsay Davenport, who had been overweight as a teen but was smart enough to whip herself into shape and claim three Grand Slam titles, was my roommate and we had a great time together. For two weeks the world comes together to embrace the true international spirit of sportsmanship and athleticism. Rising above politics in the name of something greater had been the theme of my dad's artistic work, and I was so proud to have the chance to participate in something as important as the Olympic Games. But I couldn't give myself permission to be in the moment, to lose myself in the full life experience. I was thirty pounds too heavy and I was mortified that I'd let myself get to that point. So I ate to temporarily forget how disappointed I was in myself.

The 106-degree southern heat was stifling, but the cafeteria was a haven of high-powered air-conditioning. It was open twenty-four hours a day and featured every choice under the sun: Chinese, pizza, gyros, ice cream, McDonald's. And it was all free. To make matters worse, it was the nerve center of socializing. Every ten minutes someone new was stopping by our table to hang out. I'd be finishing one meal just as an interesting discus thrower from Bulgaria pulled up a chair. That's all it took for me to get up for seconds: I don't like leaving people to eat alone. Atlanta showed me why the average college student puts on the "freshman fifteen." Unlimited access to a cafeteria plus constant chitchatting equals weight-management disaster. The highlight of every day was when the U.S. water polo guys stopped in to eat. They were gorgeous and sweet and had Adonis-like swimmer bodies. They'd competed earlier in the Games, so they spent the rest of their time hanging out and having fun. I loved talking to them but I wasn't flirting like I had when I was teenager. Long gone were the days when I felt cute and attractive, when I'd walk into a party and feel good about myself. I had turned into "one of the guys." I wasn't in the "potential girlfriend" category anymore, I was strictly in the "friend" box. I could put on a good face and smile and laugh but I had an impenetrable barrier around me. The bigger I got, the stronger the barrier became.

The cafeteria food and gabfest hadn't affected Lindsay—she took home the gold medal—but I remember being more focused on food than on my matches, and my non-medal-winning results proved it. I barely took advantage of everything the Olympics had to offer. Instead of being inspired by all this phenomenal athletic talent, I was intimidated and self-conscious. And I was angry that I couldn't put the same amount of devotion into my workouts as, apparently, everyone else did. There was a fantastic, fully outfitted gym in the Olympic Village that I never set foot in. I was so paranoid that people would stare and gossip about how big I'd gotten that I was paralyzed. So I'd skip the team workouts and tell my coach that I'd go running by myself, which I never got around to doing.

The only happy memories I brought home from Atlanta were of gorging in the food court. And souvenirs: I brought home an extra seven pounds. I'd have preferred an eight-ounce medal. What a waste. By October the weight still hadn't come off. Enter the lemonade diet.

I'd never been on a diet before and I had no idea how these things worked. *Am I supposed to be starving? Is it normal for my stomach to be growling this loudly?* I saw the recipe for the lemonade diet in a fitness magazine, one featuring an insanely toned cover model and a headline that promised *Lose ten pounds in two weeks!* I was convinced it would work for me. I diligently bought all of the items I'd need for my fast and went into it with huge expectations. I lasted two days, and I was absolutely miserable the entire time.

I resumed my track workouts with my dad. He was receiving treatment again but he had decided—with a vengeance—that he wasn't going to let it get in the way of his life. When he saw my hundred-meter sprint times he was in shock: they were slower than when I was ten years old. I went into the November 1996 WTA season-ending championships desperate to salvage something. It was the premier tour event and I'd won it from 1990 to 1992. It was the site where Gaby and I had fought through our grueling five-set match. I loved the season-ending championships and I wanted to end the year as strongly as I'd started it. The crowd was at full volume at Madison Square Garden, waiting to watch the top sixteen players duke it out. As I sat in the locker room before my first-round match, I told myself that if I could pull out a title, like I had so many times before, then I'd prove to everyone that I wasn't a lost cause. Halfway through the first set against Kimiko Date my foot started killing me and I had to retire. I went back to my hotel room devastated. I'd started the year by winning a Grand Slam, had been plagued by my injuries and inconsistent results, and had ended the year with a whimper. Then I got mad. I knew I could do better. I was better than that. I made a resolution: If I was going to accomplish one thing in 1997, it would be to lose thirty pounds. I liked the sound of that. *Thirty pounds.* That was how I'd get my life back. If I was going to do it, then I was going to do it big. Anything less would be a failure.

# – 20 –

# A Phone Call

I got home from New York and started making my usual Christmas Day travel plans to Australia. I was ready to head to Melbourne to defend my title but there was a problem: my rotator cuff was in bad shape and I couldn't raise my left arm above shoulder height. I went to therapy every day to stretch it and get laser treatment but it wasn't healing fast enough. My foot was still bothering me too. Oh, and that resolution? I hadn't lost an ounce in a month.

My weight wasn't just taking a psychological toll on me, it was starting to affect me physically. My body couldn't take the extra forty pounds of pressure and it was starting to break down on me. I wasn't going to be able to defend my title in a place where I hadn't lost a match in the four years I'd played there, and I was making frequent trips to the mall to buy size fourteens. I was miserable.

On Christmas Eve, the day that I should have been packing up for Australia, my beloved Astro died. Just seven years old, he had suffered a freak heart attack. The cloud that had been following me was getting darker. The little guy had been my best friend since I was sixteen years old. Almost every memory of being a wide-eyed teenager winning tournaments all over the world includes his furry and always-smiling Yorkie face.

With the exception of Australia, England, and Japan, Astro had gone to every tournament with me. He was by my side after I won my first French Open, the second, and the third. When I bought my first car I chose a Ford Explorer, mainly because Astro would have room to romp around in it during our drives to the beach. In the surreal adult world of media requests, high-stakes endorsements, and pressure-filled matches, Astro kept my teenage self grounded more than anything else. Frustrating defeats and brutal practice sessions meant nothing the moment I saw Astro's wiggling dance of joy. Every morning, whether I was in Florida or a hotel room in Europe, I'd wake up to see him bounding around on my bed as if to say, "Get up, lazybones! We have a lot of playtime to catch up on!" He was the best alarm clock I ever had.

I was devastated when he died and sat around my house not knowing what to do with myself. Then the phone rang: some friends were calling to invite me to Saint Bart's for a little beach vacation while my shoulder was healing. *Why not?* I thought. *I have nothing else going on.* I packed my suitcase with long, gauzy tops that billowed around me so you couldn't see the shape of my body. I also brought a dozen different sarongs. My favorite refrain of the week, when everyone was frolicking on the beach in tiny bikinis, was, "Oh, I don't need any sun. Honestly, I've gotten plenty already." And I'd spend the rest of the day sitting under an umbrella hiding under my billowy caftans. At the time I was well aware that I was being an idiot. I was on a gorgeous beach surrounded by friends and I had a rare week away from tennis. *Have some fun!* I told myself. *Just let it go!* But I couldn't. All I could think about was the dimples of fat on my butt. I'd done a careful rearview inspection before leaving my hotel for the beach and there was no way in hell I was going to be prancing around in the waves that day—or any day that week.

At eleven p.m. on New Year's Eve, I called my mom's cell phone to wish my parents a happy New Year. I didn't know if they were out celebrating or going to bed early and I wanted to catch them before 1997 hit. It had been a long year for our family and I was happy to see it behind us. The phone rang four times before my mom answered.

"Hello?" She sounded tired. Maybe I'd woken her up. But it sounded noisy in the background.

"Hi, Mom. Are you guys out celebrating?"

"Oh, no, honey, we're not." Something was wrong. She sounded strange.

"Mom, what is it? What's going on?" I held my breath as I waited for her answer.

"It's your dad," she answered. "He's not doing well."

"Where are you?" My heart started jumping around in my chest. I couldn't believe what I was hearing.

"We're in the hospital. He's in the emergency room. Monica, he's in bad shape." The next morning he was scheduled to fly back to Minnesota to start chemo at the Mayo Clinic again. I told her I'd meet them there as soon as I could. While my friends went out to ring in a new year, I stayed in my room making arrangements to fly out in the morning.

Nineteen ninety-seven was looking grim and it hadn't even started yet. What else could the universe throw my way? At least I got some press. While I was waiting for my flight, I was browsing through an international paper at the newsstand when I saw an article with a photo of me taken from an unflattering angle (to be fair, most of my angles were unflattering then). It had been taken a few days earlier when my friends and I were tanning on the deck of a boat. I was covered up but it didn't help. The caption read: "It's game, set and crash for tubby tennis champion Monica Seles who looks like she's had a serving too many during a diving holiday in the Caribbean."

*And the hits just keep on coming*, I thought.

I got to the hospital in record time, my body in shock from the sixty-degree temperature change. I was back in the middle of a Minnesota winter. As soon as I saw my father I started to cry. He looked so pale and weak. I couldn't believe how much he'd declined in only a week. He hugged me and told me not to be silly. "I'll be fine," he insisted.

I went to the cafeteria to get a Diet Coke. I needed some energy—I was exhausted from the frantic trip north—and I'd been relying on soda more

Working out on a balance beam in our makeshift training facility in Novi Sad. I spent most of my childhood winters in there, since it was too cold to train outside.

The 1985 National Junior Tournament, Yugoslavia. I won the tournament, but my most vivid memory is waiting in line to get the much-anticipated ice cream dessert. I took two helpings!

Being named Sportswoman of the Year in Yugoslavia in 1984. The ceremony was in Belgrade, the capital, and dozens of government officials were in attendance. I was ten years old.

After winning the national tournament in Yugoslavia, at age nine. I was always playing against girls who were twice my size. My mom did my pigtails for me, and I loved them.

Training during our
annual summer vacation
in Dubrovnik, Croatia.

Playing on a hometown
court in Novi Sad. I think
I was born with that
determined grimace.

With Michael Chang (future French Open champ), Natasha Zvereva (future French Open finalist), and Tommy Ho (top junior player in the world) at the 1985 Sport Goofy Junior World Championships in Orlando. I had the best time umpiring Michael's match.

A break from practicing at the Academy, in my stylish flowered outfit. At fifteen, I was still very much into pink. Check out the racket.

New Orleans, 1988. Playing against Amy Frazier in my third pro tournament, when
I was fourteen years old. As usual, we played a long, hard-fought three-setter.
*(Photograph by Carol Newsom)*

Training at the Academy while Nick Bollettieri and my dad give me advice.

Having fun on the court with my dad in Tampa, 1990.
(© 1990 Art Seitz)

A celebratory dinner after my first French Open win, in 1990, with family friend James La Vea and IMG founder Mark McCormack. I am wearing my favorite dress.

Standing on our hotel balcony after winning my first French Open title. I held on to that trophy for hours after the final match.

With Gaby Sabatini in Buenos Aires in 1990. We'd just played in an exhibition in front of twenty-five thousand fans. I was admiring her brand-new Porsche convertible.

ABOVE: Hanging out with Astro, my best travel buddy, after a tournament in Germany in 1989. It was my first pro year, and I finished the year ranked sixth. I was thrilled.

RIGHT: In Vail a month after the stabbing. Astro and I head into the mountains for one of our daily hikes.

In Toronto in 1995, playing
in my first professional
tournament after the
stabbing. I'd just won the
opening-night match. I was
so happy and relieved.
(© Alese & Morton Pechter /
Pechter Photo)

In my bridesmaid's dress, after
many last-minute alterations,
at Mary Joe and Tony's wedding,
in 2000.

Playing doubles on Court One with Mary Joe at the 1999 French Open.
One of the few times you'd ever see me at the net.

With Martina and K.D. (Killer Dog) in 1994. Martina was playing in
an exhibition in Florida and came to visit me during my recovery.

My dad proudly holding
the Palme d'Or trophy
that he was awarded
in 1976.

At a luncheon in Orlando in early 1998, standing in
one of my favorite places—a buffet line.

Toronto, 1995, in my comeback tournament. The fans were tremendously supportive, and their enthusiasm confirmed my decision to return to the tour. (© Alese & Morton Pechter / Pechter Photo)

With my dad in December 1997, five months before he passed away. The more weight he lost, the more food I ate.

Playing in a tournament in Oklahoma in 2000. I have my classic playing face on.
This was a "thunder thighs" phase, and I hated seeing photos of myself.
*(© 2000 Richard T. Clifton / RTC Photography—Oklahoma City)*

Riding a horse in Bahia, Brazil, in 2001. One of
my first steps toward a life outside tennis.

ABOVE: With my good friend Mel Jones
after my first skydive, in New Zealand
in 2005. The jump was terrifying, but I
loved every second of it!

LEFT: In Doha, Qatar, at the time of
one of my last professional tournaments. I
took advantage of everything I could
during that trip—riding horses, holding
falcons, having lunch in the desert, and
dressing up in traditional robes.

Before each big tournament my dad wrote down all of my planned training sessions. The cover of the packet was always a cartoon that represented my goals for those weeks. This was for the 1992 Australian Open.

With my mom, Ester, at a game reserve near Johannesburg in 2006. Cuddling a litter of puppies kept us happily occupied for most of the afternoon.

At Victoria Falls in Zambia in 2006. I was finally
starting to feel comfortable in a bathing suit.

With my dancing partner,
Jonathan Roberts, before our
final performance on *Dancing with
the Stars*. I was more nervous
before that show than before
any Grand Slam final.

and more. On my way to the elevator I ran into his doctor, the same one who had treated him the last time. I asked him to tell me the truth: What were my dad's chances?

"The tumor is aggressive," he said. "We've already started him on chemo."

"I know, but what are his chances? Will he be okay?"

"He didn't tell you?" he asked.

"Tell me what?"

"He's looking at a few more months, four at the most."

If at any time I could have passed out cold, it was right there, standing in that hallway. The cancer had kept coming back over the past four years but he'd beaten it into submission every time. He was bigger than life, a force of nature who had taken care of our family through everything. The concept of mortality had never hit me as hard as it did at that moment. Even after my stabbing, I had the option of getting better. I was miserable and I'd missed death by a few millimeters, but I had survived and had many years ahead of me. But my dad's prognosis didn't have any hope in it. There was a rapidly approaching deadline and his life would be hell until then. I didn't know how we were going to get through it, but I knew that if I was going to stay on the tour, I had to get on a plane as soon as possible.

Wimbledon, 1997. The dawn of a new era of hotness on the court. Hotness as in sex appeal and marketability. Martina Hingis, Venus Williams, and Anna Kournikova arrived at the All England Club and turned the old guard of tennis on its head. While I'd been off the tour, the game had not only become faster and more powerful, it had also become sexier and perfectly toned. For the first time in my life, at twenty-three I was the "old" player who was on her way out to make room for the pack of new and improved girls.

I'd spent all of March at the Mayo Clinic with my parents as my dad gave his battle against cancer one last courageous shot. One more round of pumping poison into his body, destroying his healthy cells along with the cancerous ones. My mom and I rented an apartment nearby as we waited to hear news about the three surgeries he had to undergo. He never uttered a word of complaint. In between sessions of chemo he'd come back to the apartment to rest and watch the Food Channel. The sounds of sizzling pans and voices giving gentle cooking instructions were sooth- ing to him. He couldn't keep anything down, but he got his food vicari- ously through the television. While he was learning how to bake the perfect blond brownie, I was sneaking into the tiny kitchen to stuff my face with real ones. If I kept my hands busy with opening wrappers and crumpling up empty bags into tiny balls that could be hidden in the trash, I could keep the tears at bay.

By the time Wimbledon rolled around, I could barely run a mile with- out killing my knees. Playing a Grand Slam at my heaviest, I was lugging a 174-pound body around the fast-playing grass courts that were a chal- lenge even when I was in the best of shape. And the all-white rule did not help matters much. An all-white ensemble is about as slimming as walk- ing around in a jumpsuit with huge fluorescent horizontal stripes.

Every morning on my way to the stadium, I'd catch a glimpse of the London tabloids as I hurried past the Wimbledon Village newsstands on my way to get coffee. For two weeks they plastered a photo of all the top players' butts lined up next to one another and asked the public who had the best one. Needless to say, I wasn't a winner. I looked enormous next to the tanned and toned backsides of the other women. And I wasn't a winner on the court, either. After a bad line call ruined my chance to serve for the match, I lost in the third round to Sandrine Testud, a player I'd beaten twice before the stabbing. After we shook hands, I fell apart in- side and rushed off so I could be by myself. When I got to the locker room I called my dad. He was at home in Florida watching the match on televi- sion, and even though he sounded weak, he spent the whole conversation trying to cheer me up. My dad's health was deteriorating at the same rate as my inner strength. I hated being on the tour without him and felt guilty not being home with my family where I belonged. I wanted to be there, but my dad's wish was that I go on and live my life.

I didn't want to. I flew back to Florida the next day.

# On My Own

The rest of 1997 went by in a blur of plane rides and postmatch phone calls to my dad. He was on heavy doses of morphine and there was nothing the doctors could do anymore. He'd already outlived his prognosis by several months and it was just a matter of time before I'd have to say good-bye. It was excruciating. My dad kept his sense of humor through it all and continued to coach me via hurried cell phone calls and faxes to my hotels. I flew back home every chance I got but I felt torn apart by guilt. I was traveling to Los Angeles, Toronto, Philadelphia, Atlanta, and Tokyo for matches, but my head wasn't 100 percent in the game and it wasn't 100 percent with him. I was floundering in the middle, not doing a good job with either.

I was doing my best to keep up with my business responsibilities. In 1996, I'd become an investor in the Official All Star Café chain, which meant going to new restaurant openings with the other investor athletes: Tiger Woods, Andre Agassi, Shaquille O'Neal, Wayne Gretzky, and Ken Griffey Jr. Hanging out with those guys gave me some of the only light-hearted moments of that year. Tiger had just won his first Masters Championship, and the crossover between Hollywood and the sports world was at its zenith. Restaurant openings were A list celeb–studded affairs. Sylvester Stallone, Bruce Willis, Demi Moore, Brooke Shields, and Wesley Snipes were all regulars at the parties. I became an expert at donning my "just one of the guys" persona by slipping into a long and flowing, waist-less size-fourteen dress. It was easy to disappear into the background. That style became my uniform whenever I had to go out.

My schedule was crazy, but I talked to my dad at least twice a day and flew home to Florida whenever I had more than twenty-four hours off. But it wasn't enough. After losing to sixteen-year-old Serena Williams in the quarterfinal of a tournament in Chicago, I returned home and told my dad I didn't want to play for the rest of the year. I just wanted to spend time with him. It was already November, so I'd only be missing a few tourna-ments, but he thought my idea was ludicrous.

"Monica, your life must go on. Go out and live it now. I am happier seeing you like that, not like this."

I couldn't answer him. I was biting my lip to keep myself from crying. He hadn't been able to eat anything substantial in months, while I was eating everything in sight to suffocate my sadness. He'd been so strong and I felt so weak. I didn't want to break down in front of him.

"And you have to promise me one thing," he continued. "You must promise that even when I am gone, you will keep living your life. You have to: there is no other choice." He shrugged his shoulders and smiled at me. He made it sound so easy. Just go live.

My dad knew I'd need a little help to keep going. As he grew weaker, we both knew I needed another coach. I couldn't handle the upheaval going on in my life while trying to figure out how to operate on my own at the same time. It was too much. "Just go live" was easier said than done.

Gavin Hopper was the perfect solution to pick up the pieces of my game and get my butt into shape. An Australian fitness buff with a sense of adventure, he'd whipped Amanda Coetzer into extraordinary playing shape, and his fitness skills were legendary. He would be my answer. On a bad day his body fat was 4 percent. He was regimented and unyielding in his workouts but, like my dad, did his best to squeeze as much fun out of them as possible. And the best part was that whether he told me to run a one-hundred-meter sprint or go for a hard sixty-minute run, he'd be doing the exact same thing next to me every step of the way. Not many coaches will do that. I'd never heard of a protein shake before he came into my life. Suddenly I was drinking them twice a day, one for breakfast and one for dinner. They were disgusting. One morning I tried to sneak sugar into it but he was too quick.

"Absolutely not, Monica. No sugar."

"Ever?" I asked. Surely I'd be allowed some every now and then. Sugar was good and it seemed like it was in everything. How could I avoid it? Didn't it give me energy?

"Never," he said adamantly. But he promised me that if I followed his every fitness commandment, I'd get back into the shape I wanted to be in.

I bought every book that promised to give me a new life, a new body, or both. I was obsessed with losing the weight. I was convinced I'd be happy again if I could just get rid of it. My self-help library was born that year and I digested all the advice I could get my hands on. There had to be a solution. A magic answer was hiding somewhere within those pages.

I tried meditating to my ideal weight. I spent a week eating unlimited meat and cheese until I was too grossed out to continue. I counted carbs obsessively. I tried visualizing my hunger as a shrinking blue square. I ate carbs before noon and protein until bedtime. I food-combined like a mad scientist. I ate what I thought my blood type wanted me to. But when I got home after a typical day with Gavin—four hours of hitting and two hours in the gym dividing my time between sweating on the elliptical and being miserable on the treadmill—I was too exhausted to care. The minute he left my house every night at eight o'clock I'd take to the couch, armed with bags of chocolate-covered pretzels, and nibble right through them as I read a book or watched NBC's "Must See TV." That was my world, and knowing I could retreat into it was the only way I could get through my workouts during the day. Besides, I felt like I deserved it. I'd been perfect all day long: it was impossible to maintain that kind of willpower around the clock.

That's not entirely true. Gavin could keep it up. I would have given anything to have his discipline, and I was convinced that some of it would rub off on me. It never did. "Just chew some gum if you're hungry," he'd offer. Or my favorite: "Pour yourself a glass of hot water and put some lemon in it for a treat." Yeah, right. That sounds delish. I spent three days doing that after a minor injury prevented me from practicing. I wasn't ex-pending calories on the court, so I wasn't permitted to consume them at home.

Gavin was hard-core. He had no emotions attached to his eating. It was cut-and-dried: Don't sabotage an entire day's work in one sitting. But by the time eight o'clock in the evening rolled around I'd go crazy, giv-ing in to my hunger pangs and roiling emotions. I had a million justifica-tions: I was tired, I was sore, my dad was dying, I was lonely. And night after night I'd consume thousands of empty calories while barely tasting a single one.

This unconscious eating was destroying all of my progress to fight the extra lumps and bumps that had settled onto my pear-shaped body. I worked so hard in the gym, but I'd mess it all up in one binge. My dad was getting worse and I didn't know how to handle my emotions. They were too painful to confront, so I ate more. I'd go to bed feeling numb and with a stomach stretched to capacity, and I'd wake up the next morning furious with myself and with a wicked food hangover, thinking, *Now I have to work out even harder to make up for last night.* I'd angrily put my gym clothes on and storm out the front door. I'd train harder to compensate, then go home and do it all over again. It was madness.

When winter gave way to spring, I had to make a decision. In between my torture sessions with Gavin I'd played in only a couple of tournaments, so I could spend as much time as possible with my dad. But the European swing was about to start—the most important part of the season—and I hadn't made up my mind about going. My dad couldn't speak anymore, so he wrote down a few words on a piece of paper. *Don't be silly. Get on a plane to Rome now.* I did what he wanted me to do, but my heart was breaking as the plane took off.

My first day in Rome, I was inundated with my memories of being there with my dad. It just didn't feel right to be walking along the Viale dei Gladiatori heading toward the stadium without him next to me. So I threw all of my energy into obeying Gavin's dietary commands (I'd had an unprecedented two-week spell of pretending carbs didn't exist and managed to lose eight pounds) and killing the ball in my first match. It worked: I beat Silvia Farina, a Milan native who was in the midst of a breakthrough year, in two sets, 6–2, 6–1. Anytime an Italian player took the stage at the Italian Open, the crowd lost its mind. Even though they weren't in my corner, I loved it. My adrenaline was pumping just the same.

The next day I got up early to get ready for my match. I was pitted against Sandrine Testud, the hard-hitting righty from France whom I'd fallen to in a humiliating early exit from Wimbledon the year before. But before I could leave my room, the phone rang. *Don't panic. It's fine. It's nothing. It's probably just Gavin telling me to get a move on.* But it was my brother, and right away I knew it was the call I'd been dreading.

"Monica, it's Dad. He's bad." The phone started shaking in my hand.

"How bad?" I didn't know if I wanted to hear the answer.

"Get on a plane as soon as you can," he answered. His voice was deep and croaky from exhaustion. It was too late to catch a flight home that day, so there was no point in defaulting. Even though my head was already on the other side of the Atlantic, I went ahead and played the match. I don't remember much about it. Sandrine beat me in three sets and I had to bite my lip during the changeovers to stop myself from crying. I struggled to find sleep in my hotel bed that night. It felt too stiff, then too soft, then too cold, then too hot. I was a grief-stricken Goldilocks in Rome.

The trip home took over twelve hours, but it felt like twelve days. I'd never felt so alone. Replaying every moment I'd shared with my dad, I was in a panic trying to commit them all to permanent status in my memory.

He spent thousands of hours hitting with me when I was little—not because he wanted to groom a prodigy, but just because he saw how much I loved it. Even after a long day at work, when most of the dads in my neighborhood were reading the newspaper or enjoying a cold beer, the moment my dad walked in that door he was ready to play. He'd change into his workout clothes and I'd tug on his arm all the way down to the parking lot, where he'd once again set up our makeshift net. I thought about how happy he looked at the restaurant in Paris after my first Grand Slam win. He and my mom were bursting with pride. We laughed through the whole night as my dad whipped out a cartoon of me holding the trophy above my head and Astro's face popping out of the huge silver cup.

Drawing was his work, but he never left it at the office: he took that talent everywhere. Even after I'd left my childhood far behind, my dad still used cartoons to get his coaching points across. When he was sick and could barely talk, he'd communicate with me no matter where I was in the world by faxing drawings of me with a racket and my little dog somewhere in the picture. My cartoon self was unfailingly happy—much happier than the live version of me—and his pen usually caught my dog in midair antics. Along the margin he'd scribble match pointers like *Move your feet* and *Bend your knees*, and at the bottom of the page he'd always end with *Good luck!* and *Have fun!* A few days before I received the call from Zoltan, the concierge had stopped me in the hotel lobby and handed me a fax. It was from my dad. Another note of coaching advice, but I couldn't make any of it out, his hands were now so shaky. But he'd insisted on sending it to me just so I'd know he was with me no matter how many time zones away tennis took me.

I didn't want to forget a moment of it, so I replayed every thought over and over in my head. It was the longest flight of my life. After arriving home, I was able to spend six days with him before he passed away. It wasn't nearly enough.

# – 22 –

# C'est la vie

Sitting on the bed in my hotel room in Paris, I was trying to muster up the necessary focus for my first match. For the past year I'd been logging thousands of air miles while crossing back and forth between Florida and the rest of the world to spend as much time with my dad as possible, while still trying to hold on to a top-five position. The ranking system is an unforgiving mathematical equation that leaves no room for family emergencies or time to grieve. When my dad was sick, I didn't care about falling rankings or losing endorsements. I just wanted to be with him, even though he was trying to push me back out the door, telling me not to worry. Telling me, for the hundredth time, to go live my life.

When he passed away I didn't know what to do. The French Open was less than two weeks away and I knew that, more than anything, he would have wanted me to play in it. Gavin was already in Paris helping Mark Philippoussis, a fellow Aussie, prepare for his first match. I'd originally planned on arriving in Paris on Thursday so I'd have four days to get acclimated. But Thursday had come and gone and I was still sitting at home. On Friday I called Gavin and told him I still didn't know what to do. We'd just had the memorial service for my dad and I didn't know if I was up to playing in such a high-pressure environment. What if I broke down in the middle of a match?

"Just sleep on it," he told me.

I did. And when I woke up on Saturday morning, I knew I had to leave Florida. I wasn't being brave; I wasn't that strong or unselfish. I hopped on the plane for one simple reason: I couldn't stand staying in our house a minute longer. The memories kept flooding back and I felt like I was being suffocated. No matter where I looked in the house, something reminded me of him so much, it felt like the air was being sucked right out of my lungs. So, just like I did for years after my stabbing, I ran away from my feelings by rejoining the tour. New cities, new people, new food, new hotels—everything. I needed a major distraction and I needed it immediately. I kept pushing forward so I wouldn't have to stop and think that I'd just lost my father, best friend, and coach all at once.

My brother couldn't come, so my mom, who had just lost her husband of thirty years, packed up a suitcase and came with me. My dad was the gregarious life of the party who could make light of any situation, but my mom has a quiet, steady inner strength that I know I can rely on. There was no way I could have gone to Paris alone. We arrived at the hotel, and as we were getting out of the taxi she slammed the door shut on her finger. *Snap!* It broke and we had to get her to a doctor before we even unpacked! I spent all day Sunday stretching and hitting, psyching myself up for Monday's match. I wanted to lose myself in tennis.

The next morning I put my dad's wedding ring on a gold chain around my neck and tucked it inside my shirt. Despite the media's predictions, I steamrolled through the competition and found myself facing a semifinal match against Martina Hingis, number one in the world and a ferocious player who had beaten me the last five times we'd faced each other. I had been practicing hard for the past few days with Gavin, but the odds weren't in my favor. I didn't care. This was nothing compared to what I'd gone through with my dad. I was ready to play.

I went out with an aggressive game from the first point. I capitalized on her inconsistent serves, nailed my own, and kept my unforced errors to a minimum. The game I brought was calm, controlled, and strong—the exact traits I'd been missing in myself. I could tell it was getting into Martina's head. She started scolding herself and angrily bounced her racket off the clay. I knew I had the match if I wanted it. It was over in two sets, 6–3, 6–2.

The final was waiting for me, as was the possibility that I could win a tenth Grand Slam. Gavin told me the power to accomplish what others had considered impossible was in my head. If I decided I was going to do it, I would. My prospects looked good. The championship duel was against Arantxa, a player I'd beaten fourteen out of our last sixteen matches. *I can do this*, I thought. *I might actually have the happy ending.* It was too much to contemplate so I didn't let myself think a minute past the present.

The first set went to a tiebreaker but it flew by in an instant, and before I knew it I was down a set. The French fans' support of me was as loud as the Italians rooting for a hometown player in Rome. You can't get much better than that. Anxious to get the momentum back, I came out charging in the second and took it 6–0. Then my happy ending flew right out of my hands.

I still don't know why it happened. Maybe the adrenaline I'd been existing on for the past two weeks finally ran out. Maybe I didn't think I deserved a good ending. Maybe I was just burned out. Maybe I didn't want it as bad as I'd thought I did. I lost the third set 6–2 and with it my last chance at a Grand Slam. It was like watching myself in a bad dream. I saw the set slipping away, and no matter how hard I tried to bear down and focus on getting it back, I couldn't. I didn't have anything left.

The entire stadium gave me a standing ovation as I packed up my bag and waved my thanks. During her victory speech, Arantxa apologized for beating me, saying, "I wish you could have won, Monica." You don't hear that in professional tennis very often.

I survived the postmatch press conferences without breaking down. I saved that for the hotel. My heart was so broken, I didn't know which piece to triage first. Thank goodness my mom was there; we went straight to her room, where I cried for hours until I was out of tears. If there was one thing my dad's long, painful battle had taught me, it was that life isn't fair. And it's too short to sit around brooding about it. Just pick yourself up, dust yourself off, and go forward.

# – 23 –

## The Search Continues

Dave was in perfect shape. And I'm not using the term "perfect" loosely. He was Michelangelo's *David* perfect but better. Ridiculous, actually. I didn't think it was possible to beat Gavin in the race to the bottom of the body-fat chart, but Dave left him in the dust.

We met at a charity fund-raiser in New York in the fall of 1998 and I liked him instantly. He was warm, funny, helped me put on my coat at the end of the night, and hailed a taxi for me. All marks of a good man. Who says chivalry is dead? An incredible athlete who took care of his body like it was a sacred temple, he'd be a good influence on me, I thought. A baseball player who was battling it out in the minor leagues, he did everything he could to be ready when his big break came. He lived down in Florida, so we spent time together whenever I was in town. One night, after going to a movie (he didn't order popcorn, so I didn't either), we went back to his place. I was starving and I opened up his hulking Sub-Zero fridge expecting to find a bachelor's trove of greasy takeout and frozen burritos. Perfect midnight snacks. Instead I was faced with shelves lined with bottled water, containers of green vegetable juice, cut-up melon, and Tabasco sauce, which, he informed me, was for his eggs. His theory was if he doused the eggs with enough Tabasco, he'd eat less.

"Want to order a pizza?" I asked. I liked mine straight up, but if he wanted something healthy on his like mushrooms or spinach, I was willing to compromise.

"No, thanks, I'm good. I'm still full from dinner." But we'd eaten hours ago, before the movie. We had salads with grilled chicken, hardly enough to get me through until tomorrow, when I'd have to face yet another excruciating workout with Gavin. He must have read the disappointment all over my face. "But you go ahead and order one," he offered. Yeah, that's just what I want to do: pig out on a pizza by myself in front of my new boyfriend. Sexy.

"No, that's okay. I'm fine." We hung out on the couch talking and flipping through late-night talk shows until I couldn't take my stomach growls anymore. I jumped up, thanked him for the night, and told him I had to get home to grab some sleep before my morning practice. He seemed startled by my sudden departure but I didn't stick around to explain. I rushed home and inhaled two peanut butter and jelly sandwiches, half a bag of chips, and a Diet Coke. I should have known it was never going to work out. We were just too different, but I convinced myself that being around his "good" eating habits would help me develop my own. As he geared up for spring training, he tried to keep me on the diets Gavin issued weekly. He'd even eat the dinners of salads and raw vegetables with me, insisting they were enough. Food, he explained to me on umpteen occasions, is just fuel. He never ate pasta and he mixed his protein shakes with water instead of milk. It was like spending time with a food monk. The more restrictive the diet, the more he thrived on it.

I once asked Dave what he did when he got stressed out. How did he resist the urge to reach for a candy bar at the end of a horrible day?

"Candy bar?" he asked. "Why would a candy bar make me feel better? I just go to the gym and sweat it out. I love the gym. It's like my sanctuary."

In a flash, I saw the vast difference in the way we approached food. Dave may have been extreme, but I was totally dysfunctional. He used food as energy to accomplish what he wanted to achieve in life. I used food as a drug to help me forget about the bad things in life. Instead of fueling me, food was hindering me from reaching my goals. Working out was a sanctuary for Dave. Working out was a much-dreaded necessity for me. He used food to get through the workouts. I used food as a reward for surviving the workouts. Dave was giving everything he had to achieving his dream and I was throwing mine away. His simple answer to my candy bar question woke me up. I knew that my approach to food needed to change but I didn't know where to start. I wanted to be more like him, but I wasn't willing to subsist on egg whites and watered-down protein shakes. Was there a middle ground? How was I going to find it?

By the spring of 1999, my travel schedule and Dave's devotion to training for his season kept our relationship from progressing. Instead of rubbing off on me, his restrictive habits pushed us further apart. My tendency toward excess was just incompatible with his way of life. I was awed by his dedication but I knew that I was incapable of giving up my extreme for his. Food was still my solace, and I knew that I couldn't give up pasta forever.

I also parted ways with Gavin. Throughout 1998 he'd done his absolute best to get me back to my Grand Slam winning form, but we fell short of our goal. My ranking was still bouncing around in the top five but I couldn't reclaim the dominance I once had, no matter how hard I tried. After my French Open heartbreak, I didn't come close to making it to another Grand Slam final.

By July, I was fluctuating between being twenty-five to thirty pounds overweight. I was out in the quarterfinals of Wimbledon and the U.S. Open and made it to the semis of a couple of Tier I tournaments. There were two victories in the fall: I won the Canadian Open and the Toyota Princess Cup in Tokyo. Guess who my opponent was in both finals? Arantxa. Why couldn't I have done that in Paris?

Gavin had done everything he could to get my mind focused on tennis, but I actually thought about food all day long. The more restrictive the diet, the more I obsessed over it. From the moment I woke up in the morning I was thinking about what I'd eat for breakfast, how I'd be able to last through a practice until lunch, and then how I could exert enough willpower to make it to dinner without hitting the vending machine. My existence was divided into making it to three different four-hundred- to five-hundred-calorie meals a day. I'd find myself looking at the clock at three in the afternoon, mentally urging it to go faster so I could have my dinner of half a potato and a piece of steamed salmon.

Gavin had even taken to issuing strict instructions to the hotel kitchens not to bring me any food when I dialed room service. There went my evening entertainment! And I'd grown accustomed to walking into my hotel room accompanied by the manager, who would then swiftly empty out the minibar. Gavin was doing my body and my wallet a favor: I'd left countless tournaments with an astronomical minibar charge to my credit card. Gavin knew me and was well aware I was not to be left to my own devices.

We didn't part over my failure to get ripped; it was just a matter of logistics. While Gavin had been coaching me, he continued to work with Mark Philippoussis, a top player on the men's tour, and it was becoming increasingly difficult to balance his duties to both of us. There are very few tournaments that overlap between the men and the women, so Gavin was running around like a madman. The second he'd leave to meet Mark at an ATP tournament, I was like a kid whose strict parents had gone out of town for the weekend. My rebellion consisted of refusing to do the five-hundred-sit-ups/one-hour-bike-sprint series he'd given me and chucking my diet right out the window. We parted on good terms and I decided I'd had enough of coaches who worked me to death. I needed something new. I needed to go back to basics.

In 1999 I went to Australia alone. No coach. No hitting partner. The previous year had been a nightmare and I just needed some solitude. Shortly after I lost my dad, my beloved aunt Klara, the talented seamstress who had made me dozens of beautiful tennis dresses when I was little, succumbed to cancer as well. There had been so much death, sadness, and tragedy. I needed some quiet. I needed some time that was free of drama, with nobody telling me what to eat or what to do or how many more reps

I had to churn out until I could leave the gym. I just wanted to be alone to collect myself and to hear myself think. I needed a window of calm. Once I arrived in Melbourne I hired a local pro to hit with me. There wasn't any pressure; I was there because I wanted to be there. Nobody was relying on me to win. If I did well, it was going to be for myself.

My run through the tournament went smoothly until I met Martina Hingis in the semifinal. She was seeking redemption after my Roland Garros victory the previous spring, and she got it. She beat me 6–2, 6–4—my first loss in Melbourne. During the plane ride to Tokyo for another tournament, I started to think that maybe this was how I was supposed to be. Maybe I would never get my old body back. Maybe I'd never get my old career back. I'd never reach the number one spot again and I would be wearing those formless size fourteens for the rest of my life. I didn't want to accept that as my new reality, but maybe it was just the way my life was going to be. I wanted to look like the other girls, but I didn't know how to get there. So I just kept trucking along with the tour schedule, pulling my baseball cap down low and trying to fade into the background.

When I got back to Florida, I recruited two old friends from my junior playing days in Europe to be my hitting partners and coaches. The guys and I went way back and I knew I could trust them like family—not to improve my game, necessarily, but definitely to improve my mind-set. They encouraged me to work out with them but never said a word about my fitness or my weight. We were like kids again, joking around on the tennis court and keeping each other in stitches. I hadn't laughed that much in a long time. I'd been so down in the dumps, I needed to have a little fun.

My friends had been on the ATP tour, so they knew the traveling drill: sleeping in different hotels from week to week didn't faze them in the slightest. And they were the hottest guys in tennis. But that's not why I hired them, honestly. After our morning warm-ups at tournaments, players who had never said a word to me in the locker room were suddenly hit with an infusion of friendliness. "Hey, Monica! How's it going? I was just wondering, um, who are your hitting partners these days? Are they single?" they'd ask. I thought it was hilarious. I'd never been so popular.

For a couple of months I added one more person to our little laid-back crew. I wanted to approach my tournaments feeling more relaxed, but I still didn't know how to eat on my own. I wanted to be in decent playing shape before the French Open, so I hired a nutritionist to monitor me. Peter had come highly recommended by a few tennis coaches and I was excited to learn everything he had to teach me. The first thing he did was put me on a very restrictive diet of no more than 1,200 calories a day. No sugar, no white flour, no soda. It was just like the days of Gavin. I still thought that if I surrounded myself with the right people—healthy, spartan types—their good habits would eventually become mine. Peter calculated every calorie and had meals planned out in great detail. When he freaked out every time I reached for the butter, my first reaction was to be annoyed and resentful. Then I'd remember that I'd hired him for exactly that reason. I was paying him to keep the butter away from me.

But Paris would be our undoing.

"Whole wheat. You know, it's brown and grainy. Not like this," Peter said, picking up a croissant and looking at it as though it had just insulted his mother. The waiter stared at him. "Whole wheat," Peter enunciated slowly. "Do you have any whole wheat bread?"

"Non, monsieur." The waiter shrugged his shoulders and walked away. I don't know if he misunderstood Peter's question or he was just tired of being barked at in English.

I focused on stirring my cappuccino. We'd tried to order one with skim milk and had failed just as miserably. We were sitting at a café close to the hotel and I was trying to focus on my third-round afternoon match against María Antonia Sánchez Lorenzo, a righty from Spain who was one of the few players to have a two-handed grip like mine. I looked across the table at Peter, who had pushed his flaky white croissant to the side. I knew better than to ask him if I could have it. Peter hadn't done much traveling before, so he was thrown into an absolute tailspin when we left the States. He looked pretty miserable. I didn't know how much longer he could take staying in cities that didn't have air-conditioned rooms and skim milk at the ready. As it turned out, not long at all. After I won my third-round match, he'd had enough. He packed up his suitcase and returned to the States.

When Peter left, I briefly panicked. I'd been playing well throughout the tournament and I didn't know if I could control my eating on my own. *Just relax*, I told myself. *It will be fine.* I knew I'd lose my willpower as soon as I stepped into a restaurant, so I stuck to room service because I knew the menu backward and forward. I cruised through the next two rounds and made it to the semifinal, where I had one of the best matches of my life against Steffi Graf. It was our last classic battle. Like Hingis, she was a tough competitor who always brought her A game to every meeting. Looking every bit like the model track athlete, she could get to balls that the male players couldn't. Just one point could decide the entire match, so I had to stay focused and aggressive the entire time. It was the usual hard-fought back-and-forth duel that we'd been waging for a decade. We always played long three-set matches and the winner was anyone's call. That day it belonged to her. After winning the first set in a tiebreaker I ran out of steam. She took the next two sets 6–3, 6–4. It was the last time we ever played each other. Over the years people have asked me how I viewed playing her. Was it different facing her because of the stabbing? Did I take any of that emotional pain onto the court with me when she was standing on the other side of the net? The answer is no, I never did. I never went into our matches angrier or more emotional than I did others. I couldn't. Tennis forces you to leave all of your issues off the court. It doesn't matter if you have a migraine or your period, it doesn't matter if a family member just died, it doesn't matter if you just had a fight with your boyfriend; you have to put your game face on the moment you step onto that court. It is just you out there and you have no excuses.

That semifinal loss was an interesting end to our history. Steffi and I had met on the courts of Roland Garros a total of four times. In my first semifinal appearance when I was fifteen, she beat me. In the next two matches we met in the finals and I won them both. And finally, in our last match in the stadium that I loved so much, we met again in the semifinal, just as we had a decade earlier. It seemed a fitting conclusion to our rivalry, which—although it never reached the level everyone had thought it would—was always hard fought by both of us.

I had a decent run at the end of the year: appearances in the finals of the Canadian Open and the Toyota Princess Cup. Serena Williams took me out in the quarterfinals of the U.S. Open, and Mary Joe Fernandez and I were steamrolled by the Williams sisters in the doubles quarterfinal match. Serena went on to win the tournament—the first Grand Slam for either of them. Their stranglehold on the top of tennis was rapidly taking shape.

# — 24 —

# The Virtues of the Peanut

*February 2, 2000*

*Dear Monica,*

*I've been a fan for years . . . ever since you won the French Open in 1990. Your power game is thrilling to watch. I have a favor to ask: I'm trying everything to bulk up. I've been drinking tons of protein shakes and lifting weights until my body is exhausted but I just can't seem to put on the mass. Over the past few years, I've noticed that you've bulked up quite a bit. You're a strong, heavier-set woman, which I find very attractive, and I'd love to know what your secret has been to getting bigger.*

*Many thanks,*
*Bob*

I threw the letter down on the couch. It landed on top of the bag of peanut-butter-filled pretzels that had been keeping me company all afternoon. I didn't know whether to laugh or cry. Was this fan asking me what my secret was to being overweight? Did he think I was *trying* to look like this? I suppose the note was intended to be complimentary—he said he was a fan and that he found me attractive—but the only words that leapt from the page were "heavier-set" and "bigger." They might as well have been in capital letters and highlighted in bright pink with arrows pointing to them, because my brain zeroed in and obsessed over them immediately. I'd never met the guy in my life, but suddenly I was worrying about what he—and every other tennis fan—thought of me. Was Bob calling me fat? No, of course not. But that was how I interpreted it. "Heavier-set" didn't translate into hitting the ball with more power. "Heavier-set" meant fat. Was my changed body shape the first thing people noticed now? Was my tennis secondary? In my mind it had been prioritized like that since my stabbing—first fix my body, then worry about tennis—but I'd had no idea that the public thought that way too. *Great*, I thought, *now I'll have to find even baggier outfits to wear during tournaments*. I wrapped up my beloved pretzels, got out a pen and piece of paper, and wrote my great admirer a reply.

*Dear Bob,*

*The best advice I can give you is to eat peanut butter. Make it your best friend. Nothing will put on weight faster than that. Good luck with your mission!*

*All the best,*
*Monica*

That fan letter was par for the course at the beginning of 2000. The year hadn't gotten off to a great start. I spent the first two months nursing a stress fracture in my foot. It was awful. Stress fractures are notorious for coming back over and over again, so the only thing to do was to stay off it. And staying off your feet is a great way to pack on the pounds.

To top it off, my ranking had taken a beating during my months away and I'd dropped out of the top ten. For most of my career I'd been in the top three, so dropping down to the double digits took a toll on my ego. On the court it meant I was far from dominating the game the way I used to, and off the court it meant dwindling money in sponsorships. By February my foot was ready to play but my mind wasn't. I was tired: tired of watching the scale, tired of watching the rankings, tired of packing up and heading to a new city every week. The thought of returning to the grind of the tour and fighting my way into the top ten again was just too much. I picked up the phone to call my agent.

"Tony, I don't think I can do this anymore."

"What? Are you talking about your foot? I thought you were ready to go."

"I am. I mean, it is. My foot is ready. But I'm not. I think I'm done."

There were a few seconds of silence. He could tell I was serious. He could hear the exhaustion in my voice. As a front-row witness to my battles on and off the court, Tony knew that I wasn't saying I was finished with tennis just to be dramatic or just because I was having a bad day. He knew I meant it. I told him I wasn't having fun anymore. The burning fire to play tennis that had been in my belly since I was six years old had disappeared and I didn't think I could find it again.

"Monica, before you make this decision, do me a favor. A friend of mine is putting on a tournament in Oklahoma City next week. It's a Tier III, so it will be mellow. No pressure. Just pack a bag, get on a plane, play the tournament, and if you don't have any fun at all, then retire. I won't even try to talk you out of it. But just go to Oklahoma first." It wasn't too much to ask. Tony had been a great agent. I'd do this for him, and if I was as miserable as I predicted I'd be, I'd retire after the tournament. I got off the phone and booked my ticket.

Over the past twenty years I'd been to hundreds of tennis tournaments and I'd never, ever gone to one in the United States alone. But I got on that plane to Oklahoma by myself. It wasn't symbolic of closing one chapter of my life, nor was it a grand gesture of claiming a newfound independence. It was a matter of last-minute logistics: after my dad passed away, I didn't have a steady coach or practice partner on call, so I hit the road solo.

Tennis is a profession that demands a lot of alone time. Once you set foot on that court, your fate is in your own hands, so traveling alone shouldn't have unnerved me. But it did. It was eerie. After so much time with trainers, coaches, hitting partners, and family members, I didn't know the game without all of those distractions. I drove myself to the airport, parked in the long-term lot, threw my tennis and overnight bags over my shoulder, and headed for the terminal. Surprisingly, I didn't feel lonely. I didn't even feel like I was in my own body. It was like I was watching someone else checking in at the counter, exchanging pleasantries with the woman behind the desk ("Monica Seles? Wow, I didn't know you were still playing tennis." "Yes, actually I am." "Well, good luck, then!"), putting my rackets through the security X-ray, and getting on the plane. From the time I was fourteen years old, I'd always had several people traveling with me. For years I couldn't even conceive of going to a tournament without being flanked by my dad and a hitting partner. Once I settled into my seat, I felt a strange sense of being bare, in both a physical and an emotional sense, like I was a stripped-down version of me. I was going to Oklahoma to make a decision about my future. Without the pomp and media hype of a big Tier I tournament, I was hoping my head would be clear enough to gauge whether I wanted to leave tennis in the past or not. When I left my house that morning, I was pretty convinced I knew what the answer was going to be—it was time to move on—but with every minute that ticked by, I was feeling less certain. I buckled my seat belt, took a few deep breaths, and told myself everything would be okay.

Within an hour of landing in Oklahoma City, I realized it was a lot different from the other cities on the tour; but I didn't need the excitement of New York or the glamour of Roland Garros right now. I needed something safe, welcoming, and pressure-free. Oklahoma's IGA Superthrift tournament was perfect. I unpacked my things at the hotel and asked the tournament directors if they knew of a hitting partner I could use. They were extremely helpful and found a local guy to warm up with me before my matches. That was a relief. A hitting partner is an integral piece to the pro tennis puzzle of success, and normally I'd never go to a tournament without a trustworthy and proven one. But Oklahoma was different. As long as the guy could hit the ball back to me, my warm-up would be fine. To get back to basics, all I truly needed was me and my racket. If I could reconnect with a tiny part of what it felt like when I was seven years old, hitting a ball against the wall of my apartment building in the early morn-

ing hours before school, the trip would be worth it. I didn't need a seasoned, longtime hitting partner to find that.

My first opponent was Francesca Lubiani, a twenty-two-year-old lefty
from Italy whom I'd never played before. When I walked onto the court
at Abe Lemons Arena, I had no idea of what to expect. It had been five
months since my last match, and even though I tried not to put any personal hopes on the line, my stomach was a jangle of nerves. Even if this
was to be my last tournament, I still wanted to play the best that I could.
As I walked to my chair to put my bag down, the audience's cheering
grew thunderous. I glanced around and saw that they were getting to their
feet. The energy of a standing ovation rained down on me from every angle. Goose bumps spread down my arms. I was overwhelmed. In a town
that was far from being a tennis mecca, the audience couldn't have been
more enthusiastic and supportive. I was humbled. As I double-tied the
laces on my shoes and unsheathed my racket, I felt a little surge of adrenaline. That old edge of competitiveness that had been my trusty companion for so long began to peep its head up to quietly say, *I'm still here.* I won
the first set 6–3 and comfortably eased into a victory after racking up another 6–3 in the second set. One match down, three more to go. The
crowd was generous in their wild applause and reporters surrounded me
afterward asking how it felt to be back. "Good, really good," I said. And I
meant it.

I went to my hotel that night with a small glimmer of satisfaction.
The match had gone by in a flash, and despite the expectations I'd had
when I left Florida, I even had a little bit of fun on the court. After changing into my pajamas, I called room service and collapsed onto the bed
with a big sigh. A grilled chicken sandwich and an inner feeling of satisfaction filled me up enough to ward off the minibar that was taunting me
from the corner of my room. There had been times—oh, so many times—
when I'd succumbed to the temptation of attacking it after a long day of
playing. But the anxious, empty feeling that could temporarily be numbed
by gorging on junk food wasn't there that night. Instead of ripping through
bag after bag of potato chips, I replayed some of the points in my head,

relishing how good it had felt to hit the ball with everything I had. Sending it down the line with a force that vibrated down to my very core was one of the best feelings in the world. I hadn't realized how much I'd missed it. I fell into a deep sleep.

The next day I faced Sarah Pitkowski, a player who'd given me a brief scare three years earlier during our second round at the French Open. This time it was easier. I found my rhythm early on to beat her 6–0, 6–0, and went into the semifinal against Amanda Coetzer with more confidence than I'd had in months. *Yes*, I thought as I walked into the noisy stadium anxiously awaiting our arrival, *I am still a tennis player. I can still do this*.

Amanda, a powerful blond spark plug from South Africa, had been a top player on the tour for years. We'd met on the court many times before and I had a record of 7–1 against her, but I never, ever counted a victory before it happened. "Stay in the present" had been my motto since I was fifteen years old. I did my best to live up to it by not obsessing over my opponent's game before a match. Amanda's five-foot-two-inch frame was not representative of her ferocity on the court. Nicknamed "The Little Assassin" by the media, she had a startling ability to take down players of higher ranking and status. Months earlier she became the only player to defeat Steffi Graf, Martina Hingis, and Lindsay Davenport while they were ranked number one, and she had won a two-set victory over me the previous year in Tokyo. She was on a tear and I was ready for a good battle.

By the end of the first set I was feeling strong and connected to my body. I fired my trademark baseline shots over and over, gaining momentum with every point. The months away hadn't damaged my fundamentals, but by the time I won the match, I knew my physical conditioning needed a major overhaul if I was going to keep playing after Oklahoma. Amanda had incredible athleticism on the court, and even though I won the match 6–1, 6–2, I had to work my ass off to do it. I was struggling to reach balls that used to be easily retrievable. It was the slowest I'd ever been. I knew I had to get into shape, but I didn't know how. I'd tried for four years and nothing was working. How did all these other players run around on the court lunging for balls without an ounce of fat on their bodies? Where was my magical solution?

After the match a sportswriter who was surprised to see me at a less-than-flashy tournament asked me how long I thought I'd keep doing this.

"This?" I asked him.

"Yeah, the tour. New cities every week, nights filled with the obligations of sponsor dinners, days at home that are few and far between. When do you think you'll have had enough?" It was a good question, and it was the main reason I was in Oklahoma. Had I had enough yet? I thought about it for a few moments and looked him straight in the eye.

"The day I stop thinking I can win majors is the day I stop playing." It was the truth. Somewhere inside I knew I could still win one.

A sense of calm engulfed me on the day of the last match. Oklahoma was a far cry from Paris and London, but my game was coming back. I couldn't wait to face Nathalie Dechy later that day. A long and lean twenty-year-old from France who was the embodiment of the new hard-body look on the tour, she had made it to the final sixteen at Wimbledon, recently upset Arantxa Sánchez-Vicario, and was riding the invaluable wave of momentum. *Just play every point like it's your last*, I told myself. It worked. I took the first set quickly at 6–1, but Nathalie wasn't going to give up that easily. We took our places on the court for the second set and I could tell something had changed. She looked more determined, more steely. She came at me with everything she had.

I didn't want to go to a third set. After winning the first, you know you can beat your opponent and you've got tempo on your side. You should do everything in your power to close out the match after the second. Losing focus during the second can make you lose an entire match. The momentum switches to your opponent and it's suddenly anyone's game in the third. I didn't want to go there. *Dig deep; find that fire*, I commanded myself. We went to a tiebreaker and I asked myself whether I wanted this—really, truly wanted this—or not.

The fire that had driven me to the top of the tennis world wasn't raging like it used to, but I could definitely feel a flicker. It was enough to make me launch shot after shot, corner to corner, that had Nathalie running back and forth across the baseline. With gritted teeth and an unwavering focus that kept me from feeling the sweat pouring down the sides of my face, I knew I wanted to keep playing. I won the tiebreaker and the crowd erupted into a roar. Well, it wasn't the roar of the U.S. Open—it was short by about twenty thousand people—but it made me just as happy.

Sometimes you find what you're looking for in the most unlikely of places. I found it in a small stadium in the Midwest. After months of questioning my ability while waiting to heal, I surprised myself with how well I played, even without the support system I had become so reliant on. Being alone had worked to my advantage. Instead of feeling lonely, I felt unguarded and open to whatever emotions were going to come my way. I got back to basics, back to the raw feeling of playing tennis for the sake of playing. I wasn't playing for sponsors, coaches, friends, money, fame, or rankings. As I had when I was seven years old, I was just playing for me. There was solace in that realization, and I needed it after losing my dad. Two years earlier I had tried to distract myself by jumping full force into the tour right after he passed away, but my premature reentry had caught up with me. I hadn't dealt with the grief of losing him and I wouldn't fully deal with it for a few more years. But when I got on that plane to Oklahoma I was taking a step toward reclaiming who I was on my own and why I had fallen in love with tennis twenty years earlier.

It was the reminder I'd been desperately searching for. I still had some tennis in me, if I could just lose the weight.

# – 25 –

# A Hag with a Frying Pan

When I got back to Florida, Tony hooked me up with a new coach. If I was going to make a serious run toward reclaiming a top-five spot, I needed to get back in shape and I needed a support system. Going to Oklahoma on my own was a necessity, but I couldn't pull something like that at a Tier I tournament. Those were a whole different world. The prize money is higher and the caliber of players shoots way up. Tier I's have a higher point value in determining the rankings, so the top players always show up. Coaches and hitting partners form a buffer for a player, and at high-profile media events like the Grand Slams an intermediary is essential. The pressure is amped, the fans are in the tens of thousands, and the pressroom is filled with journalists looking for a story. In between going to mandatory sponsor events and signing autographs for fans, players have no time to handle media requests on their own. They don't even have the time to secure their own courts for hitting. Without a team behind me I'd burn out by the second round. I'd always had structure and I thrived on it. I missed that. I couldn't replace my dad but I could try to instill some structure again. Enter Bobby Banck.

Bobby had been my good friend Mary Joe Fernandez's coach for years. After an incredible career, she had recently retired and was now busy planning her spring wedding to my agent, Tony. Top coaches are rarely available—a precious few pop onto the market with the start of every year, and we were almost in March—so I jumped on the opportunity. I was sure Bobby, a fitness fanatic with a tireless work ethic, would be my golden ticket to losing weight. A hard-core, take-no-prisoners approach was what I needed. At least that's what I told myself, and that's what I told Bobby. We dove right in. His main concern with Mary Joe had been getting her to gain weight and strength. That was most certainly *not* my problem, and Bobby came prepared. He knew my weight was my greatest handicap, so our first goal was for me to drop twenty pounds. He put me on a diet of early-morning workouts, steamed chicken breasts, and intense five-hour hitting sessions. For a month I was a model athlete. I counted every calorie (1,200 a day) and pushed myself to the brink during our workouts. I memorized every word of the book *Body-for-LIFE*, elevated the author Bill Phillips into godlike status in my mind, devoured the before-and-after photos of dramatically transformed women who looked like Linda Hamilton during her *Terminator* heyday, and became obsessed with the potential power of protein powder. In the mornings, while I poured scoops of the grainy white stuff into the blender, I convinced myself that it was the long-sought-after elixir that would melt the pounds off my midsection. I was doing the same thing I'd done with Gavin two years earlier, but I'd convinced myself that this time I really wanted it. Oklahoma had made me realize I still wanted to be a tennis player. This time I was serious and I'd succeed. The weight wasn't flying off, but by the time I was gearing up for the Miami Open at the end of March, I was five pounds lighter. Small progress, but progress nonetheless.

There was another reason I wanted to slim down. Miami was a doubleheader of sorts. Mary Joe's wedding was a few days after the end of the tournament, and I was a bridesmaid. It was going to be a lavish affair filled with the tennis world's elite. If a wedding doesn't motivate you to lose weight, then nothing will. I was a woman on a mission. I wanted to win in Miami and I wanted to look damn good walking down the aisle in my pink and white bridesmaid's dress. I hit the gym with a vengeance and

kicked the calorie counting into high gear. Another short-term solution to a long-term problem. I was setting myself up for failure yet again.

⚙

Key Biscayne, Florida. A tropical island paradise of stunning beaches and the longtime venue for the annual Miami Masters. A prestigious and glamorous event, it is often referred to as the "Fifth Grand Slam" and is a mandatory stop on the WTA schedule. In 2000 it was renamed the Ericsson Open but for years it had been called the Lipton Championships and it had always held a special place in my heart. When I was a gangly sixteen-year-old with stick legs and an incurable case of the giggles, I won my first Tier I title on that hard court. But that was a decade ago and it felt like I'd lived a lifetime since then. A month had passed since my Oklahoma revelation and I'd been a "good girl" in my eating and working-out habits—meticulously recording every bite of food and form of exercise in my journal—and I had high hopes for a solid performance in the tournament.

The first few matches went by quickly. I faced Anna Kournikova in the fourth round and she pushed me to three sets. I'd lost to her at the same tournament in 1998 and didn't want to do it again. Here's the quick rundown on Anna: Behind the swimsuit calendars and men's magazine covers, there is an incredibly hardworking tennis player. When she busted out of the Nick Bollettieri Tennis Academy, she was touted as the next big thing, and sponsors were falling over themselves trying to get a piece of the Russian stunner. With her model good looks, the fifteen-year-old turned everyone's head when she first played at Wimbledon in 1997 and quickly became the hottest ticket on tour. It was during that tournament that I realized there was a major changing of the guard under way. Not just in the way tennis was being played, but more dramatically in the way it was being presented to the public. The *Express* stated that "tennis knickers promise to be the smash hit of Wimbledon," while the *Daily Mail* asked the burning question: "This year, will all the talk be about sex and the singles girls?" As it turned out, yes. While the press was foaming at the mouth over Anna and a couple of other young ones, I faced endless post-game questions about my thirty-pound weight gain. One article compared my look on the court to "a hag with a frying pan." Ouch. The WTA's bevy of hot, young leggy girls with exotic accents wasn't the greatest for my self-esteem, but it was undoubtedly the smartest and quickest way to draw legions of new fans to the sport. People who hadn't given tennis two minutes of their time became glued to the TV set during Grand Slams and ESPN highlights. It was a new era and I was desperately trying to find a way to avoid it while still being a part of it.

That was the official beginning of the "Russian Gazelle" phenomenon. A mysterious creature with a powerful swing and bronzed legs of epic length, the Gazelle usually sported a long, silky ponytail and traded track-suits for trendy sports bras and Lycra shorts during public warm-ups. This new type of player used her sex appeal to increase her visibility on the court and her income off of it. She was a marketer's dream and I was nowhere close to it. Agents checking out prospective clients at junior tournaments were no longer talking about a devastating backhand or lightning-fast foot speed. They were discussing players who had "legs that went on for miles" and who were "uncommonly beautiful." As long as a player was "infinitely marketable" she would attract serious interest from management companies. Being good at tennis wasn't enough anymore: agents and sponsors wanted the whole package.

Anna wasn't just a good tennis player, she was also smart. She had blasted open the financially lucrative door by making tennis sexy, and dozens of girls followed in hot pursuit. Suddenly players were showing up for matches with flawlessly applied makeup and carefully coordinated out-fits that flashed as much skin as possible. While I'd been away from tennis in the mid-1990s, it had turned into a speed game and I was still trying to catch up to it. There was no way I had the time or energy to bother with applying lip gloss and smudge-proof liquid eyeliner before a match. The tour was going in a completely new direction and I was firmly entrenched in the old school. Not that I wouldn't have loved to walk onto center

court for a hitting session feeling confident in a skimpy outfit and smiling flirtatiously at the guys in the crowd, but my head and body were in no condition to do so. That tracksuit was staying on during my warm-ups, thank you very much.

It would have been easy to dislike Anna. She was the anointed golden hottie of tennis. When our coaches paired us up to play doubles in Tokyo in 1998, I didn't know her very well and I braced myself for the media hurricane I suspected would accompany her. She surprised me. One of the first things she told me was that I had been her idol when she was growing up. At first I was incredibly flattered but a few moments later I thought, *Oh my God, am I getting old already?* The second thing she told me was that she'd forgotten her shampoo, had to use the generic brand in the hotel shower, and hadn't had any time to blow-dry her hair before our match. I took one look at her just-stepped-out-of-a-salon blond mane and bitterly thought about the four types of frizz control serums, detanglers, and conditioners I carried with me to every country in my vain attempt to keep my poodlelike hair under control. I told you it would have been easy to dislike her. But I didn't. She was never anything other than professional on the court and kind off of it, and she always gave me credit for showing her a new level of work ethic.

We won the Tokyo tournament in a final against Mary Joe and Arantxa and played together a few more times. Of course, it took quite a while to stop comparing myself to her. It was like being thrown back into the awkward adolescent years of standing on the sidelines while the cool girls sashayed down the hallways flirting with the varsity football players making plans for the weekend. I spent very little time in a "normal" high school but I've seen enough angst-filled teenage movies to imagine that hanging out with Anna was a very similar experience. I wasn't happy with myself, and I finally chalked her beauty and body up to genetics. Instead of using her as inspiration for stepping up my fitness and whipping myself into shape, it was easier and more comforting to blame her ultimate lottery-winning genetics. Nothing she could do about it, nothing I could do about it either, so why even bother trying.

Back to Miami. Anna, whose reputation as an "overrated" player is unfair—she's beaten Hingis, Graf, and Davenport, was a strong top-ten player for years, and dominated the doubles world—had beaten me in Miami two years earlier, so I wasn't taking anything for granted. I took the first set 6–1 but struggled in the second. It was the first set I'd lost at that tournament. I shook it off and was relieved to take the third 6–0. In the quarterfinals I beat Amy Frazier, a flat-hitter who excelled on hard courts, but the victory carried a hefty price. During the second set I lunged to reach the ball and sprained my ankle. The pain shot up my leg and I immediately knew what I'd done. Pushing far out of my comfort zone, I ignored the pain to close the match. The moment I got to the locker room I wrapped my ankle and began to mentally prepare myself for playing Martina Hingis in the semis the following day. It wouldn't be pretty. Even on my best days, Hingis could beat me—she'd done it just two weeks earlier at Indian Wells—and I certainly wasn't feeling at the top of my game when I woke up the next morning with my ankle throbbing. I shouldn't have been playing, but I didn't want to pull out. Sponsors were depending on me, fans were excited about the match-up, and major money is lost when a televised match is canceled at the last moment. My people-pleasing personality and my donkeylike stubbornness kicked into overdrive. It was a mistake.

Right away I knew I was in trouble. My lateral movement was practically nonexistent and I couldn't reach balls that should have been easily in my range. Frustrated, I started to take stupid chances and hit risky angles I had no business trying to pull off. I felt suffocated in the humid air—normally it never bothers me one bit—and the wind never let up. The first set was over in a flash, 6–0. I tried to make adjustments in the second but my feet felt like lead and I couldn't make anything work. The match was a lost cause and my game was in shambles. When I reached deuce at the end of the match, a few of the ten thousand spectators tried to rally me, but I quickly silenced them when I double-faulted. You can't get much worse than that. Hingis served me a humiliating double bagel, 6–0, 6–0. A total shutout. It was the worst defeat of my career and the quickest:

a measly thirty-nine minutes. I was mortified. The fighter in me had refused to default even though it would have been the smarter choice. As the crowd threw raucous catcalls, boos, and whistles at me, I could feel my face flushing with embarrassment and I hobbled off the court as quickly as my ankle would let me. For the first time in my career I had failed to win even one game. Not one. The last time I'd lost that badly was at Wimbledon in 1989. I was only fifteen and Steffi had seriously schooled me in how to play a Grand Slam, but at least that match lasted fifty-five minutes. At least I'd taken one game. And I got to play in front of Princess Diana, so it wasn't a total waste. Miami, on the other hand, was a complete waste. But when I was questioned by the reporters who were referring to me as "woefully out of shape," I insisted that the loss was no big deal. A combination of denial and wishful thinking made me want to pretend it had never happened. But it *was* a big deal, and when a reporter asked me whether I still had passion for the game, I stumbled over my words. I said that it was a tough question and I wanted to keep the answer to myself. It doesn't take a genius to read between those lines, and the media jumped on it. Rumors of my retirement picked up speed, and in between preparations for the Italian Open I had to work overtime to quell them.

At twenty-six I was still considered young for most professions, but not in tennis. Tennis is like gymnastics or swimming for women: It is a warped aging universe where you hit your prime around sixteen and have your best years before you can order a drink in a bar. After that, you are old news, both from a performance standpoint and from a marketing one. People want you to step aside for the "new meat" on tour, and with the transformation of tennis into a sexpot sport, the pressure was beginning to reach a fever pitch. Meanwhile I was rapidly being left behind in the race to the top of the conditioning mountain. I was still hanging on to my top-ten ranking—number nine after Miami—but I knew that if I was ever going to see another Grand Slam final, I had to do one thing and one thing only: get rid of the weight. Tennis was too fast and athletic now. Having the strongest ground strokes on tour wasn't enough. The bigger I got, the faster I could see my career slipping away. To be back at the top, I had to lose my ass.

In thirty-nine minutes, my Miami nightmare had erased all the hope I'd gained in Oklahoma. I had to do something drastic. The Williams sisters were like chiseled goddesses shooting around the court and they were dominating the game. Lindsay Davenport and Martina Hingis quickly understood the urgent fitness message and had acted on it. With a six-week countdown until the Italian Open, I issued a challenge to myself to get into the best shape possible. Twenty pounds in six weeks? I could do it. It would take ironclad willpower and Ironman workouts but I could do it.

Well, I didn't. At least not for the first nine days.

The second part of my Miami doubleheader was just around the corner. Mary Joe and Tony's wedding. If I'd been smart I would have spent those nine days getting a jump-start on my fitness for Rome with the added benefit of looking and feeling good in my bridesmaid dress. Can you guess what I did instead? Here's a hint: It didn't involve protein shakes or interval sprints. Instead, I obsessed over the Miami loss. And I ate. And then I obsessed some more. And followed it up with eating more. Thinking, eating, thinking, eating, on and on and on. It is mind-numbing to think about it now. How much time I wasted punishing myself by sabotaging all the gains I'd made! A huge part of my brain was taken up by my food plans. What was I going to eat for breakfast? For lunch? For dinner? When could I fit some snacks in? It was just like when I was in serious training—obsessing over every little calorie—but now I was aiming that focus in the opposite direction. Instead of thinking about how little I could eat, I twisted it into thinking about how much of every forbidden food I could eat. I went out to dinner with friends, gorging on pasta dishes and indulging in the desserts I'd banished during my diet for the previous month. Nobody said anything to me, although I'm sure they wanted to. Then I went to my hotel, turned on the television, and relieved the minibar of every salty and sweet item it held. If it hadn't been refilled I'd go back out and buy chips, cookies, and soda at the closest convenience store.

After working my butt off for that month before Miami, I sabotaged all of my progress in what had to have been some sort of record. The bowls of spaghetti and bars of chocolate didn't erase my memory of the loss, but they did an incredibly efficient job of erasing my waistline. I knew I was hurting myself but I couldn't stop. I wanted to feel better . . . *right now*. And food was my solution. Never mind the extra workouts that lay ahead or the slim chance of winning in Rome with the extra weight; just eat now and worry about all that stress later.

The bridesmaid's dress that had been so carefully tailored had to be let out not once but twice during those nine days. Twice! The first time the entire bridal party was together for our last fitting. I was embarrassed but laughed it off with a quip. "I guess eating pasta isn't the best way to train for the Italian Open!" Ha, ha. Not so funny. No sooner had I gotten the newly altered dress back than I knew I'd need it readjusted again. I called the seamstress in a panic and asked if she could fit me in for an emergency fix. *In Style* magazine was covering the wedding and I knew those pictures would be around forever. The last thing I needed was a public record of my dress splitting down the back as I walked down the aisle. The seamstress told me to come right away and with nimble hands she quickly made the delicate fitted bodice even bigger. I was so embarrassed—why couldn't I stop myself? Why couldn't I get a handle on my emotions? What was wrong with me?

As three hundred people waited for the ceremony to begin, the bridal party was a jangle of nerves and excitement. We made some last-minute adjustments to Mary Joe's tiara and told her how stunning she looked. She was like a princess in her strapless Vera Wang dress and I felt like a blimp next to her. As I stood in line waiting for my cue to walk down the aisle, all I could think about was how big I looked next to the other bridesmaids. It was a lineup of perfect size zeros and the last thing I wanted to do was stand right in the middle of them for the next hour. As a professional athlete, I should have been the one in shape. I wasn't and I was overcome with anger at myself for not holding it together over the past week. Then the music started, the church doors swung open, and we were off. I plastered a smile to my face, but my brain was crowded with destructive thoughts. *I look huge. Everyone is staring at me. Everyone thinks I look fat.* Talk about egomaniacal. There I was, at the wedding of two of my closest friends, and all I could think about was what everyone was thinking about me. It was madness. It should have been a day full of happiness, but I couldn't get out of my own head long enough to enjoy it. After the ceremony we all headed to the beachfront reception for a sunset cocktail hour and one of the most incredible buffet dinners I've ever seen. I didn't touch any of it. I didn't want to eat in front of anyone, so—over the rumblings of my stomach—I insisted I wasn't hungry. A Latin band was in full swing and guests were twirling around the dance floor. I wanted to be right in the middle of it, feeling confident and carefree and having as much fun as everyone else, but I couldn't. My ankle was throbbing and I was furious with myself. I spent the evening chatting with the other bridesmaids and counting down the minutes until I could go back to my hotel room. The wedding had been another opportunity to lose weight and I'd blown it. Put another check in the failure box. By the time they cut the cake I was starving, so I let myself have a piece. It was my first bite of food all day. Rum cake with vanilla icing. It's still my most vivid memory of the wedding.

# – 26 –

# A Girl's Best Friend

Do you know who doesn't care if you lose a match, get roasted by the press for being past your sell-by date, and can't fit into your fancy dress? A trusty four-legged furball. Throughout my playing days, friends never understood why I spent my few weeks off at home instead of jetting to exclusive and far-flung places like Mustique and Fiji. They just didn't get it. My life was spent on a nonstop treadmill of airplanes, cabs, and hotels. The only thing I wanted to do during those treasured days away from the tennis world was *nothing*. I was yearning for something that had eluded me for years—normalcy. For me, sitting on the couch in my own house with my dog was the finest form of luxury in the world, a luxury that no five-star resort could offer.

So when I wanted to erase the memory of my Miami defeat and those horrendous dress fittings, it only seemed natural to seek refuge in the company of my canine. For a while a couple of concerned friends called to check in on me, but I never felt like talking. I just wanted to decompress and go on walks with my dog. The year after Astro died, I got another little fur buddy. Ariel was the best-behaved dog in the world and her impeccable manners earned her the honor of being the first canine to get press badges on the WTA. Quite a feat. Martina Navratilova had a three-legged Chihuahua named K.D. (short for Killer Dog) who was as fierce as Mike Tyson in his heyday. At every tournament you knew you had to watch yourself in the players' locker room. K.D. protected Martina's locker with devoted ferocity. Some players got freaked out but I thought it was hilarious. Seeing K.D. absolutely lose it always broke the tension in the room and never failed to make me laugh. "Okay, okay, K.D. I'm staying waaaaay over here!" I'd yell across the locker room. I don't think K.D. was ever a serious contender for press badges. Ariel was (and still is) as sweet as K.D. was loyal.

As soon as I got home after Mary Joe's wedding, I told my mom and Ariel to get ready to hit the road. The best way to forget a bad tournament is to conquer the next one. It was a week away and in one of my favorite places to play: Amelia Island. I was due for some good luck. No, I was past due. Way past due.

Take one part Victorian elegance, two parts laid-back island living attitude, throw in some marine life (sea turtles and manatees galore), add a dash of southern charm and a pinch of country-club flavor, and the result is Amelia Island. The streets are lined with Queen Anne–style houses and enormous live oak trees, and the vibe is both romantic and fanciful. Walking around the old district made me feel like I was in the middle of a scene from an illustrated storybook. You can almost feel the ghosts of Victorian past elegantly strolling the sidewalks. There is a town legend that I love. In the early 1900s a local woman named Kate Bailey was so taken with the gigantic tree on her street that when she heard city workers were coming to chop it down to pave the road, she sat on her veranda with a shotgun in hand. The workmen took one look at her determined stance and promptly left. Now, that's a woman who knows how to get what she wants. The majestic tree still stands there today. Coming to Amelia Island as the defending champion, I was determined to channel some of Kate's bravado into my own performance. This title was my territory and I was going to defend it for all I was worth.

To be a threat on the professional tour, you are forced to be selfish and to put yourself before all others. At the end of a match there is only room for one winner. Being—and staying—in the number one slot intensifies it even more. That inescapable fact has always bothered me. Having a tight-knit group of friends on the tour simply wasn't compatible with being a top player. Mary Joe and Betsy were the only tennis friends I had during my playing days. Betsy's singles career had come to a close by the time I turned professional, so our interaction on the court was limited to pairing up for doubles, which I loved. Mary Joe, on the other hand, had been a force at the top of the rankings for much of my career and over eight years we played each other sixteen times. I dreaded our matches. One of my worst experiences was during our quarterfinal match in the 1997 French Open. In the third set there was a terrible line call. We were tied and I felt bad arguing the call but I needed that point. Mary Joe needed it too. It was awkward and uncomfortable and I tried to move past it as quickly as I could by closing out the match. Playing her was never fun and I swore to myself I wouldn't make any other friends in tennis until after I retired. When you are down 5–3 in the third set and you have to pull out all the stops to harness the kind of aggression it takes to beat the player on the other side of the net, it is much easier to do if you know you aren't going out for dinner together afterward. If your goal in life is to make friends, the professional tennis circuit is a poor career choice.

Amelia Island was the tune-up for the start of the European season; playing well would make my life easier on the other side of the Atlantic. Within two weeks I'd be on a plane bound for Italy, then France, and then a quick hop over to England for the most famous tournament in the world. If I put on a solid performance now, my seeding would be lower at the French Open and Wimbledon, allowing me to put off playing my strongest opponents until later matches. It was important to show up with my A game all week long. In between sips of my tasteless breakfast protein shake (I'd have much preferred French toast with hash browns, but I was hell-bent on doing everything on Bobby's list, at least for that week), I envisioned myself stepping foot onto the clay court.

Clay. It's right up there with dogs and sugar on my list of all-time favorite things. Feeling the soft crunch of earth beneath my feet sends primal chills down my body in anticipation of playing on what feels like home to me. To get tennis-geek technical, Amelia Island uses the American version of clay called Har-Tru, so it's a little different from my beloved gritty, dusty French Open turf. That crushed red brick in Paris is the backbone of the European and South American tennis landscape. Kids there grow up with their legs covered in beautiful burnt sienna dust—the dirtier your clothes, the stronger a testament to a hard-played match. But American clay is different. First, it's green. Second, it plays harder and faster than the red clay. European and South American players tend to excel on clay courts, since they grew up with them. I moved to the U.S. when I was still a kid, so I grew up playing on all kinds of surfaces. But I'm a baseliner, so the slow nature of clay suits my game perfectly. Once the ball hits the ground, the clay grabs it and causes it to sit up. The ball gets a high bounce, dangling in the air just asking—no, *begging*—to be pounded with a power ground stroke. There aren't any fast, tricky, fancy points to be played on clay. You can save that stuff for Wimbledon's grass (by far my least favorite surface). Clay is a grueling test of endurance. Players either love it or fear it. I'm afraid of an all-you-can-eat Italian dessert bar but I'm not afraid of grinding out excruciating long points; it's my specialty. Clay is a very old, very good friend.

Instead of staying in a nondescript hotel room, I spent the week at a house close to the tournament site so I could cycle to the courts. Jumping on my bike brought back the best memories from my childhood. After downing my protein shake, I kissed my mom and Ariel good-bye, grabbed my tennis bag, and hopped on my bike. The wind was whipping through my hair as I cruised along the streets. The sun was warm on my bare arms, and for just a moment I felt like a kid again. I felt like I was on my way to meet my friends for a game of soccer. For one moment, maybe just a fraction of a moment, I felt like everything in the world was okay. Then the stadium courts came into view and I was jolted back to reality. I had matches to play and a title to defend. It was time to put my game face on. My first match was against Anna Smashnova, a player I'd never faced before; but if her name was any indication, I was in for a good fight. I mean, come on, *Smashnova*? You couldn't invent a better name than that for a tennis player. The only thing I knew about Anna was that, like me, she was a baseliner who was at home on clay courts. I also knew that she was from Israel and had gone to military school. Having a soldier's mentality was sure to add another layer to her game. And she had a tactical edge. Her husband, Claudio, had briefly worked with me in 1997. I'd known him from our junior playing days at the Orange Bowl tournament, which he'd won. He was a friend of mine and he knew exactly where my balls would be landing. Anna, known to be one of the nicest and most professional players on tour, would be well prepared. She came out for our warm-up and I was struck by her size. With eight inches in my favor, I towered over her; but I'd soon find out that, like Amanda Coetzer, her height was no indication of her power. Her arms were absolutely ripped. I could've done triceps dips eighteen hours a day and I wouldn't come close to looking like that. She was a powerhouse waiting to burst onto the court. And that's exactly what she did, coming at me with everything she had.

I had to struggle to stay focused in the first set. It was close, but I managed to bear down and take it 7–6. When you battle it out so hard and the set comes down to a single point, the person who ends up on the losing side often feels mentally destroyed. Once that momentum is snatched right out from under you, the adrenaline that was coursing through your veins moments before takes a nosedive and it is painfully hard to get back into the match. Anna couldn't and I took the next set 6–0. I did my job for the day and headed back home for—at Bobby's request—a meal of steamed chicken and spinach. I still had four more matches to get through.

That night the rain started and it didn't let up for two days. When tennis tournaments are rained out, there is a lot of sitting around. Because all the tournaments are scheduled back-to-back, if a few days are missed due to bad weather, the tournament organizers have to squish all the remaining matches in as quickly as possible the moment the rain stops. I sat around for two days looking at the gray clouds, flipping back and forth between the Weather Channel and the local news, and doing my best to stay away from the kitchen. Is there anything better than a huge bowl of popcorn and a mug of hot chocolate to keep you company during a storm? If there is, I have yet to find it. Exerting superhuman willpower, I left the bags of Newman's Own Butter Popcorn sitting unpopped in the cabinet and continued my workouts and hitting sessions with Bobby while we waited out the storm. The thing about rain delays is that you have to maintain a constant state of focus. You get very little notice before your match starts, so you stay in this no-man's-land of being in a highly competitive state of mind without knowing when the heck your match is going to start. Sitting around waiting for a match can be more exhausting than playing it. By Friday evening the forecast for the weekend looked promising.

"Are you going to be ready tomorrow?" It was Bobby calling to check in on me after our last hitting session of the day.

"Yes, I'll be ready."

"Make sure you eat right tonight."

"I've got it under control." I glanced at the water boiling on the stove and the stalks of broccoli waiting for their scorching steam bath. A sad, limp little chicken breast was lying on the counter. The thought of eating that food for the umpteenth time depressed me. Especially when I knew there was a fantastic steak-and-seafood place with a stunning view of the ocean just a few blocks away. *Fuel, Monica*, I told myself. *It's just fuel. Don't get all emotional about it. You aren't here on vacation. You're here to work.*

"All right," Bobby said. "Get a good night's sleep. See you in the morning."

I tossed and turned that night, unable to quiet my mind over the constant rumblings of my stomach. *You aren't hungry*, I repeated to myself like a mantra. *You aren't hungry.* But my stomach wouldn't listen to me. It felt empty and lonely and abandoned. *Where are my good friends? Where are my loyal chocolate chip cookies and barbecue chips and fettucine? Where did everyone go? I miss them!* Those were the wrong questions. What I should have been asking had nothing to do with food and everything to do with my father and my future. *Will I ever fill the void left by my dad's death? Will I ever be the tennis player I once was? If I'm not, what will that mean? Who will I be?* But I didn't ask those questions that night and I wouldn't for a few more years. All I could hear was my stomach. I glanced at the clock. It was 4:30. I was relieved. Only two more hours until I could eat breakfast.

Mornings were always easy for me, dietwise. I was an impeccable eater from the moment I got out of bed until the early evening. But as soon as the sun started to set, I was in my danger zone. I turned into a food vampire. My hunger was insatiable. So when I woke up a minute before my alarm went off, I felt unusually hopeful and optimistic. I practically skipped to the kitchen in hot pursuit of my protein shake, which I drank down with a good dose of self-righteous pride. I felt far more proud of myself for making it through the night without cracking for carbs than for winning my first match three days earlier. Disordered eating had turned into disordered thinking.

The rain delay meant there were only two days left in the tournament. Which meant I had to play my third-round match in the morning and, hopefully, get to the quarterfinal in the afternoon. Sunday would be a doubleheader of the semis and the final. That was a lot of tennis to plow through in two days. I charged over to the courts, ready to take on my next opponent. Corina Morariu had won the Wimbledon doubles title with her best friend Lindsay Davenport the previous year, so I was ready for a strong competitor right out of the gates. I was so ready, in fact, that I took the match 6–3, 6–1 and immediately started thinking about my afternoon with Arantxa Sánchez-Vicario. We'd played against each other dozens of times, starting way back in 1989 when I was a clueless, gawky fifteen-year-old and she was a seventeen-year-old hotshot from Barcelona who had just stunned the world by upsetting Steffi in the finals of the French Open. Over the years, I had a very good record against her with the 1998 French Open final as one of the only glaring failures.

Maybe I was channeling my frustration at not beating her at Roland Garros. Maybe I was in a hurry to get the match over before the skies opened up again. Maybe the protein powder from my second shake of the day had a little more kick than normal. Or maybe I was just having a plain old good day. Whatever the reason, I went out on the court and forced my legs to do battle for the second time that day. I beat her 6–1, 6–3 and got ready to set my sights on the next day's repeat of back-to-back matches. But not just yet. The press had to pepper me with the same old questions one more time. It would have been much easier to walk around with a sign that said, NO, I AM NOT RETIRING. Instead we went around and around in the same circles we always did in the postmatch press conferences.

Them: "How is your foot?" (Translation: *You looked sluggish out there.*)

Me: "Fine, thanks."

Them: "How's your ankle?" (Translation: *There must be some reason you looked slow on the court today. What was it?*)

Me: "It's doing much better."

Them: "How much longer do you think you will put up with these injuries?" (Translation: *Can you give us a firm retirement date?*)

Me: "As long as I feel like I can play—which I do—I plan on doing just that."

Them: "How's your fitness coming along?" (Translation: *Are you ever going to lose the weight?*)

Me: "I know I have to work at it. My coach and I are making it our main focus right now."

Them: "Do you think your fitness is affecting your game?" (Translation: *If you dropped twenty pounds, you'd run a heck of a lot faster on the court.*)

Me: "Again, I know my fitness is something I need to work on. I've been spending tons of time in the gym, something I've never done before."

Them: "Monica, you've already won nine Grand Slams, the last one in '96. What do you think your chances are of capturing another?" (Translation: *Face it, honey, your glory days are long gone. Can't you get into commentating or something?*)

Me: "Well, if I didn't think my chances were good, I certainly wouldn't be out here."

Them: "Have you thought about settling down?" (Translation: *Retire already!*)

Me: "Settling down?"

Them: "You know, getting married, having kids, that sort of thing."
(Translation: *Okay, seriously, it's time to get off the court.*)

Me: "No. That isn't what I'm thinking about right now."

They could have recycled the transcripts from every press conference over the past three years and it would have been exactly the same. Maybe one or two questions would be about the match. The rest were about the shape I was in or when I was going to retire. It didn't matter that I'd just won two matches against extremely strong opponents. Instead of focusing on what I was accomplishing in the present, they were focusing on what I wouldn't accomplish in the future. Retire, retire, retire. It became the dreaded *R* word for me and I eliminated it from my vocabulary. Nevertheless, I was constantly reminded of it whenever a journalist crossed my path.

As soon as I hit twenty-two I felt like people were just waiting for me to step aside. I'd already been at the top, won the prestigious tournaments, and being in the top ten, or even the top five, wasn't good enough. If I wasn't winning Grand Slams like I used to, then it was assumed I was on the downward slope of my career arc. And if I wasn't going to be at the very top, then I was taking a coveted top-ten spot from an up-and-coming, more promising, and more marketable teenager. But I wasn't ready to retire at twenty-two, and four years later I still wasn't ready. I've never been a quitter. It's not in my DNA. After getting through the stabbing and my dad's death, I knew I could withstand a lot. A group of journalists that was impatient with my playing form and my inability to recapture the glory of my Grand Slam days wasn't going to pressure me to close the chapter on my tennis career. I wasn't going to quietly ride off into the sunset of Floridian recreational club tennis until I was good and ready.

When I woke up on Sunday morning, I thought about one thing: the booing of the crowd in Miami after Martina Hingis had wiped up the court with me. It still made my cheeks flush with anger and embarrassment. I wasn't going to let that happen again. Paola Suárez, a twenty-three-year-old from Argentina, was waiting to take me on in the semifinal. Over the next few years she would crack the top ten and be the number one doubles player, but at Amelia Island she was a new opponent for me and I didn't know what to expect. My goal was to win the match as quickly as possible so I could rest before the final later that day. I won the match 6–3, 6–2 and immediately went home to regroup. Playing three matches in twenty-four hours is hard on your body and even harder on your mind. As I stretched my hamstrings on the floor of the family room, Ariel came up to lick my face. "Hi, girl." I ruffled her fur. "Just one more to get through. No problem right?" She gave me an excited little bark and ran back and forth across the room. I took it as a good sign.

The final was against Conchita Martínez, a Wimbledon champion and patient baseliner who was notorious for ruining her opponent's rhythm. She had the ability to mix up the pace and spin of her shots at a dizzying rate, leaving the player on the other side of the net scratching her head and wondering what had just hit her. Like Arantxa, she and I had a long history, so I knew exactly what was waiting for me. Before I set foot on the court, my mind wandered again to Kate Bailey, the local woman who had stood guard over her beloved tree. Kate had claimed guardianship over that ancient tree, looked the townsmen in the eye, gripped her shotgun a little tighter, and stood her ground until they left. That was exactly what I had to do today. The court was my tree, the impatient journalists the townsmen, and my racket my trustworthy weapon. The analogy was a bit of a creative stretch but tennis is such a mental game. You have to play games like that in your head to keep you focused and in the moment. Besides, it worked! I took the match with the same score as the semi, 6–3, 6–2.

If this was my official kickoff to the European season, then the future looked brighter than it had in a long time. Just three months earlier I had been playing in a Tier III tournament, thinking it was going to be the last time I'd lace up my shoes as a professional. With this win, the horrendous memory of being booed off the court in Miami quickly faded into the distance, and I could see Rome on the horizon. Four weeks until the Italian Open. It was time to get ready to take on Europe.

# The A-Team

Amelia Island gave me a desperately needed shot of confidence. If Oklahoma City had been a small nudge on my long, steep climb back, Amelia Island had given me a sizable push. But it wasn't necessarily indicative of how things would shake out once I got to Europe. The season over there is three months long. Twelve weeks of living out of my suitcase, packing, unpacking, and packing again, eating in a different restaurant every night, and getting on another plane every seven days. The list of tournaments reads like a college grad's dream backpacking trip. It also reads like a gourmand's menu of gastronomic delights: Budapest (Castle District and cabbage rolls with loads of paprika), Berlin (Brandenburg Gate and apple strudel), Warsaw (beautifully restored Old Town and cheese and potato pierogi slathered in sour cream), Rome (Coliseum and gnocchi with Gorgonzola sauce), Antwerp (Rubens House and chocolate, chocolate, chocolate), Madrid (Retiro Park and arroz con pollo), Paris (Champs-Élysées and hot, flaky croissants with a cup of *café con crème*), London (Bond Street and Yorkshire pudding with gravy), and Prague (Gothic towers and apricot dumplings).

Unfortunately, the tournament schedule is so tight that all I saw in these incredible cities was my hotel room and the tennis court. And my clothes were so tight I wasn't allowed to indulge in most of the international delicacies. Ordering skim milk or fat-free anything in countries that pride themselves on culinary excellence—*real* food—would be blasphemous. Simply unheard-of. A fat-free cappuccino in Rome? Good luck. I'd already run into that problem with Peter the year before in Paris. But every hotel restaurant can whip up a plate of tasteless grilled chicken (no oil) and steamed vegetables. So that's where I ate every meal. My inner foodie was screaming out in protest. The itinerary was amazing, but I didn't see it from a tourist view. When you have the blinders of professional tennis permanently attached, it doesn't take long before every city looks the same.

Case in point: The first time I played in Paris was in 1989, and it became one of my favorite stops on the tour. I can't get enough of that Roland Garros clay. Every year, after I'd return home from the European swing, my friends would gleefully ask, "How amazing was Paris? Don't you just *love* that city? Did you go to Versailles? Montmartre? The Musée d'Orsay? Did you see the *Mona Lisa*?" I'd just smile and repeat for the millionth time, "Yeah, I didn't really have time to see that stuff. Maybe next time!" But I knew that wasn't true. I knew that as long as I was playing tennis, I wouldn't have a life outside the daily grind of workouts, matches, sponsor obligations, and diets. The moment the French Open was over, I was headed to Eastbourne, the British warm-up tournament for Wimbledon. There is a mere two weeks between the Grand Slam on clay and the Grand Slam on grass. You have to transform from an endurance monster on clay to an agile rabbit on grass, so there isn't any time for sightseeing in the Latin Quarter. Within hours of leaving Paris, I'd be practicing on one of Eastbourne's grass rectangles.

I could find my way from the hotel to Roland Garros with my eyes closed, but I'd never seen Notre Dame or the Louvre. During the car ride from Charles de Gaulle to the hotel I'd get glimpses of the city's grandeur, but I'd never really seen it up close. It wasn't until 2005—when I was taking a major break from tennis—that I finally saw Paris the way it is meant to be seen.

But in the spring of 2000, while I was enjoying my post–Amelia Island victory (it lasted about twenty minutes), being a free-spirited tourist in Paris was the last thing on my mind. At Amelia Island, when the press wasn't grilling me on the countdown to my retirement, they were peppering Bobby with questions about the shape I was in—or rather the shape I wasn't in. Over and over he patiently replied, "Our main goal is to get Monica into the best physical shape possible." The day after the win, Bobby sat me down. He meant business.

"Monica, how are you doing?"

"Not bad." It was true: I wasn't feeling bad. But I wasn't feeling good, either. My mind was already on the other side of the Atlantic, fretting over the shape I'd be in for the high-profile Italian Open and whether it was possible to be in Grand Slam shape for Paris. "Look, I know I have a lot of work to do. I know I have to work on my movement."

He nodded. "Uh-huh."

"And my conditioning," I continued.

"Yep," he agreed.

"And just, I guess . . . What's your go-to phrase? My 'overall fitness'? I know I've got to get to the ball faster."

"You know what you have to do," he said. "You just have to ask yourself one thing: How bad do you want it?"

"I want it. Bad." I did. I wanted to be the player I used to be. I wanted to win more Grand Slams. I wanted people to stop waiting for me to retire. I wanted to be proud of my game again.

"Okay." Bobby smiled with the excitement of a new coaching mission brewing in his head. "Here's the plan . . ."

He said that if I was going to make a serious run for another Grand Slam, we had to pull out all the stops. My diet had to be perfect 24/7, the intensity of my cardio sessions needed to be ramped up even further, and my off-court agility sessions had to be a daily commitment. No getting out of them—ever. We were operating on a tight deadline and there was no room for error. We were undertaking the making of a champion—or, more accurately, the remaking of a champion—and we had to do it in a month. My fundamentals were fine, but everything else had to change if I wanted to keep up with the younger girls who were dominating the top spots. The days of resting on my natural power from the baseline were long gone. I was about to log more time in the gym over the next four weeks than I had in my entire life. I was at least twenty-five pounds overweight— the Miami bulge was stubbornly staying put on my stomach—and there was no way in hell I was going to be a sprightly little bunny while lugging these unwelcome pounds around. Even with a hard-core workout routine and spartan diet—maybe if I ate like a rabbit I'd play like one too?—I didn't know how much progress I could make in four weeks. But drastic times called for drastic measures.

We put together our own tennis "A-Team," hired guns to take me to my optimum level of performance, or at least the highest level I could get to by the Italian Open deadline. It takes a village to raise a child, and it was going to take a team of athletic wizards to raise my fitness to playing level. Think about it: Tennis is the most individual of sports. Even my dad's beloved sport of track-and-field has an element of camaraderie. Athletes can train together on the track, but you'll never, ever see tennis players prepping for an upcoming tournament on the same court. And when you're performing, it's just you out there on your side of the net. Baseball, basketball, football, soccer, hockey—you've got your team and your coach to depend on (and to help take some heat when things go wrong). Even golfers have caddies to pull the right club and to talk them out of an unwise shot. If you mess up in tennis, it's just you out there. There's nowhere to hide and there's no deflecting the blame.

But behind most top players there is a small army of coaches, trainers, hitting partners, therapists, and nutritionists enabling that athlete to reach her peak performance. Every morsel of food is calculated to translate into the highest nutritional punch possible. Every exercise is planned to maximize the agility and speed of lateral movement and explosive first-step power. For decades my dad had been my coach, nutritionist, fitness trainer, and sports psychologist, and while I'd worked very hard, he always took a bit of a laissez-faire approach. He always kept it fun and free from pressure, so even when I was working seven hours a day, it never felt like work. After he passed away, tennis really became work. I didn't know the first thing about building a team around me. My dad had been my team. In two years I'd already been through two coaches and who knows how many hitting partners. Nothing was clicking and my whole tennis game was a haphazard house of cards in danger of collapsing at any moment. I had to figure out how to restructure, balance, and fortify it. I'd take help from as many different sources as possible. You can always learn something new in tennis; it is a game that is impossible to master. That's the beauty of it. Tactics are forever changing, shot placement and angle creation are forever improving; the second you think you can rest at your current level, you'll get knocked right off the podium by someone who is working twice as hard as you on the next court over.

So Bobby put our team together. Obviously he would handle my coaching. A master at technique, Bobby could discern the tiniest flaw in anyone's swing within a fraction of a second. He'd been trying to change my serve since Oklahoma, and it was finally starting to feel less spastic and more natural. Next we called up my old drill sergeant, Bob Kersee. He'd whipped my lethargic, ice-cream-eating self into shape when I was in the throes of the post-stabbing haze of depression and confusion. I promised myself that this time I wouldn't throw all my gains away. Vail was seven years ago, a lifetime in women's tennis. I was different now. I'd lost control in Miami, but I told myself that it was just a blip. I was ready to reclaim my place at the top and I'd do anything Bobby and Bob told me to do. Here was the breakdown:

*7 to 8 a.m.:* Drink my fantastic shake; bonus points if accomplished without complaining. You know how sometimes you build up a tolerance to things that you once couldn't stand? Maybe even come to appreciate or enjoy them? Like Brussels sprouts or broccoli? Yeah, that didn't happen with the shake and me.

*8 a.m. to 12:30 p.m.:* On-court hitting sessions with Jimmy Arias, a former top player who basically invented the topspin forehand in the men's game. He and Bobby had grown up together in upstate New York and he'd become a friend of mine. A tennis prodigy, Jimmy was raised by a strict and demanding father, so he took the opposite approach. Like my dad, he wanted to turn everything into a game. Whenever Jimmy and I worked together I always had so much fun. The hitting sessions always revolved around bets. Whoever lost had to do push-ups—the real kind, not the girl kind. Every morning we hit thousands of balls while I refined my angles and brushed up on my power from the baseline. This was the least daunting part of my new routine, since I had a masochistic devotion to hitting balls for hours on end. Along with adjusting to my improved serve, I was also trying to make friends with my new Yonex racket. My old one was a giant relic at 130 square inches, but I adored it and it had to be pried out of my clenched hands. Knowing that I needed more control when facing big hitters and a more powerful serve, I traded up to a smaller and more technologically advanced racket of 110 square inches. It may not sound like a dramatic change, but for the first few days I felt like my best friend had moved away and I had to hang with some new kid I didn't really gel with.

*12:30 to 1:30 p.m.:* Lunch of—you guessed it—plain grilled chicken breast with a side salad of mixed greens, tomatoes, and vinegar. No cheese, no oil, no nuts. In other words, nothing to make it taste good.

*1:30 to 2 p.m.:* Deep stretching of my back and hamstrings. Years of pounding my legs back and forth across the tennis court had given me hamstrings as tight as my size twelve pants now felt. This was also supposed to be the time for me to digest my lunch. I was already thinking about what I'd be eating for dinner.

*2 to 3 p.m.:* Step onto the treadmill—or "dreadmill," as I preferred to call it. Set the speed to 3.3 and crank the incline up to level 15. Not all treadmill programs are the same, so how can I best describe level 15? Imagine taking the treadmill and standing it up on its side so that is completely perpendicular to the floor. Now get on it. That pretty much describes level 15. Stay on it for one hour. Bonus points for not throwing up or being dragged like a pancake underneath the belt.

*3 to 3:05 p.m.:* Water break. Replenish my fluids and weigh the odds of my being able to sneak out the back door of the gym without Bobby noticing. Realize I have less than a .05 percent chance of escaping undetected. Decide my legs are too tired to try to outrun him.

*3:05 to 5 p.m.:* We save the best for last. My days ended with Kersee-created track workouts: two-hundred-meter interval sprints, fast-feet drills between orange cones, and squats with vertical jumps to maximize my core power. Throw in a medicine ball to make it super-fun. Repeat all until I can't move anymore.

*5:30 p.m.:* Return home. Walk in door. Bed seems too far away. Decide couch in family room looks exceptionally inviting.

*7 p.m.:* Ah, dinnertime. My long-awaited reward. Wait a minute, what's this shake doing in front of me *again?*

*8 p.m.:* Drag myself back to the couch, pick up the remote, find something to watch that doesn't take one iota of brainpower to comprehend.

*10 p.m.:* Go to bed. Fall asleep before my head hits the pillow. Dream sweet dreams of pancakes drizzled with syrup. Start all over in the morning.

✳

While every meal and workout was planned for minimum caloric intake and maximum $VO_2$ expenditure, what was to keep me from screwing up at home?

My A-Team was one step ahead of me: before we even embarked on the first workout of the new regime, they had a food sentinel standing guard, ready to tackle any salty fat-loaded carb right out of my hands. Chris, a ripped-beyond-belief testament to the value of fitness and a severely restrictive diet, had worked with Kersee for years and was assigned to my troubled case. He was officially in charge of "monitoring my nutrition," but really he was a food babysitter whose sole responsibility was to make sure no unapproved calories passed my lips. He weighed all my food and we ate—or, more often than not, drank—every meal together. Instead of resenting this new shadow in my life, I was relieved that the pressure was off me. I didn't have to exercise my own willpower; I left it up to Chris, my food warden. Every minute of my life was planned out for the next four weeks—he even stayed in a guest room at my house so that midnight runs to the kitchen would be impossible. It wasn't a coincidence that I gave him the room that was right next to the kitchen. I needed that kind of deterrent. Missing a workout would be a catastrophe, a personal shame that would disappoint everyone trying to help me. So I showed up with my game face on every single day. I didn't want everyone else's hard work and dedication to go to waste. Besides, it was only four weeks. I could get through it.

My mission impossible became possible. I was, far and away, in the best shape I'd been in since my stabbing. Score one for the team! In one month I lost eight pounds and had broken that impenetrable twenty-pound barrier. I was now only 19.5 pounds over my target weight. I really counted that .5 pound: it was of the utmost importance and I even did two extra miles on the track and twenty minutes in an unbearable sauna the day before I left for Rome to reach that elusive number. Italy, here I come!

Curled up in my airplane seat on Alitalia, I fluffed the tiny pillows, wedged them in between my head and the window, and settled in for a good night's sleep. I don't need three Tylenol PMs and two glasses of wine to get through a long flight. The moment the plane hits its cruising altitude, I am out like a baby. Airplanes are a quiet bubble of peace for me, an isolated sanctuary at thirty-five-thousand feet. Instead of counting sheep, I thought about Rome. And I thought about my dad. While Paris owned the biggest share of my best championship memories, Rome laid a sentimental claim to a big piece of my heart.

# – 28 –

## *Roman Holiday*

I've never done a "real" spring break. I've never been to Cancún or gone on a booze cruise with a crew of giggling girlfriends. The closest I got to wet T-shirt contests and trays of Jell-O shots during my teens was watching snippets of MTV's *Spring Break* while I was kicking back in a hotel room during some tournament or other. Instead, from the time I was sixteen, I did spring break Roman style, with my family. An extra scoop of gelato after dinner was as crazy as I ever got in Rome, but it was a fantastic place to play. As the first stop on the European swing, it was where I greeted my old friend—real red clay.

The first time I went to Rome I was, like every tourist, awestruck by the magnitude of its, well, its *everything*. In most cities I never had the chance to see the sights, but in Rome I couldn't help it. Everywhere I looked, my senses were assaulted with the sultry, sophisticated, over-the-top grandeur that is the Eternal City. Over here, look, the Spanish Steps! Over there, see, that's the Pantheon! The Forum! The Coliseum! and just try walking twenty feet without running into another famous fountain or mosaic. It was beauty overload, and it stretched beyond the city's architecture and swept up its inhabitants too. Impossibly chic women teetered down the ancient streets in five-hundred-dollar stilettos while the men strutted by in designer sunglasses and expensive loafers. A lingering glance and hint of a smile was considered flirtatious without being slimy. Italians just appreciate beauty.

In late spring, the rising temperature brought a burst of flowers and a flood of people to the outdoor cafés. Why be inside when there is so much beauty to be appreciated in the Piazza di Spagna? It was a perfect time to be in Rome. I didn't spend many hours indulging in the café life, but I did spend an awful lot of quality time with some chiseled Roman studs. During the tournament my dad and I always set up shop in the Stadio dei Marmi (Stadium of Marble). With his track-and-field background, my dad had a nose for sniffing out the nearest training facility no matter where in the world we were. But in Rome, he didn't have to go very far. The tournament is held in the Foro Italico, an enormous sports complex on the banks of the Tiber River. Amid the tennis courts, swimming pools, and cavernous Olympic Stadium sits the majestic—and almost always empty—Stadio dei Marmi.

I've worked out on dozens and dozens of tracks—some were devoid of lane lines and overgrown with weeds, while others were impeccably cared for under the watchful eye of big university sports programs—but nothing compares to the sight that greets you in this stunning Roman stadium. The bright green field is encircled by a dusty red track. The marble stands can seat twenty thousand spectators, and at the very top there are sixty white marble statues of athletes perched on individual tiers. Some are nude while some are covered with a discreet fig leaf, and all of them are engaged in some sort of physical endeavor. Representing the sixty provinces of Italy, they make an intimidating group of twelve-foot-high übermuscular specimens of athletic greatness. If that doesn't channel your inner gladiator, I don't know what will. It did the trick for me: some of the best workouts with my dad happened under the haughty gazes of those frozen-in-time athletes.

When I made my first appearance there at sixteen, I was at the start of a massive winning tear. It turned out to be the longest winning streak of my career: thirty-six matches in a row. Six straight tournament titles. I'd made somewhat of a splash the year before when I reached the semis of the French Open, but veteran players could easily dismiss that as a one-off, just another teen phenom flash in the pan. You don't gain respect by having a single extraordinary tournament run, especially at such a young age. The road to the coveted top five is littered with early peakers and those who burned out from the grind. What would you call that? A ground out? So, to prevent being an early peaker or a ground out, and to gain the respect of other players, you've got to do two things on your way to the top: win consistently and win a Grand Slam.

I've always had a problem with the way the points system works in tennis. It's possible to be ranked number one *without ever winning a Grand Slam*. That's never made much sense to me. Regardless, I'd been winning for most of 1990 when I arrived in Rome for "Spring Break: Extreme Tennis Version." My dad told me to focus on this tournament, to put the French Open out of my mind. He counseled me not to think about tomorrow, let alone a few weeks ahead. *Stay in the moment, Monica,* he said. Easier said than done, obviously. But he made a good point: if I played Rome while my mind was already going north up to Paris, there was no way I'd make it past the quarterfinals—or even past the second round. I had to play Rome for Rome, not in anticipation of hoisting my first Grand Slam trophy into the air.

Rome is considered the most prestigious clay tournament after the French Open, so it wasn't like I'd been planning on breezing through it with my head in the clouds. The trick was to focus on playing my best game possible, one match at a time. If I went far, great. If not, I'd have another chance to prove myself in Paris. But here's the kicker: Tennis is more a game of the mind than a game of the body. You can have the best serve, the strongest fundamentals, a lethal drop shot; but if your head doesn't believe it, your body will follow suit and obey the command to lose. Momentum is everything in a game, in a set, and in a match. It is also everything on the travel schedule. If I did well in Rome, I'd feel like the wind was at my back on the way to Paris.

So I got to work. With complete focus, I churned through my matches one at a time, and the moment they were over, I'd head to the practice courts to hit or I'd practice my sprints and quick starts and stops in the Stadio dei Marmi. We'd stop by one of the pizza joints on the way back to the hotel for a quick slice. Every day we'd try a different topping: potatoes, sausage, olives, red peppers, even figs and smoked salmon. Later that night, a big plate of pasta at the hotel restaurant fueled me up and got me ready to do it all over the next day.

My one-track mind had worked, and before I knew it I was in the semi-final against Helen Kelesi, the fierce baseliner whom I'd played my first professional match against two years earlier. As I had through the whole tournament, point by point, game by game, I took the match in two smooth sets, 6–1, 6–2. For the final I had to face the one, the only Martina Navratilova, truly a legend. She'd beaten me twice the year before, so I was more than a little nervous walking down the long, long hallway. Rome has the longest walk from the players' locker room to the court of any tournament. The first time I did it I thought I was lost! I had to look at a tournament official for reassurance that we were, indeed, still heading for the court. It actually takes about five minutes to walk to Court Centrale. When you are fighting off the butterflies in your stomach, that five minutes seems like an eternity. *Stay focused, Monica. Stay in the moment.* My father's words from that morning's hitting session were ping-ponging back and forth in my head. After setting up my gear on the player's chair, I stole a quick glance at Martina. She looked loose but focused, an air of calm that surrounds a player who has proven herself over and over again.

The match went by in a flash as I played my heart out amid cheerings of *"Andiamo!"* and *"Forte!"* I was on my game, in my zone, and I beat one of the best players in the history of the game 6–1, 6–1. *What? How'd that happen?* For a split second I was whisked back in time; I was eight years old and, not knowing how to keep score, had to look at my dad to find out whether I'd won the match or not. At sixteen I knew I'd won but I still searched him out in the crowd to get some reassurance that, yes, I'd just beaten one of my idols. There he was in the player's box, clapping and bursting with pride. At the postmatch press conference, Martina said she felt like she'd "been run over by a semitruck." That wouldn't be the last time I'd be compared to a hulking truck, but it was definitely the only time it was meant as a compliment. So, with my first major clay court victory in Europe stuffed into my professional pocket, the momentum was on my side. Rome gave me the mental surge I needed. I could do it. I could win at Roland Garros. Two weeks later I did it.

Some people have a lucky penny, a silver locket, or a pair of worn-out socks that they keep around for good luck. Other than the bizarre line phobia that used to make me hop, skip, and jump all over the court, I've never let superstition color my game. At least I never thought so, but that was what Rome ended up being for me. A good-luck stop, a geographic talisman that made me feel both at home and psyched to hit the road with my A-game intact. After that first win, I went back for the next two years in a row and, had it not been for the stabbing, would have kept going back every year.

Have you ever been to a city where you feel instantly at home? A place where everything is foreign—the language, the food, the customs, the taxis—but nothing seems strange? Where you don't feel out of place? That was Rome for me. It has some sort of energy that pulled me back again and again. When I'm hopping around from city to city, it always takes some time to settle in to each new place. But in Rome, the second my plane touched down, I was raring to go. Arriving was like finding an old pair of softly worn-through jeans: *Ah, there you are, old friend,* you think as you button them up and admire the rear view. I knew what I'd be eating, where I'd be staying, where I'd be working out, and I had a pretty good idea that I'd play well on those red courts and be adequately psyched for Paris. After that first victory, I made sure it was on my schedule every year. Gaby Sabatini beat me in '91 and '92, and I'd lost in the third round in '97 and '98. But it was still one of my favorite places to play. Was it superstition? Maybe. I wasn't going to label it or question it. Maybe it was just that I loved working out with my dad in an empty Roman stadium and heading to the nearest trattoria to discuss the next day's match strategy over a long dinner.

Players usually jet out of town the second they lose their match, but I was never in a hurry to leave Rome. The pace of life, the beauty of the buildings, the warmth of the people, and the food, oh, the food! All of it made me want to stick around. Every spring, after I played my last match, I had three choices:

1. Hit the road and hustle to fit in another tournament before the French.
2. Pack my bags and, along with the advance press corps team, get to Paris early.
3. Stay put and continue my Italian rhythm, free from the obligations of tennis as a business.

In a world where staying in one place for two straight weeks is a treat, staying for three weeks is an unheard-of luxury. It wasn't a difficult decision. I always decided to stay. Once the traveling circus of the tour left town, it was just my dad and me. We got to take a breath and we got to eat a lot of pizza.

But even in Italy, reality finally intruded. The phone call I received from Zoltan telling me to get on the next flight home to say good-bye to my dad still haunted me. And now here I was again, two years later, heading back to Rome.

"Pasta or chicken?"

"Hm?" I was shaken out of my state of semi-sleep and looked up from my pillow to see a flight attendant bending toward me.

"Would you like pasta or chicken for dinner?"

"Oh, um, neither. Thank you anyway." I stole a glance at my team. My mom was reading next to me. Chris and Bobby were sitting in the same row, casually looking in my direction to make sure I didn't order any of the sodium-laced caloric monstrosities lurking in the attendant's cart. I reached down to my tote bag and pulled out a small bag of trail mix and a bottle of water that was almost as big as I was. Dinner was served. I ate my itty-bitty portion of nuts and dried fruit and stared out the window at the endless black sky until sleep came. I kept thinking of long walks down gladiator hallways, the marble statues at the stadium, and the sound of my dad's laughter ringing across the field.

― 29 ―

# The Wolf's Mouth

There's a saying in Italy that I have a love/hate relationship with. "*Fare una bella figura*"—literally, to make a beautiful figure. There is no exact translation in English but "to make a good impression" comes close. The phrase compresses all that is good in someone's appearance, style, charm, ability, and poise—things that can be gleaned at first sight. A perfect manicure, gorgeous clothes, salon-fresh hair, and an attitude that says you know how good you look without being arrogant about it. It can also mean putting on a great show, excelling in whatever you are doing beyond everyone's expectations. When you *fare la bella figura* you can leave opponents shaking in their shoes on the court and men salivating as you walk by. You look put together and exude confidence with every gesture, every movement. When I'm at the top of my game, I can *fare una bella figura* with the best of them on the court. But with an extra 19.5 pounds still hanging on, I knew my *figura* wasn't so *bella* off the court. I'd lost my Miami midsection but I knew I still had work to do. The match was going to be televised, but that wasn't what had me worried. I knew that Enzo would be there.

Ah, Enzo. How do I explain the allure of dating an Italian man? It's like skydiving: no words can adequately describe the firsthand experience. But

I'll do my best. Enzo and I had been casually dating for about a year. You can approach dating on the tour in one of two ways. First, you can date someone on your team—a coach, a therapist, a trainer, a hitting partner, etc.—but mixing business and pleasure can be hazardous to your playing health. From a logistical standpoint, it is the easiest choice, since you are with each other all the time. But from an emotional standpoint it has the potential to get dicey. Lines get blurred, feelings get hurt, and painful departures are forced. It's a scenario I've always avoided. Choice number two: date a guy who doesn't care if you call every day, who is comfortable with your success, who understands that he comes second, third, or sometimes fourth on your list of priorities, and who thinks that seeing you once every couple of months is plenty of quality time. On the men's tour it is common for girlfriends to give up their jobs to travel with the guys. This almost never happens on the women's tour. It's too hard on the male ego. On tour, it is about me: getting my practice time in, meeting with sponsors, eating the right food before a match, doing interviews, and signing autographs. It can be difficult for a boyfriend to take a backseat to that. And traveling eleven months of the year is expensive: most men aren't comfortable having a girlfriend pay their way. So my relationships usually ended up being long-distance, which had its own complications.

Enzo fell under the second option. A friend who worked for the tour introduced us in Paris the previous year and we hit if off instantly. Tall, dark, and handsome, with an air of mystery, he was like a character out of a romance novel. We kept in touch by e-mail and whenever I was in Europe he tried to meet up with me to watch my matches and take me out to dinner. My schedule, my bedtime, my matches—how many guys are ready for that? But Enzo was confident and laid-back and could handle it. He was a lovely and much-needed diversion—I couldn't wait to see him in Rome.

As with most Italian men, he was blessed with genes that enabled him to keep a lean, wiry frame even though he never went to the gym and had a habit of indulging in gnocchi by the pound. I loved the long conversations we had over our dinners together: our latest music obsessions, the best beaches for scuba diving, the intricacies of Italian culture (like why it's perfectly normal for a thirty-five-year-old man to still be living at home with his mom cooking and cleaning for him; not that he was one of those guys, but he knew *lots* of them). But there was something I loved even more. Enzo was a walking Zagat guide—a living, breathing, well-coiffed resource to the best dining in any European postal code. It was uncanny. Best risotto in Venice? He knew it. Best manicotti in Florence? No problem— the owner was a good friend! Freshest octopus in Barcelona? He didn't know the address, but he drew a detailed map on the back of a napkin using Gaudi buildings as landmarks. Some women swoon over diamonds; I swoon over a man who knows his way around the food world. And, like me, Enzo preferred the mom-and-pop joints over the highly touted establishments written up in magazine articles. It was a match made in foodie heaven.

I met him at a restaurant a few hours after my plane landed. Dressed in my usual flowy outfit that revealed nothing (but down to a size ten now), I was thankful I was wearing flats as I navigated my way through the uneven cobblestone streets. After a couple of wrong turns, I finally found the restaurant. Its location was stunning, set on the banks of the Tiber with Rome's ancient buildings as the backdrop. I felt like I was on a movie set. A shiver of excitement ran up my spine and I felt good, even a little bit glamorous. Here I was, twenty-six years old, healthy, having a good-hair day, not feeling jet-lagged, and about to meet a dashing Italian for dinner in one of the most beautiful cities in the world. Who cared about a few pounds? I was Audrey Hepburn in my own version of *Roman Holiday*, out on my own, looking for adventure in one of the world's most breathtaking cities and forgetting about all of my responsibilities. *Come on, Monica*, I told myself as I entered the restaurant, *you are lucky to have this life*.

Our table was outside on the terrace with a 180-degree view of the water. Spring blossoms were spilling out of the crystal bowl placed in the middle of our candlelit table. Enzo looked more debonair than ever. He smelled good, looked good, and—with that accent—everything that came out of his mouth sounded good. Just asking for a bottle of mineral water sounded exotic and captivating. When the antipasto was set down before us, I tried to focus on what he was saying (something about art), but my eyes kept darting toward the platters of vegetables and meat drenched in olive oil. His lips were moving but I wasn't processing anything he was saying. I was fortifying myself for the battle of wills that was about to take place. He flagged down our waiter and made a request in rapid-fire Italian. Was he ordering another bottle of wine? We'd barely made a dent in the one we already had. I was allotted one glass with dinner, so I was taking the tiniest, slowest sips imaginable. Within moments a plate of lettuce, tomatoes, and shredded carrots was placed in front of me. It looked pathetic next to the brightly colored antipasto platter. Guess it wasn't wine he'd ordered.

"Is this for me?" I asked.

"*Si, bella.* I am under strict instructions to not let you indulge your appetite tonight," he said as he put a generous helping of melon with prosciutto on his plate. Strict instructions? The last time we'd gone out on the town I kept up with him bite for bite. He'd told me it was sexy that I loved food. But Bobby hadn't been pleased. Apparently Enzo had been given the nutritional smack down by Chris and was now on their side. Damn. There were eyes everywhere now. I tried to make my salad interesting by dousing it with vinegar. Enzo had moved the bottle of olive oil to his side. How romantic. My date with the dreamy Italian was quickly turning into a battle with the food caribinieri.

Warm plates of fresh pasta were followed by heaping mounds of fried prawns and calamari. It was a continuous parade of my favorite foods, all of which were strictly off-limits. I tried to focus on the romantic view in between bites of steamed zucchini.

"Please, do not look so sad," he said.

"Oh, I'm not. I'm fine. Great, in fact. Just thinking about my matches." My first match was three days away and I'd gone to the tournament site before meeting him for dinner. The draw was posted on a window and I had scanned down the list of my potential opponents to see what I was up against. I didn't care how good they were: I was worried that they would walk out on the court with unbelievable bodies and Enzo's attention would go straight to them.

He put a minuscule refill into my wineglass. "Let's make an agreement."

"An agreement?" A small piece of grilled chicken was set in front of me.

"Yes, an agreement." Enzo pointed to my chicken. "If you need to add some flavor, use the lemon." He looked quite pleased with himself. He honestly thought he was being a big help to me.

"Yeah, thanks for the tip." I took the yellow wedge and squeezed it with exaggerated force.

"The agreement is a good one," Enzo continued. "You will like it, I promise."

"I'm listening."

"If you win the tournament, we will come back to this place and you will eat anything and everything you want. Without feeling bad about it."

*Hmmm, not a bad plan*, I thought. Artichokes swimming in butter, hot crusty bread, a cheese platter to finish it all off. That was my kind of agreement. Too bad my chances of having this dream dinner were slim to none. Hingis was skipping the tournament after getting hurt in the German Open the week before, and Serena was out with a bad knee, but all the other top girls were entered and—oh, that's right—I hadn't won it in ten years. Capriati, Pierce, Mauresmo, and Venus (the defending champion) were all going to be there. I was convinced I wouldn't be sitting in this beautiful restaurant a week from now. But I accepted the challenge anyway. I offered my hand to Enzo so we could seal the deal with a handshake. He took my hand in his, placed a gentle kiss on it, and in his incredibly alluring voice said, *"In bocca al lupo."* I hadn't the slightest idea what he said, but it sounded lovely.

"What does that mean?" I asked.

"It means 'Into the mouth of the wolf,'" he answered. "It is what we say when we are wishing someone luck when they are about to embark on something important. It is to wish you courage on your journey."

"Into the mouth of the wolf?" It sounded ominous, but I guess "break a leg" isn't much better. "Oh, well, thank you."

"No, no." He shook his head emphatically. "When someone says this, you must answer, *'Crepi al lupo.'*"

"*'Crepi al lupo'*?"

"Yes. It means 'May the wolf die.' Or you can just say '*Crepi.*' That will work too." He poured some more wine for himself and gestured to my glass. I shook my head. I'd already cheated by having an extra half glass. I'd never sipped anything as slowly as I nursed that Chianti. I raised my glass and finished the last few drops of wine I'd have that week. Into the mouth of the wolf I went.

Seven days later, to my complete disbelief, I was standing on the brink of my all-you-can-eat Roman buffet. In true gladiatorial spirit, the tournament had turned into a war of attrition and upsets. Lindsay Davenport pulled out before the third round with a lower-back strain; Venus, who was battling the lingering effects of a six-month layoff thanks to wrist tendinitis, lost the chance to claim back-to-back titles after a third-round loss to seventeen-year-old Jelena Dokić; Capriati surprisingly fell in the first round to thirty-first-ranked Anne-Gaëlle Sidot; Mary Pierce and Arantxa both fell victim to a battle-ready Amélie Mauresmo, who was playing like she was unstoppable.

I'd been on my best behavior all week. The constant presence of Chris and Bobby was doing wonders for my playing and my weight. I'd even managed to lose another pound or two; it was probably just water weight from sweating so much, but who cared? A pound was a pound was a pound. I hadn't gone off my diet once all week; the unlikely bet I'd made with Enzo was lurking in the back of my mind. With every round's victory, it was becoming more real until, on the morning of my final match, I could practically taste the eggplant lasagna. I'd had a brief scare during my quarterfinal match against Dokić, who had beaten Venus in straight sets the day before. I took the first set easily, 6–1, but for some reason completely lost my concentration in the second. It was surreal.

I was watching myself play, but I didn't feel like I was there. I was thinking about everything but tennis. *Is my shoelace loose? It feels loose. No, it's fine. Wait, no, it's too floppy. Yeah, I should retie it. Oh, my serve already? Hmmm, do I need to get more dog food for Ariel? The bag looked a little low this morning. She really likes the new brand I bought before we left Florida. Seems like a good product. Is it organic? I think that's what it said on the label.*

*What does "organic" even mean? Is it vegetarian? No, I think it has to do with pesticides. And maybe preservatives? Does that mean no preservatives? Or they're organic preservatives? Do those exist? I'm not even sure. Well, it must be better for her anyway. Oh, damn, did I just lose my serve? Oops. I wonder what movies are playing on TV at the hotel. Do they have the original American versions or are they all dubbed in Italian? I really hope they have some in English. That would be so great to unwind with room service and a movie tonight. Uh-oh, did I just hit that into the net? Weird. This new sports bra is really comfortable. I should tell Nike I want some more. Wait, the set's over? Are you serious?*

I don't remember playing any points, just losing them over and over until the set slipped right out from under me, 3–6. Panic that I might not make it past that day set in. What was going on? *Get your head into the game! You took the first set, now do it again! How hard can it be?* Angry at myself, I went into the last set with new aggression. It wasn't aimed at Dokić, it was aimed at myself: I was frustrated that I couldn't hold my game together long enough for consistent results. That second set was a microcosm of what had been plaguing me on and off for the past several years. As soon as I was in the flow, feeling good, I couldn't trust it. I couldn't let myself go; I couldn't leap forward to that sublime place of living moment to moment with the faith that my strength and skill would win out in the end. I was either analyzing, dissecting, and stressing over each mistake ad nauseam, or just not thinking about the game at all. Deep disappointment in myself and the fear of future regret helped me to buckle down and take the last set. It was much harder than it should have been.

But I learned my lesson—at least for that week it stayed fresh in my mind—and I decided to take the semifinal as quickly and with as much intensity as possible. Corina Morariu and I exchanged points evenly until I broke her serve at 3–3 in the first set. Once I broke her I knew I could run away with the match. My concentration was back and my focus was complete. In less than an hour, I emerged with a 6–3, 6–1 victory. There was only one thing that stood in the way of the title and a feast fit for champions: Amélie Mauresmo.

After steamrolling through the competition, Amélie—who could've easily been a model for one of those chiseled marble statues—was in iron-strong mental and physical shape. She also had the advantage of being twenty years old, with legs, muscles, and reflexes that were six years younger than mine. In tennis those age differences can feel like dog years. We'd never faced each other before, so I didn't know what I was walking into. And the media—ah, my fair-weather friends. Just weeks before I'd been labeled a has-been and "past my expiration date," but now they were running headlines like Monica's Magic and referring to my wins as a "return to former glory." A decade after my first win in Rome, which set me up for my first win in Paris, I was trying to repeat history. Was it possible at my teetering old age? Could I do it again ten long years later? So much had happened since then. Did I have enough left in me to be able to leave my heart and soul on the court yet again? All week the newspapers kept building the drama, so I stopped reading.

A few hours before the final match, I stood in front of the mirror in my hotel room, meticulously studying my reflection. Sure, I was on the lower end of my sliding scale of extra poundage, but I wasn't about to go parading around in a bikini anytime soon. I was tired of thinking about how the match would unfold, so I started obsessing on something new and different: my body. What a surprise. The topic of the day was the size of my hips and the best strategy to employ in covering them up. I tucked my shirt into my tennis skirt and turned around, craning my neck to see what my backside looked like without the security of my shirttail hovering over it. Not the greatest. I yanked the shirt out and once again spun around to check out the front and back. Now the front looked better, but the back looked even bigger than before. Did I have a third choice? I finally settled on leaving my shirt untucked, hoping I wouldn't have to hit any shots that would make it fly up and expose my far-from-toned stomach. Bobby knocked on the door.

"You almost ready?" he asked.

"Yeah, I'll be in the lobby in ten." I took off my outfit, threw on a baseball cap and tracksuit, and took one last look in the mirror. It would have to do for now.

# – 30 –

# Gladiator

I could hear the crowd from fifty yards away: a low rumble at first, increasing in volume and vibration with every step I took forward. Thunderous clapping, chanting, singing. The Italians know how to be a theatrical audience, no doubt about it. The day was brilliantly sunny and clear; just ahead of me at the end of the tunnel I could see the light pouring in. I was a gladiator heading into battle against a French player with insanely good passing shots. I was on a direct route into the mouth of the wolf. *Crepi, crepi, crepi*, I mumbled under my breath for extra insurance.

I didn't mess around. Shot after shot went exactly where I wanted. The zone I couldn't find during the quarterfinal was back and I wanted to stay in it for the duration. The first four points went unanswered in my favor: down the line or corner to corner. It had been a long time since I'd had such a loyal arsenal at my disposal. I was pulling off angles I hadn't had the confidence to execute in ages. Using my army of ground strokes, I took the first set 6–2. Then I got scared. Nerves and anxiety disarmed my game and—*poof*—my focus was gone. *Again.* I served at match point at 5–4 and Amélie broke back. The same thing happened at 6–5. I have no idea where my focus goes when it takes off on those little solo jaunts, but it doesn't even leave a note. I started to panic and knew I had to calm down before it was too late. During the water break I took out the piece of paper Bobby had slipped to me before the match. On it he'd written down three things:

1. Fast first step
2. Sacrifice
3. Believe

There it was: two months of blood, sweat, and tears distilled down to three tiny items. A mini grocery list of everything my workouts had been about. Looks easy when it's put like that, doesn't it?

*Fast first step:* All the track workouts and agility sessions were done to make me faster. And the difference between running down a ball and losing a point is a direct result of how quick your first step is. One half of a second can be the difference between winning and losing an entire match.

*Sacrifice:* All the nutrition plans, "training" food, and general abstaining from anything remotely appetizing was my definition of sacrifice. Give me the interval sprints, the super-sets, the squats, the lunges, and the bench press, but please, I beg of you, please don't take away my salt and vinegar chips and chocolate-covered graham crackers. Sacrifice off the court was what it took to get me here, and sacrifice on the court was what it was going to take to win. I had to go for every ball no matter how unlikely I was to reach it. I couldn't give up on a single point. Taking the easy way out was not an option.

*Believe:* There was no point in running down a ball if I didn't believe I could hit it right back. Believe without a whisper of a doubt in my mind that I could launch it into the farthest corners and at irretrievable angles.

I took a last sip of water. *All right, three things. Just do these three things and I'll get through this match without falling apart.* I had to close it out in the tiebreaker. Going into the third set was too risky; I didn't want to self-destruct after getting this far.

The crowd was going crazy. Winds were swirling around the court, making my new serve even harder to pull off. The butterflies in my stomach were jumping around like they were on supercharged pogo sticks. *Just keep breathing.* We traded points back and forth until I burst ahead to 6–4 after Amélie hit a forehand long. One more point was all it would take to get to the magic tiebreaking number: seven. I had two chances to do it and to prove to everyone that I still belonged out there, that my best days weren't behind me, that I didn't have an expiration date . . .

It was my serve. I pulled my baseball cap down as though ensuring a snug fit would fortify me to power through the next point. I bounced the ball a few times, collected myself, tossed the ball cleanly into the bright sky above my head, and *bam!* I hit it right into the net. Not a problem. Just do it again, but preferably over the net this time. I cleared my head of everything. I wasn't thinking about dog food, shoelaces, or what I'd be doing later that night. I was just thinking one thing: hit the ball like you mean it. My second serve was good. Amélie returned it to my backhand, I hit it crosscourt, she returned it, I hit it again with everything I had, then she hit it down the line and had me on the run to my forehand. *Fast first step. Sacrifice.* I hustled as quickly as I could and lunged to get my racket on the ball. It was too far for me to use my usual two-handed grip. I had to hit it with one hand. *Believe.* Stretching as far as I possibly could, I felt the ball hit my racket. *Whack!* I got it over the net in an awkward lob and immediately prepared myself for the overhead that I'd set up for Amélie. The few seconds of waiting for your opponent to hit a smash are torture. Where is it going? How hard is it going to be? Will I be able to handle the angle? Do I have a chance in hell of returning it? Waiting, waiting, waiting . . . Amélie positioned herself, wound up to pound it right past me, and hit it with all of her force. It was long.

It took me a moment to register what had happened. The crowd erupted into applause and everyone was on their feet. I threw my arms in the air and a laugh of joy bubbled up from deep inside me. I'd done it. It wasn't a Grand Slam, but to me it was just as important. I'd won in the stadium that had set me up for tennis stardom ten years earlier. I'd won in the city that was my dad's and my favorite place to be. The memories of all of our breakfasts, practices, dinners, talks, and long walks flooded through my mind. The memories of Rome were so thick, I could practically hold them in my hand.

I met Amélie at the net and she was gracious in congratulating me. I ran over to the players' box and was engulfed in hugs by my mom, Bobby, and Chris. It had been a team effort, no doubt about it. For a precious few minutes I let myself enjoy the victory. The crowd was still on its feet, and shouts of congratulation were falling all around me. I wasn't thinking about Paris, I wasn't thinking about my next workout, and I wasn't even thinking about dinner with Enzo. I was completely filled with relief and happiness. I'd been afraid that my lasting memory of Rome would be of receiving that devastating phone call about my dad. It didn't seem fair that a city that had been our favorite would forever be associated with sadness for me. Now I knew it wouldn't.

A few hours later I was sitting at the restaurant with Enzo. It was like Christmas morning and I was about to rip into all of my presents. Actually, we never celebrated Christmas in my native country, so it was far better than that. It was like my birthday, New Year's Eve, and a much-anticipated hot date all rolled into one. I opened the menu and read through all of the options several times. It had been ages since I'd actually made a decision about dinner. Steamed asparagus or boiled spinach do not count as choices. I could order anything I wanted, so I was intent on being absolutely certain I would be satisfied. I studied the menu as if I were taking a culinary exam later. In the interest of full disclosure, I didn't *technically* have carte blanche to go hog wild. I'd told Chris and Bobby we were going out for a quick little celebratory dinner—not one word about the bet I'd made with Enzo. But they must have known I'd be indulging a little; after all, what person in her right mind celebrates with a platter of dark, leafy greens? I finally settled on the *caprese* salad and a plate of pasta carbonara. While we waited for our food, I dug into the warm breadbasket. Bread is good, but bread drizzled with olive oil is heaven on earth. I was pouring oil onto another slice before I'd finished chewing the first one. I'd played a hard match; I deserved this. I didn't feel the slightest bit self-conscious, and Enzo, my food comrade in arms, didn't bat an eye. With full glasses of champagne, we toasted to my success. I couldn't remember the last time I'd felt so happy. I could get into this lifestyle. Appreciation of beauty, food, wine. Nobody in a hurry. Learning to enjoy the moment instead of making plans for tomorrow. Maybe Rome was a turning point for me. Ten years before, my win had been a good omen for all the championships to come. Maybe this time it would be a good omen for getting my whole life back on track.

Dinner was even better than I'd imagined. The weather was beautiful, the service was impeccable, and I savored every last bite on my plate. Six weeks of deprivation had heightened my senses; my taste buds were ready to burst from happiness. And then, to put the cherry on top of the whole deliciously perfect evening, it was dessert time. Our waiter wheeled over a tray laden with the most delectable desserts I'd ever seen. But there it was: tiramisu. My all-time favorite dessert, and one that is not well replicated outside of Italy. It was my favorite thing to order when my dad and I went out to dinner and there was no way I was leaving Rome without eating it. I ordered my beloved treat of ladyfingers and mascarpone cream and Enzo ordered fruit. Wait, what? Fruit? Was he serious? Never mind, he could have his fruit. Our desserts came and mine looked divine with a delicate sprinkling of cocoa powder on top. Perfect. Enzo's cut-up fruit looked, well, it looked like fruit. I took my first bite. I fell in love. I took my second. Even better. I was about to dig in for a third bite to offer to Enzo when I caught him looking at me funny. His eyebrows were raised and his eyes were surveying me like I was a kid who'd just been caught doing something really, really bad.

"What is it?" I asked.

"Do you really want to have that?" He popped a chunk of plum into his mouth.

I laughed despite myself. Was he serious? Of course I wanted it. It was what I'd been waiting for all week! Maybe there was something lost in the translation. Maybe it was his cute way of asking if he could have some too.

"Why?" I asked. "Do you want some? Here, you should try it. It's fantas-tic." I offered my fork to him but he waved it away from his face.

"No, no, I do not care for it. I mean to say that you have had a lot to eat tonight, no? I think perhaps it is enough?"

I felt like I'd been punched in the stomach. So much for being cute. Or sexy. Or attractive in the slightest. Not even the usually disarming accent could make up for the hurt those words caused. I'd just won the Italian Open, my world ranking had shot up from number seven to number three, and with those flippant remarks he'd just sucked all of the joy out of the day. I'm sure he thought he was helping me, but I didn't take it that way. I was hurt. Who did he think he was? I'd like to see him play two minutes against Amélie without falling over from exhaustion.

"Actually, I'm really enjoying it, but thanks for the concern." That was the last full sentence I spoke for the rest of the night. I took one more bite of the tiramisu but I couldn't enjoy it. Tears began to well up in my eyes and I tried to will them away. There was no way I was going to break down over a stupid dessert and a stupid comment made by an insensitive guy. I left the rest of the dessert sitting there. I couldn't wait to get back to my hotel room, get under the covers, and forget about the entire evening. Moments ago I'd felt as invincible as the statues in the Stadio dei Marmi, and now it was like someone had taken a sledgehammer and shattered all of my pieces to the floor. Where was I going to find the energy to pick them up again?

# – 31 –

## Gold Isn't Everything

Enzo and I didn't make it to our one-year anniversary. The day after our dinner I told him I needed to focus all my energy on tennis and that we shouldn't see each other anymore. He didn't object. I think my food freakouts were too much for him to handle. There wasn't a happy medium. He was either taking the brunt of my coaches' wrath after enjoying a good dinner with me or reducing me to tears when he thought he was helping. I'm the first to admit I was not an easy case; it wasn't Enzo's responsibility to fix me and it was unfair to put that on him. The long-distance issue didn't help. It was too stressful when we were apart and the pressure to have a perfect time during the rare days we were together was too intense. It's probably why his careless comment hit me so hard. That night should have been perfect, but I'd gone back to my hotel in tears. There was no time for sad good-byes or feelings of regret the next day: I had to pack up and head to Paris.

I was still riding the media wave of the Rome win. The usual questions about retirement were replaced with questions about a "renaissance" of my career. But the momentum came to a screeching halt in the quarter-finals of the French Open. If you're going to lose early, at least fall to the eventual champion, right? It's a silly justification, but it does make losing a little easier. A little, teeny, tiny bit easier.

Mary Pierce was on fire in Paris. Even though I was playing a strong and consistent game, she was playing a stronger and more consistent one. The ten-thousand-strong crowd in the Suzanne Lenglen Court was firmly in their countrywoman's corner. (Although raised in Florida, Mary held a French passport, thanks to her mom.) After two days of drizzle and gloom, the sun was shining gloriously onto the court. With every well-played point by Mary or error by me, the spectators went nuts. It sounded more like a raucous soccer game than a genteel tennis match. I loved it. Tennis can be so boring when there isn't a peep from the stands, so any energy is good energy when you're on the court. Being the underdog can even make me play harder. *You don't want me to win? Well, watch this crosscourt winner!* There has to be an underdog and a favorite in every match, so you just have to roll with the fans' whims. Two years earlier, when I was playing in Paris a few weeks after my dad died, I couldn't have asked for a better crowd. I could feel their enthusiasm and support throughout every match I played. It was exactly what I needed during the most painful time of my life. So I had no hard feelings when they cheered after I launched a forehand right into the net. They pick their favorites every year and Mary happened to be it in 2000. *C'est la vie.*

At one point right before I was serving, I heard someone yell, "Come on, Monica!" After his enthusiastic outburst, he was immediately hushed up with a chorus of boos. Poor guy. I wanted to turn around and yell a hearty "Thanks, anyway!" but I had to focus on getting my still new and still out-of-control-at-times serve in. I beat Mary 6–4 in the first set, then had another case of flyaway focus, a persistent loss of confidence that kept striking at the most inconvenient times. Why couldn't it hit me when I was reading a book in bed or trying to follow an intricately plotted spy movie? I would have gladly dealt with a loss of focus then. But no, it had to hit me when it counted the most and I lost the next two sets 3–6, 4–6. I gave up match point with a double fault. Never a good way to go out. I'd gotten close, but I was playing tennis, not horseshoes. The fans were beside themselves with *une joie énorme*. Mary was one step closer to being the first Frenchwoman to win at Roland Garros since 1967 and they gave her a standing ovation to show their approval.

Three weeks later I made another quarterfinal exit, this time at Wimbledon at the hands of defending champ Lindsay Davenport. We both came out raring to go; neither one of us lost our serve in the first set, forcing a tiebreaker. We were neck and neck in racking up points until I hit a crosscourt winner and Lindsay double-faulted. The first set was mine. Struggling with my serve, I lost the second set 4–6 and the third set was like a bad flashback of the Pierce match. I totally blanked. My focus left— yet again—and this time it took along my energy. I didn't win a single game in the third. After the match, journalists asked me what happened. I didn't know. I was outplayed at the end? My serve wasn't reliable yet? My endurance wasn't good enough to pull off a third-set pounding? Take your pick.

There were a few highlights though. Pete Sampras added another Wimbledon title to his mantelpiece, giving him a record-setting thirteen Grand Slams and tying Willie Renshaw's century-old record of seven Wimbledon victories. Pete was the grass-court king. How wrong I'd been when, back in 1989, I'd seen him warming up on a nearby court at the French Open. My dad watched him for five minutes before proclaiming he'd soon be number one in the world. "Him?" I asked incredulously. "Yes, without a doubt," my dad said. "No way," I laughed, and thought my dad had a lot to learn about spotting player potential.

Venus beat Lindsay for the title, making it an all-American sweep, perhaps to make up for the dismal showing in Paris. Even though I packed my bag much earlier than I'd hoped for, there was a tiny victory. The players' facilities had undergone an enormous face-lift and the locker rooms for the top sixteen players were even more beautiful than before. For the first time since 1997, I didn't circle the multitiered silver platters of sandwiches and cookies like a starving shark. I made it through the entire tournament without even one shortbread cookie passing my lips.

I didn't have long to sulk over my earlier-than-hoped-for exits in Paris

and London. Something amazing was waiting for me on another conti-
nent: the Olympics. You can't tear me away from the television when the
Olympics are on. Is there anything better than Bob Costas narrating an
against-all-odds sports story? Some players don't think the Olympics are a
big deal; they'd much rather pocket a Grand Slam than a medal with five
rings on it. I wasn't one of those players. Since becoming a citizen in 1994,
I jumped at the chance to represent the U.S. whenever an opportunity
came my way. Fed Cup, Hopman Cup, Olympics—I'm your girl.

It wasn't easy to make the team bound for Sydney. Olympic tennis is
played as an individual sport instead of a team sport (which the Fed Cup
is), so I had to beat out Serena to nab one of the three spots. No simple
feat, but I pulled it off and our team was set: Venus, Lindsay, and me. Billie Jean King, one of my heroes and a steadfast supporter of my comeback,
was our coach, and Zina Garrison, the player I'd faced during the infamous
flower-throwing episode in Paris (thankfully my faux pas was ancient history and had been long forgotten by then), was the assistant coach. We
had a dream team and we were headed to one of my favorite cities in the
world; I was determined to make this Olympics vastly different from Atlanta. I promised myself I'd spend more time soaking up the Olympic spirit
and less time sitting in the cafeteria. Serena made the trip as well, since
she and Venus would be playing doubles together. I was happy for them:
they have a truly remarkable bond. I don't know how they've managed to
have the careers they've had without sacrificing their relationship. Most
players can't even talk to their opponents, let alone be best friends with
them. Over the years we played together I never once saw a display of bitterness or jealousy between them. Pretty impressive.

Once we arrived in Sydney I couldn't wait to get to the Olympic Village. It was like a Disneyland version of college with a bunch of incredibly
coordinated people walking around in cool tracksuits. Some athletes (the
basketball players) opted to stay in hotels, but what was the point of that?
That would have been just like any old tournament on the tour for me.
No way. I was staying in the Village.

The opening ceremony was one of the most beautiful events of my entire career. The athletes had to arrive at the stadium by two in the after-noon and we didn't get back until two in the morning. The U.S. team looked elegant and ready for the country club in our outfits. The guys were wearing dapper navy sports jackets and white hats, while the girls were decked out in red blazers, khaki skirts, and hats that matched the guys'. Wedged between the United Arab Emirates and Uruguay, we had a long time to wait before it was our turn to enter the parade of nations. Every-one was so wired. When we finally got the cue to go, nearly every athlete whipped out a camera to record at least some moments of this unforgetta-ble night.

There was a constant roar from the crowd in the stands and the crowd in the field. Massive amounts of human energy everywhere. Lindsay and I couldn't stop smiling as we waved our little American flags high in the air. Television cameras swept back and forth as we walked around the track, and all the athletes turned into ten-year-olds after a sugar rush. Waving like crazy, making funny faces, hooting and hollering, jumping onto one another's back—it was great. I finally understood the meaning of being "high on life." I wish there was a way to bottle that magic.

A week into the Games, there was a knock at my dorm room door. I opened it to see a guy who was a dead ringer for the Incredible Hulk, ex-cept for the green part. At least six feet two inches and easily weighing in at over 250 pounds, he looked like he could pick me up and toss me over his shoulder with one meaty hand. He politely introduced himself and told me he was a fan of mine. His name was Rulon Gardner and he was a Greco-Roman wrestler. Cool, I thought, though I knew absolutely noth-ing about his sport. But that was the best thing about the Olympics: you were in the company of the greatest athletes in nearly every sport from around the world. It was like getting a crash course in physical fitness, cul-tural anthropology, and geography. The following day Rulon was sched-uled to face a formidable foe, Russia's Alexander Karelin. As he was describing the superhuman greatness of his opponent—gold medal win-ner in Seoul, Barcelona, and Atlanta; undefeated in international compe-tition; had not surrendered a point in a decade—I couldn't help seeing flashes of *Rocky IV*'s ultimate matchup between Ivan Drago and Rocky. It didn't sound like Rulon had much of a chance, but that was what the Olympics were about: it was a sixteen-day period where miracles could happen.

"I wish I could come to your match, but I'll be playing in my own tomorrow afternoon," I said.

"That's okay," he said. "I just wanted to come by and introduce myself. And maybe get a little extra kick of inspiration. I've followed your comeback over the years; it isn't an easy thing to do, what you've been accomplishing."

I didn't know what to say. Standing there in my baggy sweats and messy ponytail, I didn't feel like a particularly forceful figure. And I didn't think that my comeback had been all that inspirational. I knew people had categorized it like that, but come on, let's get real. For five years I'd been trying to claw my way back to the top but had yet to regain the form and position I once held. From a purely technical, wins-based perspective, my comeback hadn't been that strong. But that didn't seem to faze Rulon. Whatever I'd done on the tennis court had been enough to spur him to knock on a stranger's door, hoping to get some advice for what was going to be the most important match of his life.

"Good luck tomorrow." I shook his hand. It's a miracle he didn't break mine. "Just give it everything you have. You never know what can happen out there. I'll be pulling for you." It wasn't the most eloquent or unique advice, but if there's one thing that tennis has taught me it is never to count yourself out before the umpire calls the final score. Not even when you are down 40–love at 5–0 in the third set. You never know what can happen. The next day Rulon did what everyone had said would be impossible (in fact, the gambling odds were something like two thousand to one): he beat the Russian. The media went crazy, hailing it as the "Miracle on the Mat," the wrestling version of the U.S. men's hockey team's legendary 1980 victory over the seemingly invincible Soviet team. Rulon, a guy who had grown up on his family's dairy farm in Wyoming, didn't compete on the high school varsity team until his senior year, and had never won an NCAA championship, had taken down the world's best on the world's stage. Talk about performing under pressure! I wish I'd seen that match.

That night there was a knock on my door. I opened it up to find Rulon standing there again, but this time he had a gold medal around his neck. I think I shrieked from excitement.

"Just wanted to stop by and show you this." His smile was nearly as wide as his shoulders. I must have said congratulations a thousand different ways. I couldn't believe he'd pulled it off, but then again, I shouldn't have been surprised. After all, the Olympics were made for victories like that. Bob Costas was going to have a field day.

In between my matches, I watched Ian Thorpe take the swimming world by storm, Dara Torres make her jaw-dropping comeback at the age of thirty-three (Who knew she'd do it again at forty-one while juggling the demands of motherhood? If I ever make a comeback I will call Dara for inspiration: she is someone you want on your team.), and Marion Jones blow by the competition (it's sad how that one turned out). I watched in amazement as Liu Xuan executed feats of glory on the balance beam, and I even fit in a tour of the Sydney Zoo. I held a baby koala in my hand; it was the cutest thing I'd ever seen. The smart little buggers sleep eighteen hours a day. If Atlanta had been my Olympics at the food court, Sydney was the Olympics of my dreams. Every time I met someone new or did something I'd never done before, I'd fill up a little inside. I kept myself so busy taking advantage of everything the city and the Games had to offer that I hardly noticed the food court.

The downside to playing Olympic tennis as an individual sport was apparent in my semifinal match against Venus. So much for patriotism: it was every player for herself. We may as well have been playing in the Australian Open. Billie Jean couldn't take having to watch two of her players thrash it out against each other, so she watched it on the television from the tennis center's dining room. Seeing her hurry away from the court, Serena said, "Now you know how our parents feel!" Her loyalties would have been even more divided if Lindsay had been thrown into the medal-contention mix, but after a back injury flare-up she was forced to pull out.

Venus came out flying and took the first set 6–1. I battled back and squeaked out a 6–4 score in the second, but Venus closed me out 6–3 in the third. My gold-medal hopes gone, I now had to gear myself up for the bronze-medal match. It's a bit of a downer, playing for the bronze, so I had to shift my mind-set. I was now competing for a medal, period. If I could walk away with one, it would be a vast improvement over my showing in Atlanta, and I didn't want to blow my only shot at winning an Olympic medal. I'd never get another chance. The match was against Jelena Dokić, a player who had also left her home country of Yugoslavia at a young age. She'd made Australia her new home, and understandably the crowd was behind her. I didn't want to start out as sluggish as I had against Venus, so I nailed down the first set 6–1 and rode that momentum to 6–4 in the second. It was quick and I had my medal. I stood on the podium— something we never get to do in tennis—and watched as our American flags rose up into the air (Venus beat Elena Dementieva for the gold). As "The Star-Spangled Banner" played over the loudspeakers, I realized with a bit of a shock that I wasn't disappointed. It had been a tremendous two-week journey. My bronze didn't look so shabby under the bright Australian sky.

# – 32 –

## Injustice Served

They're moving the championships to *where?*"

"Munich," my agent, Tony, said.

"As in Munich, Germany? There isn't a Munich, Switzerland, or Munich, New Zealand, I don't know about, right?" I was kidding—I wasn't that bad at geography—but the thought that the WTA was moving their prestigious season-ending championships to a country I swore I'd never play in again was too much for me to wrap my mind around. It was unbelievable to me. I was hoping I'd misheard him.

"Yep," he said, "as in Germany. I was surprised when I heard about it too."

I was feeling more than just surprised. Shocked, annoyed, angry, and hurt were right up there too. In 1995, after two unsuccessful appeals in the Hamburg courts, I had no further recourse. The man who stabbed me would get off without spending a single night in prison. People who have stolen a pack of gum have received harsher sentences than that. By the time the second appeal was going on, the German media had changed its tone. Newspapers were no longer calling for justice to be served; rather, they were painting Parche as a lost soul, a loner who didn't have a life and hadn't meant me any real harm. The scar on my back disagrees with that assessment. It was like a nightmare in which I felt like I was the only sane person who could see an injustice being perpetrated, but I was unable to get anyone to agree with me.

To add some salt to the wound, I was unsuccessful in bringing a civil suit against the tournament organizers for their failure to provide adequate security. The suit was dismissed and I was ordered to pay their legal costs, which had surpassed a million dollars. My sense of justice and my wallet both took a serious beating. Just add it to the growing list of money lost from the sponsors and endorsements when I was forced out of the game. With the exception of Yonex, I lost each and every endorsement contract I had worked so hard for. Yonex suspended my payments until I returned to the game, but at least they kept me on. The entire Yoneyama family (the owner) has been an incredible source of support to me over the years. I will be forever grateful to them for sticking by me when nobody else did. And they make the best rackets in the world. The other contracts disappeared while I was recuperating at home. Actually they didn't disappear into thin air: they went straight to the other players who had all just been bumped up a spot in the rankings thanks to my absence. Tennis isn't about loyalty, it's about money. For two and a half years I didn't receive a cent, and with my own and the tournament organizers' legal bills my losses were huge.

But while my financial loss can be tallied (into the eight figures), I can't put a number on the emotional and physical damages I sustained. By the time I was ordered to pay the organizers' legal fees, I'd stopped being fazed by such atrocities. I could have cried and whined and pouted and stamped my feet about it for years. Instead, I decided to focus on tennis and not return to Germany again. I caught a lot of heat for that decision and I've been offered fees that were more than an entire year's winnings just to show up to play one exhibition match within Germany's borders. My answer has always been the same: No, thank you. I made a promise to myself that not going to Germany was my small, symbolic stand against an unjust and totally irresponsible justice system. I have nothing against the people—one of my best friends lives in Munich and one of my hitting partners was from Hamburg—and I think the country is beautiful. But as long as that verdict stands, my promise to myself remains unaltered. To make a quick buck isn't worth sacrificing my principles.

That is why my jaw nearly hit the ground when I heard the WTA was moving the championships to Munich in 2001. I was on the players' council and had never been asked for my opinion. Again, money talks and Munich was offering a lot of it. One million more than the WTA was making from the championships being held in New York City. They decided it was worth it. After nearly thirty years of having the top players gather in Madison Square Garden to duke it out at the end of the season, the tour packed up and took the show on the road to Germany. I wouldn't be going with them. Besides that disappointing news, 2000 ended well. I was ranked fourth in the world, I weighed 157 pounds (a number I couldn't seem to get below), and I had huge hopes for 2001. My plan was to lose more weight by the Australian Open—at least ten pounds—and firmly put myself in the top three.

# – 33 –

# A Chemical Army

Creatine. Glucosamine. Xenadrine. Hydroxycut. MuscleTech. Muscle Milk. It was like stumbling into a science fiction movie where "real" food no longer existed. Now you could get all of your basic nutritional needs met with one cube of food a day! Ick.

As usual, I started the year off Down Under and it was glaringly obvious that the nutritional supplement craze had the tennis world by the throat. Was there a memo sent over the holidays that I missed? *Body-for-LIFE* held a favored position on my bedside table back in Sarasota, but I never took all the nutritional suggestions to heart. I was more than willing to try any exercise program and nutritional plan (with real food), but this fake, synthetic stuff freaked me out. I'd tried putting protein powder in my shakes, but suddenly that wasn't enough. Now there were all sorts of "designer" proteins on the market. What did that mean? Did they come in a stylish little Prada bag? MET-Rx bars were everywhere; I couldn't walk two steps in the players' locker room without tripping over a wrapper. Every sport drink and every energy bar had PROTEIN screaming from its label. Had we all been severely protein deprived and not known this, or was this just another food fetish? It all seemed a bit obsessive: people walking around like robots eating chemically engineered food. But maybe I was missing out on something. I was still stuck at 157 pounds so maybe everyone else had the right solution. I was confused, and I didn't have anyone to run it by.

Chris left after the close of the 2000 season and then Bobby, whose father was ill, decided to stay home to be with him. I fully understood and supported his choice. I was on my own and left to my own nutritional devices. Yikes.

The Australian hard court trifecta started out with the Hopman Cup in Perth, where I paired up with Jan-Michael Gambill to represent the U.S. in the high-profile mixed-doubles competition. No points are earned at this tournament; it is solely for your country's bragging rights. Jan-Michael is one of the only players who has the same double-handed forehand that I do, so I always got a kick out of warming up with him. It was like watching my swing's reflection. And I thrive on the competition that comes with playing mixed doubles. The men always try to nail a shot past the women and I never fail to get a thrill out of returning it just as hard. We won our first three matches but lost in the final to the mighty Swiss duo of Martina Hingis and Roger Federer. That was the first time I'd ever seen Roger play; I was blown away by his talent and skill. He hadn't yet won a title on the ATP tour and he was still over two years away from his first Wimbledon championship, but I knew that he was going to dominate the sport. His hands were unbelievable, he was uncanny in passing people at the net, and he made the entire thing look so easy. I turned out to be far more accurate in my prediction for Roger than I'd been for Pete. Two and a half years later he won the first of his five straight Wimbledon championships and soared to the number one spot, where he made himself at home for over four years. My dad would have been impressed I'd called that one.

After a stop in Sydney for the Adidas International, I headed to Melbourne for the Australian Open. Here I saw player after player chugging sugary "energy" drinks as though they had discovered the fountain of youth. They hopped around like Energizer bunnies, only to crash and go rifling through their bags in search of another bottle. It seemed so unnatural, especially as I'd always been told to stay away from sugar. Why were all the players obsessed with the new drinks? What happened to good old water? Did they know something I didn't? I flashed back to when I was nine years old and had just won a big European tournament in Italy. A man walked up to my dad and started giving him advice about all the different pills I needed to be taking in order to grow and get stronger. He even handed him a package of colored capsules. In a very commanding voice my dad said, "No, thank you. Those are not for my daughter. I will never give her anything like that." He thrust the package back at the pill pusher and took my hand as we left the tennis court.

That would explain my adult aversion to swallowing pills and taking supplements. I've never even taken a vitamin in my life. I much prefer getting my vitamins and minerals from natural food sources. Just drinking those protein shakes for Bobby was a major concession on my part. I had to fight my gag reflex each time. So this processed protein fad was not going to be my scene. I decided to leave the glucosamine, creatine, xenadrine, and all the other "-ine" foods (exceptions made for fettucine and linguine) to others.

I faced Justine Henin in the fourth round and was amazed at the agility and power she had at her disposal despite being much smaller than all the top players. I'd played her in the Fed Cup the year before but was astonished at how much she had improved. She was literally growing up before my eyes and had developed one of the fiercest single-handed backhands I'd ever seen. *Oh, great,* I thought, *another one to worry about.* I survived that match but lost to Jennifer Capriati in the quarterfinals, who went on to win the entire tournament—her first Grand Slam championship ever.

Right after my loss, Martina Hingis and I paired up in doubles. Playing with Martina was fantastic, and not just because she was brilliant at the net. Whenever we practiced together, I got great advice from her mom, Melanie, an incredible tactician who was always willing to give me tips on improving my game. Some people looked to technology to give them an edge—finding a magical stringing tension or pair of super-shock shoes—but I relied on tiny tweaks to my technique. Melanie was a huge help in that area. Martina and I made it to the semis, where we were at the receiving end of the Williams sisters' revenge. A week earlier, in our debut as doubles partners, we'd taken them out in Sydney. It had been a second-round match but all four of us were playing like it was a Grand Slam singles final. And it was at night in a full and rocking stadium. It was so intense! The harder I hit it, the harder they'd return it. We took it all the way to a third-set tiebreaker and Martina and I squeaked out a victory, ending Venus and Serena's twenty-two-match doubles winning streak. I was so exhausted I barely made it back to my hotel room that night. I did, however, have the energy to order a plate of spaghetti, a baked potato loaded with sour cream, and a piece of chocolate cake from the room service menu. I was hopeless on my own.

Understandably, the sisters wanted to prove something at the Grand Slam. They brought the heat and they brought it early. The match was over in two sets, 7–5, 6–2, quickly and efficiently erasing our previous week's triumph.

I booked a return flight to the States that night. Back in Florida and still coachless, I felt a bit lost. My momentum and mental strength were fickle friends, and I never knew when they'd make an appearance. One minute I felt like I was within striking distance of my tenth Grand Slam victory and the next I felt like I had a long, long way to go to keep up with the new power players. Bobby told me many times, "It's not your game, it's your head that needs work." Billie Jean had said the same thing at the Olympics. I knew that once my head was screwed on straight, the pounds would fall off and I'd be back in top form. But I couldn't get my head clear unless my size-ten clothes felt loose. It was a chicken-and-egg dilemma. Did my self-confidence need to return before my body got to its ideal level or was my self-confidence a result of feeling like I looked great in my tennis skirt? And where did my performance on the court fit into all of this? I just wanted a simple solution. I didn't want to trudge through the dirty, messy underbrush of my psyche.

Onward I went to Indian Wells, a Tier I tournament in Southern California that was right behind the Grand Slams in prestige and importance.

It is a mandatory tour stop for all the top players. I promptly suffered another stress fracture and an early exit after the second round. It turned out I'd have plenty of time—in fact, four months—to delve into my psyche while I waited yet again for my foot to heal. I spent a lot of time at the physical therapist's office and I read a lot of books on losing weight and achieving the best version of me. For a few weeks I lost myself in an abyss of overeating until my mom gently reined me in. As she heard me taking down a bowl to fill with ice cream, she cheerily called from the family room, "Look at the sunset . . . It's gorgeous. Let's take Ariel for a walk." The clink of the dishes in the cabinet was like a car alarm going off, warning of imminent danger or disaster. Alert! Monica is about to go on calorie overload! Act now! My mom rose to the occasion and continued to do so throughout my recovery. Knowing I had a walk waiting for me every evening calmed my nerves and prevented me from stuffing myself at dinnertime. And being outside with my dog and my mom on warm, balmy nights was a tonic for the panic that usually struck me in the evening hours. I couldn't walk very fast, but it was enough to give me a break from the thoughts racing around in my head. *How long is this recovery going to take? How much weight am I going to gain this time? How long will it take me to climb back into the top three again?* The questions were getting old. Arriving back home at around eight, I felt like I could settle in for the night without venturing into the kitchen in search of something to keep me company.

# 34

# Back in the Saddle

Roland Garros and Wimbledon went by while I sat on my couch during the summer of 2001. I could barely handle watching the matches. *I should be there*, I kept repeating as I cursed my foot. The year before I'd been right in the mix and had proven the retirement rumormongers wrong. Now they were back in full force. But the fact that I was angry about sitting there on the couch instead of warming up on center court held my answer: I still wasn't ready to retire. I just had to get over this little hurdle and I'd be back. But there was something that was bothering me more than the pain in my foot: it was the dreadful suspicion that these nasty recurrences of foot injuries were a direct result of the extra weight I'd been carrying around for the past five years. It's common for tennis players, especially those who start out early like I did, to battle chronic injuries in their ankles, knees, and wrists, but I'd been uncommonly healthy and free of injury until my stabbing. I'd never had foot issues until I came back in my supersize form. Could I really have brought this upon myself? Was my weight causing irreparable damage to my body? I was afraid to even think that it was possible and I never once asked my physiotherapist whether fat was a factor. I didn't want to know just how big an enemy I'd been to myself.

Other than a few test runs on my foot in Madrid (*no bueno*) and Hartford (better), I spent the rest of the four months hibernating in Florida and poking my nose around for another coach. My weight gain wasn't awful: about eight pounds, thanks to a handful of chocolate-covered almonds here and there and the huge drop in exercise. As summer slid into fall, I had no time to waste if I was going to play in the U.S. Open. Enter Mike Sell.

There are five things I look for in a coach.

1. **Great work ethic and impressive stamina.** If he is going to hit with me, he'd better know what he is getting into. Before hiring potential hitting partners, Tony always asked them, "Are you sure you'll be able to keep up with her? She only knows one speed." No matter what, they always said, "Yeah, yeah, of course." They were probably thinking, *Hey, she's a girl, how bad could it be?* Some guys quit after a week, some made it to two, but very few made it past the maximum shelf life of two months. If they did, they were keepers. So if my coach was going to hit with me too, he had to be in insane shape with a work ethic bordering on the masochistic.

2. **Stability.** If my coach says practice starts at 8 a.m., I will be there at 7:45 warmed up, with my shoes tied, and ready to go. The younger coaches on tour wouldn't think twice about rolling into morning practice twenty minutes late after a raging night on the town. That wasn't a good fit for me.

3. **Steady hitting ability.** See #1. If a coach can't place the ball where it will be in a match, and place it there over and over while I perfect a shot, then there's no point.

4. **Knowledge about the other players' games.** When I was younger I made a point of not knowing what the other players were doing. My theory was that I was just playing myself out there, so it didn't matter who my opponent was. If I played my best, everything would turn out fine. It wasn't that easy anymore. The technical side of the game had risen along with the physical power of the

players. I needed every edge I could get, and if that meant knowing the intricacies of my opponents' weaknesses, then bring on
the video and practice notes. I was an eager student.

5. **Willingness to make me a part of his life.** A coach has to sacrifice a lot to be on the road with me. When we're on the tour, it's
just the two of us battling everyone else. If I don't get along with
the coach off the court, it won't be a successful union. And if he
has a family, it's important that I have a relationship with them
as well. For a few hours during a professional match, tennis is an
individual sport. For all the rest of the time it is a team one.

I'd been lucky in finding a good combination of these five factors in Gavin,
Bobby, and Jimmy Arias (who graciously filled the coaching vacuum
whenever I was in need; I'm so lucky we're neighbors), and I was relieved
to find it again in Mike. Standing six feet tall and looking like he'd just
stepped out of a J. Crew catalog, Mike had been a standout player at the
University of Georgia (Go, Bulldogs!) and had played on the pro tour for
a bit. More important, he grew up with three sisters, so he was very at-
tuned to the tricky business of dealing with women. At the risk of sound-
ing sexist, this is an art form and it's not for the faint of heart. If you can't
cope with me the night before a Grand Slam, there's no point in being my
coach. That's what you're there for: to keep your player calm, cool, and
focused. Mike walked into our new situation without any fear. Nothing
rattled him, and his tranquil, down-to-earth energy worked for me. With
my foot feeling strong, I hit the ground running. In the month leading up
to the U.S. Open, I beat Jennifer, Serena, Justine, and Martina Hingis
(twice). It was a good four weeks.

But I think I used up all of my good playing karma too early. In the
midst of the electric hustle and bustle at the U.S. Open, I was handed my
earliest exit in eleven years: I lost in the fourth round to Daja Bedanova,
an eighteen-year-old Czech player I'd never faced before. While walking
around the grounds on my way to see some quarterfinal matches, I could
see that the transformation of tennis into a sport of hard bodies was com-

plete. For the first time, there was a fully outfitted gym at the tennis facilities. In the nineties, it had been impossible to find a StairMaster or squat rack in any tournament location. It had been a monumental challenge for coaches to come up with makeshift fitness routines for their players on the road. I'd done countless leg and arm workouts on chairs in my hotel room and on benches in nearby parks. And in a pinch I could always do push-ups and sit-ups on my hotel room floor. But resourcefulness was no longer needed: now gleaming cardio machines and circuit weight-training stations stood at the ready at tournament sites and in decent hotels around the world. A nonstop procession of girls wearing sports bras and tiny shorts kept these gyms hopping—and kept me out of them! Call me old-school, but I'd rather run on a city sidewalk for over forty minutes than on a treadmill any day of the week. In between tournaments, I had to log loads of time at the gym. I didn't want to spend every waking moment on the road in those sterile environments.

After my surprising loss on September 6, I headed to Bahia for the Brazil Open with the help of Michael Rodriguez, a fast-thinking USTA official who helped my mom and me secure travel visas at the last minute. My U.S. Open loss had been much earlier than predicted, so I made this snap decision to go to Brazil to help boost my ranking.

Bahia was a new event and I'd been given a bye in the first round, a common practice new tournaments use to entice top players to come. Players seeded fourth or higher usually receive a bye, which is helpful since you can scout your second-round opponent. But there is a drawback: if you lose in the second round, you still only get one point, the same as if you'd lost in the first round.

I woke up on the morning of September 11 thinking about my second-round match. My mom had gone downstairs to get breakfast for us. The local news show was interrupted to bring the footage of the second plane hitting the tower. I couldn't understand anything they were saying. Was this real footage? I flipped the channels and it was the same thing over and over but I had no context for what I was seeing. What was this? What was going on? Was this in Brazil? I had no idea it was New York City. My mom came back to the room balancing juices, fruit, and pastries in her hands. She stopped in the doorway when she saw my face.

"What is it?" she asked.

I didn't say anything. I just pointed to the television. We sat on the bed, transfixed by the images being broadcast to us down in the southern hemisphere. The phone rang. It was a tournament official calling to say we'd be going on with the matches. He mentioned something about New York.

"Wait, those planes were in New York?"

He sounded surprised. "Yes, downtown. The World Trade Center." Just then a panoramic shot flashed on the screen. I don't know why, but I hadn't made the connection between those skyscrapers and the city I'd just left. None of it made sense. Phone calls weren't going through to New York and there was no Internet connection where we were staying. When I got to the stadium, players were huddled in little groups exchanging what little information they had. It wasn't much. The only information we had access to came from the local news shows and those anchors seemed just as confused as we were. I swore I'd never take the twenty-four-hour CNN news feed for granted again.

The week went by in a blur of matches and thirdhand information from home. Everyone's head was somewhere else, and people were itching to get back. I won the tournament but it didn't mean very much. Planes weren't going anywhere, so my plans to fly straight to Japan for the Toyota Princess Cup were put on hold. Instead, the players had to cool their heels in Bahia until we were given the go-ahead to leave. It was a strange waiting game. Knowing there was no way to get to Tokyo in time for my first match, I was starting to jump out of my skin sitting there in my hotel room. I had a headache from watching so much horrific coverage on the news and I needed some fresh air. I decided to explore Bahia's coastline. We were staying in a completely rural area with just the one resort surrounded by acres and acres of white dunes and coconut groves.

One afternoon I walked down to the ocean as the sun was setting lower in the sky. I'd been there for a week but hadn't yet walked the seventy yards from my hotel to see the water. Between the incessant television watching and my matches, it hadn't even dawned on me. The Atlantic looked glassy and the water was comforting and warm on my tired feet. It was like slipping on a pair of cozy aquatic socks. I stood in the soft sand with my feet sinking deeper and deeper as the waves rolled in and out around me. Suddenly I heard a rustle nearby. A man was leading a horse up to a lean-to shack I hadn't noticed before.

"Hello!" he called to me.

"Hi, there!" Two other horses were tethered under the palm frond roof of the lean-to.

"Would you like to take a ride?" he asked.

*Would I like to take a ride?* I hadn't been on a horse since I was eight years old.

"May I?" I was already jogging across the sand toward him.

"Of course: they belong to the hotel. You may take them for as long as you like. I will be your guide."

Hotel horses? If I'd known about this little slice of paradise, I would have been down there ages ago.

"Great, let's go," I said as I stroked the silky mane of a white horse. He adjusted her harness in preparation for our ride and offered to help me up. "Let me give it a go. It's been a while, but I think I still remember how." With a steady hand on her saddle and a bare foot solidly in the stirrup, I hoisted myself up and swung my leg over. I could have sworn I heard a quiet grunt from my horse, and I was struck with the fear that I was too heavy for her. I began scratching behind her ears to make up for the burden I'd just placed on her back. But one look at the stocky figure and pot-belly of my guide atop his chestnut mare and I knew these horses were well conditioned to carrying around loads more challenging than mine.

We took off in a trot down the pristine beach as our horses weaved in and out of the incoming tide. To the left of me all I saw were rows and rows of coconut trees. To the right all I saw was the ocean. Paradise. After a few minutes my guide told me to take her into a gallop.

"What do you think, girl?" I patted her neck as we trotted in the shallow water. "You wanna run?" She jerked her head up and snorted. I took that as a yes. I gave her a sturdy but not too hard (I didn't want to hurt her!) kick with my feet and some slack in the reins. I even threw in a cowboy-worthy *Hyeeeah!* for effect. It worked. Off we went as I held on for my life. Jumping out of the water in one fluid movement, she found solid ground on the hard-packed sand. Perfect terrain for giving it her all. We soon fell into a rhythm together and I was no longer white-knuckling it on the saddle horn. I had total faith that she knew what she was doing and I was just going to trust her and enjoy the ride. The sound of her hooves hitting the ground sent goose bumps down my arms. Her power was staggering. We flew down the beach and I felt something I'd never felt before: weightless. I've heard about the healing effects of horses, the spiritual connection they have with humans, but I'd never experienced it for myself. That night, as the sun gave way to the moon, I got it. My feet felt no pain in those stirrups and I couldn't stop smiling as the sand and ocean spray hit my body. Her energy was primal and raw and I felt like nothing could hurt me from atop her back. I wasn't trying to jump out of my skin anymore; I wanted to ride her forever.

When we brought the horses back, my guide, Marcelo, asked me if I'd ever eaten a coconut before.

"Not a real one," I said. "I mean, not from straight off the tree. Does coconut cake count?" He laughed and said that it didn't.

"Here." He handed one to me. It felt heavy and scratchy in my hands. "What do I do with it?"

"You open it!" He laughed his melodic laugh again, which made me laugh too. "Like this." He took the coconut back and grabbed a narrow, six-inch, rectangular piece of wood. "Look for the happy face first." He held the coconut up to me; sure enough, one end was marked with a distinct set of eyes, nose, and what could arguably be called a little squiggle line of a mouth.

"Next, you make holes in the eyes and nose." He swiftly popped right through the poor coconut with the pointy edge of the wood stick. "Then you do like this." Marcelo slammed the coconut down into the sand with surprising force. Then he handed me the stick and showed me where the vertical "equator" of the coconut ran. "Just hit on this line until it opens for you." I kneeled down on the sand and started tapping away. There was no way this thing was going to open. It felt rock solid and stubborn and in no mood to surrender to me. Over and over I tapped along the orb's side, but there was no progress. I took a break and looked up at Marcelo.

"Keep going?" I asked.

"Yes, keep going. Do not be afraid to hit it!"

If there's one thing I'm not afraid of, it's hitting something hard. I ramped up the intensity of pounding until suddenly I heard a crack.

"There!" Marcelo exclaimed, clapping his hands together. "You are almost there. Just a few more taps, gentle this time, and you will have your coconut."

I urged the coconut on with a few subtle knocks to its shell and watched in astonishment as a neat fault line deepened along its side and fell cleanly open into two halves in my lap.

"Quick, quick!" He grabbed one half and funneled the juice into a glass bottle. I did the same with the other half. "This is very good for you, this juice. It gives you very good strength." Marcelo whipped out a pocketknife—this guy was like Inspector Gadget—and peeled off a few perfect crescent slices. "Try one." He handed me a piece. First, I heard a nutritionist's voice lecturing me about the high fat content in coconut and how, despite its benefit in replacing electrolytes after a hard workout, I should stay away from it. Then I heard myself say, "Screw it." My voice was louder than the nutritionist's. The coconut was fantastic. After a few more slices off of Marcelo's knife, I thanked him for the lovely ride and went back to the hotel.

"Do you want to go down for dinner?" my mom asked when I got back to my room.

"No, thanks. I'm not hungry." I wasn't. The coconut and horseback ride had filled me up in every way. I got ready for bed, left the television off, and picked up a book.

"Really?" my mom asked. It had been a long time since she'd heard those words come out of my mouth.

"Yeah, I think I'm just going to relax for a while."

"Okay, sweetheart." She kissed me on the forehead. "Have a good night. I'll see you in the morning."

Cuddled up in bed, I could hear the distant sound of waves crashing outside my window. I fell asleep before I turned a page of my book.

# 35

# Diet Secrets of the Sumo Wrestler

I was in Tokyo for the Japan Open, a hard-court Tier III event. I adored going to Tokyo, the headquarters of my longtime sponsor, Yonex. I'd progressed from using their rackets to being outfitted from head to toe in their gear. Jun, a Yonex representative who had become a close friend of mine, would be in town. So I went into the tournament expecting to do well and excited to reconnect with old friends. My body felt healthy, I was rested from the forced break in Bahia, and I was playing a solid game with Mike's calm and steady coaching behind me. I won all four of my matches in two sets each and in the final I defeated Tamarine Tanasugarn, a determined and gritty retriever who runs down every ball. Tamarine is from Thailand and is one of the sweetest girls on tour. We always got along well, but our matches were fiercely competitive. My victory made a small dent in the point deficit I had from missing the two summer Grand Slams. At the postmatch press conference a journalist asked me what it felt like to win my fiftieth career title.

"It is?" I asked, bewildered.

He checked his notes and nodded vigorously from the press gallery. "Yes."

"Oh, well, it feels good. I'm feeling like I'm playing solid tennis and

I'm looking forward to next season." I had no idea it was my fiftieth title. I guess that's something of a milestone in tennis but, with the exception of Grand Slams, I never kept track of tournament wins. His stat caught me off guard. After I won the tournament the Yonex group took me out for a celebratory dinner of sushi. I love sushi. It isn't an ordinary love like "Oh, I love ice cream." I love it to the point of dreaming about it. We talked business for the first ten minutes—How was the second season with my new racket going? Was I happy with my clothes? Did I need to make any changes to my gear?—and we spent the rest of the dinner talking about the dream itinerary that my Yonex friends had in mind for me; the plan included Kabuki theater and sumo wrestling.

On my way back to the hotel, I popped into one of my favorite places in Tokyo. A paragon of high culture and taste, a place that takes a special person to truly appreciate it: the am/pm convenience store. I know they have them in California, but the Japanese version is completely different. It is a fast-food temple extraordinaire. If you put them side by side, the Tokyo version would be insulted. Jun, my go-to Yonex guy, was based in California but he made frequent trips back to Tokyo to see his family. Every time he went, I asked him to bring back some am/pm treats for me. He was happy to do so and was convinced that I knew Japanese sweets better than he did.

Whenever I flew to Tokyo I'd be a wreck from jet lag for the first two days. I'd walk around for forty-eight hours barely knowing my name. When I grew tired of watching the surreal, laugh-out-loud Japanese game shows, I'd walk the city streets until I found my fluorescent-lit beacon of comfort. I'd spend an hour in the dead of night strolling up and down the aisles, not understanding a word of the packaging but loving every brightly colored cartoon smiling up at me from the wrappers. By my fourth trip to Tokyo I knew my favorite snacks by sight, although I had no idea what they were called. I'd fill my basket with little crackers, tasty pretzel sticks covered in cinnamon and chocolate, and bags of mix-and-match candies, then go back to my hotel room and nibble on my new stash like a crazed chipmunk. The next day I'd play for four hours in a panicked attempt to work it all off.

I'm not sure why I stopped at my favorite store after dinner with the Yonex crew. I wasn't particularly hungry, even though portions in Tokyo were minuscule compared to the gargantuan sizes I was accustomed to in the States. I think I was drawn through the doors out of habit. It had always comforted me before; why wouldn't it now? I loaded up my basket, just like always, and headed back to my hotel laden down with treats. I spread them out on the bed and picked up a package of cinnamon pretzels. I ate them all, then chased them down with a handful of chocolate pretzels. Then I stopped, wrapped the rest up in a bag, stuffed it deep inside my suitcase, and shoved my suitcase to the back of the closet. I didn't want to ruin a perfect night with a binge. I was getting better, but I didn't trust myself with a mountain of my favorite treats sitting out in plain sight. One day, maybe, but most definitely not yet.

The two days were a high-energy tourist's dream. Brazil had caused a fissure in my normal tennis-and-only-tennis façade. I was suddenly on a mission to see everything I could before I had to leave for my next tournament in China. I went to my first sumo match and I was in shock—these guys made my Greco-Roman wrestling buddy Rulon look like he was in junior high school. They not only had superhuman size but also the superhuman strength to back it up. After the match I couldn't wait to talk to the star wrestler. It was a huge honor to meet him and right after our introduction, I asked, "I'm sure you're tired of hearing this question, but I'm dying to know one thing: What do you eat?"

He chuckled and graciously replied, "I am on a very strict diet."

"A strict diet? How strict?" If this guy was on a strict diet and still weighed over four hundred pounds, I was going to give up all hope.

"I am on a strict diet of fifteen thousand calories."

"Fifteen thousand *a day?*" I asked. That was a whole lot of steamed spinach and egg-white omelets. Or ten cheeseburgers, three plates of pasta, an ice cream sundae, a large bag of potato chips, and a milkshake to wash it all down.

"Yes, I must eat that every day. I am not allowed to eat any less or I'll risk losing my size. And I make sure to lie down as soon as I've finished eating. That is very important in helping with fat production." *That's it*, I thought, *I'm giving up sleep.* He went on to describe all the other rules and how they helped him stay in top sumo shape. I kept a mental checklist to see how I compared:

**Rule number one:** Skip breakfast. This slows down your metabolism and keeps it down for the rest of the day, making it harder to burn off the calories you ingest at lunch and dinner.
**Verdict: not guilty.** If unsatisfying and tasteless protein shakes count, then I'm a breakfast eater.

**Rule number two:** Eat two big meals a day. Starving all morning and then gorging yourself in the afternoon is a surefire way to get fat. It ruins your energy and wreaks havoc on your metabolism.
**Verdict: guilty.** I ate next to nothing during the day and then, just as my metabolism was reaching its slowest pace in the evening, I'd consume a mountain of junk food. Living in those extremes guarantees serious weight gain.

**Rule number three:** Nap right after eating.
**Verdict: guilty.** Is there anything better than passing out after Thanksgiving dinner? Food comas aren't a good idea, but they are so tempting. It's fine to do it once a year in November, but I fell into one nearly every night.

**Rule number four:** Exercise on an empty stomach.
**Verdict: guilty.** In my extreme training phases I was down to 1,200 calories a day (before the evening binge), so even if I'd just eaten a meal, I was still starving while working out.

**Rule number five:** Eat in social settings. Sumo wrestlers live in "training stables" and eat all of their meals gathered around a communal table.

**Verdict: guilty in the past but currently recovering.** The Atlanta
food court had been a fiasco, but by the Sydney Olympics I did
prove that I'd reformed in that area.

My "guilty" tally was disturbing. Horrified, I realized that my habits
bore an eerie resemblance to sumo training. Uh-oh. But meeting that
athlete was the most educational experience of my life. I learned more
from him in twenty minutes than I had from years of reading books and
listening to trainers. I'd been living my life like a quasi–sumo wrestler!
And the most important thing I learned was that what you put into your
mouth is more critical to weight loss than how much exercise you do.
These guys were working out more than six hours a day but they were still
enormous. If you are consuming thousands of calories, no amount of exercise can burn it all off: you will be big. It takes one hour of intense exercise
to burn off five hundred calories, but it only takes one bagel with cream
cheese to add five hundred calories. Calories are easier to put on than they
are to take off, which is why one of my half-hour binges would wipe out
an entire day's worth of hard work. After my stabbing, it had taken less
than a week to destroy all the progress I'd made with Bob Kersee because
I hadn't mastered the energy balance equation. Working out hard didn't
give me a free pass to eat everything in sight, but that's exactly what I did.
I worked out in extremes and I ate in extremes. Nothing was in balance
and my body showed it.

I woke up early the next morning to go on an excursion with Mr. Yoneyama. At 5 a.m. we were in front of the fish market downtown. The
fish, gorgeous works of art pulled fresh from the ocean, were being auc-
tioned off like masterpieces. Buyers walked up and down the aisles, gently
rolling the fish onto their sides to check out the color, texture, and fat
content before the bidding started. Once it got going, it was as chaotic as
the New York Stock Exchange. Hand signals and money were flying across
the room. Several of the priciest catches were headed for a nonstop flight
to Nobu, a fancy sushi restaurant in New York.

That night the Yonex group took me to see Kabuki theater in all its splendid glory. The audience was dressed to impress. Not a pair of jeans in sight. Men wore elegantly tailored suits and women were draped in gowns of silk. I've never been able to go shopping in Japan: the sizes are tiny. In a land of seventeen-inch waists, I couldn't even get my leg through a pair of pants. Aside from the sumo guys, who had to work hard at it, I never once saw an overweight person in Japan. Despite am/pm, it is not really a culture of snacking, and it's difficult to put on weight when eating three small meals a day, made up mainly of rice and fresh fish.

The cavernous, intricately carved theater was silent as we waited for the show to begin. Like traditional Shakespeare, in Kabuki both the male and female roles are played by men, but the makeup is so immaculately applied, it is hard to tell it's a single-sex production. Thank God I had my earphones with an ongoing English translation, otherwise I wouldn't have had any idea what was going on in the story. But I didn't need an explanation for what was happening when, twenty minutes into the production, an actor with uncommonly good looks walked onstage and the women in the crowd erupted into gasps, shrieks, and applause. He was being received like Brad Pitt with the musical talent of the Beatles. The proper and reserved nature of the audience was broken for a three-minute freakout over the actor's dreamy qualities. Some things are the same, no matter where you're from.

# 36

# Call Me Ox

The Year of the Ox. According to the Chinese zodiac calendar, all babies born in the Year of the Ox have a solid and steadfast nature and thrive on taking a methodical approach to life. But these people also have a stubborn streak and hatred of failing, which often results in self-defeating behavior. And don't look for them to be the life of the cocktail party—their serious nature makes them feel uncomfortable in large social gatherings and they are frequently told to "loosen up." It is rare for ox people to try something new, though when they do they surprise themselves with how much they enjoy it. A dark cloud has the potential to hang over those born in the Year of the Ox, but if they learn to value their own positive qualities, they will see the glass as half full.

Hmmm, guess what year I was born in? The last stop on our Asian swing was Shanghai. My mom, coach Mike, and I got on a plane bound for my last official tournament of the year and my first trip to China. On the plane I found an article on Chinese zodiac signs in the in-flight magazine. Normally I don't put much stock in that kind of stuff, yet I couldn't get over how dead-on that description was. I didn't want a dark cloud hanging over me for the rest of my life.

The Shanghai Open was a thirty-two draw, a smaller tournament, which offered a good chance for some eleventh-hour points if I managed to take home the title. They'd had the inaugural tournament the previous year but it was a soft opening of sorts; this year was the real deal. The event organizer pulled out all the stops and the tournament ran like clockwork. Tennis was a new thing in China, so there was an air of eagerness and a little unease about proper protocol. For example, the court was painted red, a lucky color in Chinese culture, but it wasn't made of clay. That didn't bother me, but the incessant cell phone ringing took some getting used to. Most tournaments have a strict ban on cell phones because they disrupt play. The last thing you want to hear when serving for the tiebreaker is the electronic jingle of "Lady Marmalade"; good luck getting that one out of your head. But the Chinese had no such ban. The crowd wasn't sure when to clap or when a game was over. After I hit an impossible crosscourt backhand against Nicole Pratt to take the first set in the final, you could hear a pin drop. One brave spectator clapped, then another, then—the silence broken—the entire crowd got into it. By the time I won the final 6–2, 6–3, they had a much better grasp on the intricacies of scoring. It was a learning experience for all of us. Cell phones and awkward applause notwithstanding, the tournament went off without a hitch and Shanghai seemed to embrace this new, somewhat confusing sport of tennis.

The enthusiasm of the Chinese kids was contagious. After every match, they surrounded me like a swarm of bees. I saw many up-and-coming players hitting the ball with a two-handed forehand, including fifteen-year-old Peng Shuai, who was making her WTA debut, and I kept thinking about how happy my dad would have been to see that. His coaching method hadn't been so crazy after all.

Eating proved to be a bit difficult, since I couldn't read a thing on any menu. I lucked out with sweet rice and bean curd soup, a paper-thin pancake stuffed with chives and egg, and a carnival-worthy fried dough stick. You generally can't go wrong with sugar-covered fried dough. But my luck ran out when, on one of my last nights, I ordered what I thought was the sweet rice soup. After digging in for my first bite, my spoon emerged from the murky liquid holding an animal claw. We were dining with some of the tournament organizers and I didn't want to appear rude, so I tried to hide my shock even though my eyes were probably as wide as my soup bowl. I picked around the claw as best I could and tried not to think about what kind of animal my dinner had once been attached to. It may be close-minded and culturally ignorant of me, but I'd rather enjoy my dinner without crunching into mysterious feet!

I was pleased to win in Shanghai, especially after such a disappointing run at the U.S. Open. It was a relief to finish the year strong: three titles in one month. Not a bad road trip, but these tournaments weren't heavy hitters like the season ender I was missing in Munich, and it was reflected in my ranking: I was down to number ten. Surprisingly, it didn't bother me; in fact, it was a wake-up call that my international tennis traveling days might be coming to a close.

Instead of bolting back to Florida the moment the tournament was over, my mom and I decided to head to Beijing. I didn't pick up a racket for five days. We went to Tiananmen Square, were awed by the Great Wall, and took a rickshaw ride through the city. It was one of the best times I've ever had. I wasn't thinking about practice times, endorsements, or airline reservations: I was just being. It was calming and liberating. I thought about all the opportunities I'd passed up in other cities over the years. I wondered if I'd ever get a chance to go back and make up for lost time. I hoped so. I'd given up so much for tennis and had never mastered the art of striking a balance. I had been convinced that, to be number one, I had to eat, sleep, and breathe the game. But while I was walking along the Great Wall, I realized there was so much out there for me to see. Maybe I'd been too hard on myself over the years. Maybe I'd been too strict about my schedule. Maybe limiting myself to the hotels and the tournament sites had been counterproductive. What if I'd been able to see the world *and* play tennis? Would that have taken the pressure off of me? Would that have made my mental game stronger? What if working out so hard and restricting what I allowed myself to do hadn't been the key after all?

By the time I got back to Florida, I vowed to strike a better balance in 2002. But old habits die hard. After my Asia trip, I was tipping the scale at more than 160, so once again panic set in. I needed a new angle, a new person, a new workout; I was still searching for the magic answer. I contacted Pat Etcheberry, a renowned fitness and conditioning coach who had worked with dozens of top players, and he gave me some intense workouts to incorporate into my training. My practices were going well and my tennis was solid, but I hadn't had a food babysitter since the previous winter. New workouts wouldn't be enough. I was still too heavy, and as much as I hated admitting it, I needed constant supervision again. It is a quick jump from 160 to 170, and I didn't want to make that leap. Pat put me in touch with Lisa Reed, a trainer at the University of Gainesville who competed in fitness competitions and had one of the hardest bodies I'd ever seen. *That's it! This is my answer*, I thought. *A female trainer will be a completely different experience. This time it will work.*

# — 37 —

# A Pumpkin by Midnight

Armed with Mike and Lisa I started the season off with a bang in Australia. At the Hopman Cup in Perth, Jan-Michael and I beat France 3–0, lost to Italy, beat Belgium—despite their being aided by the fiercely good Kim Clijsters, who went on to win the U.S. Open title a few years later—and lost in the final to Spain. The highlight of the week was spending New Year's Eve at the players' ball. It was held in a beautiful and glamorous casino. I channeled my inner Cinderella and had my hair blown out and makeup done and arrived at the glittering party wearing a pink organza dress. After spending 95 percent of my time in workout clothes, it felt refreshingly indulgent to primp and devote an inordinate amount of time on my looks. When the transformation was complete, I hardly recognized the girl in the mirror. I even felt—dare I say it?—*pretty*. And, like Cinderella, I really did have to get home by midnight. Our second match was at 10 a.m., which meant a 7 a.m. wake-up call. All the players had been keeping their fingers crossed that they wouldn't have to ring in the New Year with a morning match, but in a draw of just five teams I knew there'd be a decent chance we'd have to cut our New Year's celebration short. Like a good girl, I took my leave early, just before the dazzling fireworks display.

Two weeks later at the Australian Open, I shocked every prognosticating journalist by beating Venus in the quarterfinals. She was going for her third Grand Slam in a row, and it had already been six years since I'd last taken home that honor. I was seeded seventh, she was seeded second, and I was 0–6 in our past meetings. On paper, my chances looked bleak. But I still had hope. I knew I could defy the odds if I was on top of my game and able to take advantage of any weakness Venus might show. The problem with Venus is that she is rarely off her game, so going in I knew I had to immediately neutralize her take-no-prisoners serve. Her serve turns the ball into a bullet: it regularly reaches a speed of 115 miles per hour and has been clocked at 129 miles per hour, much faster than the serves of most of the men on tour. Mike told me my only goal was to hang in there for all three sets; if I could do that, I'd have the opportunity to end her twenty-four-match winning streak. The hard court in Australia produces higher bounces and is my favorite surface after clay; if I was going to beat her, this was an ideal situation.

I got off to a fast start. I won the first eight points to charge to a 2–0 lead, but I didn't get ahead of myself. *Play every point,* I thought, *the games and the sets will take care of themselves.* Venus broke back and we eventually went to a tiebreaker, which she grabbed with a backhand volley that I didn't have a prayer of getting. *No problem: new set, new game, new chance to take the first point.* I stayed calm like the old days and sailed through to tie the match by taking the second set 6–2. It all came down to the third set. I'd never kept up with Venus like this. All six feet two inches of her looked powerful on the other side of the court, but I now knew that she was not invincible. *Could I do it? Stop. Don't ask questions right now, just play.* And so I did. I was up 4–3 and, after Venus failed to capitalize on three break points, managed to scrape my way to 5–3. *Almost there.* On the second match point Venus hit a backhand into the net. It was over.

There was some postmatch press conference chatter about it being a weird match, not representative of how we usually played because Venus was dealing with a hamstring problem and I was combating a fever, but that was becoming the norm on the tour. Long gone were the days when everyone was playing at her optimum health. Workouts were more intense, the current serves could blow away ones from a decade earlier, and the traveling was even more constant than ever. It was bound to inflict a beating on a player's body and immune system. Playing with an injury or a nasty virus was becoming the rule instead of the exception. But beating Venus showed me that the magic that I'd been able to find on the courts of the Australian Open for so many years hadn't disappeared completely. In fact, it lasted just long enough for me to take the first set in my semifinal against Hingis, but it didn't stay around to get me to the final. Hingis came back swinging in the second set and won the match 4–6, 6–1, 6–4. I left without my fifth Australian Open title but with a small reprieve from the bombardment of the retirement rumors.

# – 38 –

# *Live to Work or*
# *Work to Live?*

After our first week together I should have known that, even though she was a woman, Lisa's approach was exactly the same as the male trainers I'd worked with: extreme and unyielding. I'd been hoping for a confidante, but she was just as hard-core as the others. I was doing the same thing I'd always done and expecting different results again. Lisa was amazing: her disciplined food intake was unmatched. I thought if I spent every meal with her, studied the way she approached food, and copied exactly what she did, I'd eventually adopt her habits on my own. It didn't work. If we were on the road, I made up excuses about where I had to be. I'd say I had to meet a Yonex representative, but I'd really go to the grocery store and buy chips and cookies. If we were home in Florida, I'd wait until Lisa went to bed to make my move. I'd quietly tiptoe past her bedroom door, get in my car, and head to the nearest drive-thru. I'd binge on all of the forbidden foods and not say a word about it the next morning. I kept the anger and frustration buried deep inside me.

While my food intake was still out of control, the last few months had been good on the tennis front. I'd made it to the finals of a tournament in Tokyo and won a title in Qatar. Before the start of the European swing, we returned to the U.S. for the Indian Wells tournament, where I lost to

Martina Hingis in the semifinal, and the Miami Open, where I lost in another semifinal, this time to Jennifer Capriati in a nail-biting, pushed-to-
the-limit third-set tiebreaker. I was having my best start in years, making
it to the semis or better in seven straight tournaments. My body was holding up injury-free despite my still being twenty-five pounds overweight. I
was beginning to think, *To hell with it. I'm just meant to be this big forever*.
But then I'd see a size four walk by and I'd be struck with an undeniable
pang of envy. *I used to look like that*. I hated that I cared that much,
but I did.

Before we got to Paris at the end of May, we had a stop in Spain for the
Madrid Open. I loved Spain for many of the reasons that I loved Italy: the
warm, laid-back people, the food, the history, the parks. But there was one
thing I didn't like: the obscenely late dinner hours. When I got there I
walked from restaurant to restaurant, searching in vain for a dining room
that opened before 10 p.m. It seemed like there were two siestas, one in
the afternoon and another from 7 to 10 p.m., when—finally!—the restaurants would throw open their doors and the night would officially get under way. Sure, it sounded sexy and sophisticated to say, "Meet you for a
midnight dinner," but there was no way that could be part of my routine
when I had a 10:00 a.m. match.

The tournament went great. My semifinal against Paola Suárez was the
only match that went to three sets. I beat Chanda Rubin in the final, 6–4,
6–2. It was my first clay court title since Rome in 2000 and I felt good going into Paris. I was having little flashes of hope that I had another Grand
Slam in me. I was playing solid tennis and had some momentum on my
side. Being on the tour didn't feel like such a struggle this time. What had
changed? A tiny spark had been lit in me. It was nearly a year since my
Bahia beach ride, and I was taking baby steps to make my life more whole,
reaching outside the confines of tennis. In Qatar I rode a camel (harder
than it looks) and slept in a tent under the stars in the middle of the desert. In Madrid I went to the Prado, one of the most impressive museums
in the world. I am about as far from an artsy sort of person as you can get,
but I stood completely transfixed in front of all the Velázquez master-

pieces. Being around such beauty, created by a pair of hands and some paint nearly four hundred years ago, gave me a jolt like the one I had experienced when I saw the Great Wall. It made me realize that I'd been missing out on so much. For thirteen years I'd been lucky enough to travel through five continents and visit some of the most culturally and historically rich cities in the world. But I couldn't remember a thing I'd done or seen that wasn't colored in some way by tennis. Walking around the grand rooms of the Prado, relishing every minute of the art and solitude, was like discovering a whole other layer of life.

On the evening of my final match victory, two cool local girls who worked for the tournament took me out to dinner. "You need to get out of the hotel. We'll show you the real Madrid!" they promised. We had a drink in Las Cuevas, one of the oldest taverns in Madrid. The bar was at the bottom of a set of creaky stairs in a dark cave. It seemed like a strange place for an establishment, and I almost asked them if we'd taken a wrong turn somewhere. As soon as we rounded a corner I knew we were in the right place. The bar was packed with locals, and flickering candles lit the room as pitchers of sangria were passed around from table to table. The three of us sat on an old wooden bench, and they kept me enthralled with stories of growing up in Madrid and how the Spanish way of life differs from the American.

"It is quite simple," Caterina said. "We work to live while Americans live to work." Teresa nodded her head in emphatic agreement. Well, yes, that was true. But I'd always considered myself a citizen of the world. I could get along in Tokyo just as well as Melbourne and Dubai. On an analytical level, I knew how other cultures embraced life and stressed quality over quantity, but on an emotional level I hadn't yet figured it out.

Next we hit a tapas bar, where we ate no fewer than twenty-one tiny plates of delectable dishes. I'd escaped Lisa, telling her I was going out with some friends. Maybe she thought I deserved one night off after winning the tournament. I certainly thought so. The cuisine was entirely new to me, so I didn't recognize half the things put before me. But I did know two things: each plate was more delicious than the last, and Lisa would not have approved of any of them. We left the restaurant at one in the morning and I could barely keep my eyes open. If I ever moved to Spain, I'd have to completely revamp my body clock. I said good-bye to my new friends and walked through Plaza Mayor on the way back to my hotel. The girls told me that it was similar to the Place des Vosges in Paris: surely I'd been there? No, actually I hadn't. I didn't have the slightest idea of what they were talking about. Plaza Mayor was majestically lit up and full of people eating and drinking at outdoor tables. Everyone looked so happy to be where they were in that moment. *Yeah,* I thought, *me too.*

The next day Mike, Lisa, and I headed to Paris. It was time to get ready for my favorite Grand Slam. We went for runs under the leafy overhanging trees in the Bois de Boulogne, the same park my dad and I had walked through on our first visit to Roland Garros, a lifetime ago. The thought that I could make a run for another French Open title was so strong, I could practically taste it. I beat Daniela Hantuchova in the fourth round and was on my way to the quarterfinals, against Venus. Uh-oh. My win over her in Australia had proven to me that I could do it, but she was still one of the only players I dreaded facing. When her game was on, she was unstoppable. Unfortunately for me, her game was more than on, and I kissed my hopes of another French Open title good-bye with a 6–4, 6–3 defeat.

Mike told me to shake it off and focus on Wimbledon. "Don't let it get into your head. There's a lot more tennis to be played," he told me about a dozen times. His quick-reflex game was good preparation for the fast playing surfaces awaiting me. Lisa did an amazing job of coping with the full-fat European food. She never once freaked out or complained about the lack of skim milk. We ate every meal together and I kept my secret binges to a minimum.

I worked my butt off going into London. I wasn't going to let the loss to Venus derail the momentum I'd had all year. The Williams sisters and Jennifer Capriati were holding on to the top three rankings with tight grips, but I was hanging in there at number four. It wasn't high enough for the media, and as soon as I entered the All England Club, the rumors of my imminent retirement started again. One mathematically astute journalist pointed out that at twenty-eight and a half years old, I was exactly twice the age as when I'd turned pro. Did I see a date for retirement in the near future? No, I didn't, I said. Truthfully, the concept of ending my pro career was starting to pop up in my consciousness, but I wasn't the kind of person to go on a farewell tour. I knew that one day, when I was sure, I'd just stop. I didn't need to give the world advance notice.

Most interviews over those two weeks focused on these questions:

"If it hadn't been for Hamburg, how much more do you think you could have accomplished?"

"If you were playing now like you were playing before the stabbing, how do you think you'd fare against the Williams sisters?"

"If you hadn't stayed away from the game for two and a half years, would you be in a better position now?"

I tried to be as polite as possible, but I absolutely hated answering those questions. I was so tired of asking all of the what-ifs; I'd been doing it myself for years and I didn't want to do it again. There was no point. What happened in Hamburg wasn't my choice; it wasn't a stupid mistake or a lapse in good judgment on my part that took me out of the game. There was nothing I could have done about it then and there was nothing I could do to change it now, almost ten years later.

Why, on the cusp of turning thirty, was I still trying to win Wimbledon, the only Grand Slam that had eluded me? Easy: I'm stubborn. I was still playing great tennis, and back in 1992 I'd thought I'd have plenty of time to win on those grass courts. Time slipped away faster than I ever could have imagined, and I wanted to try again. I didn't want to live with the regret that I didn't at least try.

I got through the first four rounds without much trouble, but knew I was in for a fight in the quarterfinal. The field of top ten women was so strong, if I made it to the final eight, I'd face a battle no matter who I was matched up against. The draw put me against Justine Henin; I'd beaten her in every one of our last four matches. She took an early lead and had me at 2–4. I rallied and advanced to 5–4 before giving up three straight games. After losing the first set, I tried to banish the negative thoughts from my head. I didn't want to give up before the match was over. The thoughts stayed anyway. *You're getting too old. She's faster than you are. Come on, do you really think you can win another Grand Slam?* I couldn't get them out of my head. I couldn't access the focus, and my confidence was shot. Amid rain delays that pushed our match into the cold night, I blew a 4–1 lead in the second set and lost 7–6. The last chance I'd probably ever have to make a run in Wimbledon was over. The crowd gave us a standing ovation. I packed my bag and hurried off the court, furious that I'd sabotaged myself again.

# A Well-Timed Rain Delay

Summer came to a close and I packed my bags for New York City. I was still disappointed after my Wimbledon loss but there was one good thing: I was going to New York with zero expectations. I had no pressure and I decided I was just going to give it everything I had.

The crowd, which is always rowdy, was tremendous through all of my matches. New Yorkers break every rule of tennis etiquette, and I love it. One of the best parts about playing in New York was that my honorary coach would be there. I'd met David Dinkins, the mayor of New York City, in 1992 when I received an award for being the WTA's Player of the Year. After my stabbing, he had written me a heartfelt letter and called to check on me. It meant a lot during a time when I felt incredibly alone. Since my return to tennis, "Coach" Dinkins had been my most loyal supporter and hadn't missed a single one of my U.S. Open matches. Throughout the years, he has always given me the same advice: "Everything comes and goes in life. Nothing is permanent, so don't get upset about things that don't matter. Your only responsibility is to make sure you spend as much time as you can doing something that you love. If you do that, it will all work out in the end."

There was another reason I was excited to go to New York that August:

Benjamin, a guy I'd met at a friend's engagement in Boston when I got home from London, was going to be there. At the engagement dinner party, my friend had slyly seated us next to each other. While we were the only single people there, and her plan was pretty transparent, it worked like a charm. Benjamin was a world-traveling corporate type who loved food. The first night we met we spent most of the evening arguing over whether poor restaurant service can be made up for with exquisite sauces. I said of course it could; he disagreed. It was a very obnoxious foodie conversation that bored everyone around us to tears, but we had a great time. And he had something going for him that no other guy I'd ever dated had: he was overweight. His less-than-ripped physique was comforting to me; I interpreted it as a silent acceptance of how I looked. The European trip had taken a lot out of me and, despite Lisa's vigilant eye, I'd put on another eight pounds. My size twelves were starting to feel tight.

With Coach Dinkins cheering me on even louder than the enthusiastic New Yorkers, I got through the first couple of rounds without much trouble. Then, in the third round, I blew a 6–1, 5–1 lead to Yoon-Jeong Cho. I wasn't playing in the moment and she capitalized on it. I lost the second set 7–5 and I was furious. I pulled out all the stops and threw my rarely used drop shot into the mix to steal the third set.

Hingis was waiting for me in the fourth round. We'd been going head-to-head since 1996 and I knew what to expect. She'd have me running back and forth until my legs turned to Jell-O. One of the smartest tacticians on the tour, Martina was brilliant at keeping me on the run, something I despised. It was hard enough when I was skinny; it would be nearly impossible now. Our scheduled match was rained out and Mike wanted me to rest, so I went back to the hotel to kill some time. Lisa made sure there wasn't any food in the minibar. I was flipping through the television channels when I saw that a tennis match was on. *That's weird. I thought everything was rained out.* Then I recognized one of the players: she was a younger, fitter me, and she looked fierce. CBS was broadcasting the epic duel between Jennifer and me from the 1991 U.S. Open semifinal. We were just two kids with our careers in front of us. It felt like ancient history.

I hate watching videos of myself and I can count on one hand the number of times I've done it, so I reached for the remote to change the channel. Suddenly I stopped. My youthful clone had just hit a game-winning killer forehand right down the line, and the camera panned to the crowd. There was my dad, clapping and smiling and looking so much, well, so much like *himself*—the version I remembered most vividly—that I felt like I could reach into the screen and hug him. I sat on the edge of my bed with my eyes glued to the set. I'd never seen my dad's reactions during that match. As usual, he cheered for my opponent whenever she hit a nice shot—he'd done that since I was playing in twelve-and-under tournaments in Europe, and it used to drive me crazy—and looks of elation and determination crossed his face, depending on how I was doing. My heart jumped into my throat every time the camera panned to him. But I also couldn't believe I was the same person as the one I was seeing on the screen. She seemed so intense and focused. It had been a decade since I'd last won the U.S. Open. I wasn't a hungry teenager untouched by the sadness and tragedy of life anymore, but I knew I could get some of that focus and intensity back if I really wanted to.

Riding a high from seeing that match, I walked into the stadium with renewed purpose. On my way in, I glimpsed a huge sponsor ad from a camera company. It was a photo of me from that 1991 victory. I had my hands thrown up in the air in celebration, and a smile had taken over my entire face. "Take home a memory," the caption said. I was going to do my best. I came out on fire. I played aggressively and didn't let go. I think Martina was thrown off balance. Her winning record against me was close to 75 percent, but I wasn't playing like it. I won the match 6–4, 6–2 and advanced to the quarterfinal match against—take a guess—Venus Williams. Seriously? Again? These Grand Slam brackets were killing me. She was going for her third straight U.S. Open title and she looked unstoppable. Her 115-mile-per-hour serves had been blazing trails all week long. But I had hope, and it was buoyed by the great run another member of the old guard was having on the men's side.

Pete Sampras, at a rickety thirty-one years of age, was on the unlikely mission to add a record fourteenth Grand Slam title to his résumé. He was deep in the muck of a thirty-three-tournament losing streak and was the seventeenth seed coming into the tournament. Journalists dismissed him: Sure, it'd be appealing in a sentimental way, but come on, what are the chances? Funny thing is, it didn't seem anybody told Pete he didn't have a chance. He soared through the first several rounds and was playing like he was a decade younger. I saw him in the players' lounge before the quarterfinals after his fourth-round win and wished him luck. As always, he was incredibly gracious and I couldn't get over how amazing his wife, Bridgette, looked. The players' lounge at Grand Slam tournaments was a constant parade of the gorgeous girlfriends and wives of the guys on the ATP. Feeling like a gigantic clod who'd just walked into a fashion shoot, I usually spent no more than five minutes in there.

*If he can do it, then I can too*, I thought. *We're not out of the game yet.* Pete made a phenomenal run to the final against Agassi. It was like the clock of professional tennis had just been rewound twelve years. In a fantastic four-set match, Pete emerged victorious and left prediction-making journalists all over the world stunned. I didn't have as much luck. Venus consistently held her serve and I never really got in the game. She beat me 6–2, 6–3 and I beat a hasty retreat to meet Benjamin at my favorite Italian restaurant on Manhattan's Upper East Side.

Lisa gave me a pep talk before I headed out. I wasn't going to drown my frustration in pasta. At dinner I followed her instructions. Benjamin looked at me like I was crazy when I ordered steamed fish with a side of spinach. I was so tempted to share his fried calamari, but the anger over losing in the quarterfinals was still fresh in my mind. If getting back into Grand Slam final winning form meant starving myself, then screw it. That's what I would do. But my resolve only lasted until dessert. I ordered cheesecake, had half of Benjamin's gelato, and ate more than my fair share of the sugar cookies that were placed in between us. I went to bed feeling guilty, angry, and disappointed.

# – 40 –

# A Passing of the Grunting Torch

I ended the year with another quarterfinal loss to Venus at the season-ending championship. After one year in Munich it had moved back to the States and was being held in Los Angeles. After my loss to Venus, my rank dropped to seventh. Mike had just gotten married and decided he didn't want to travel anymore. I couldn't blame him; the last year had been crazy. We'd gone from Australia to Japan to France to Qatar to the United Arab Emirates to California to Miami to South Carolina to Madrid, then back to Paris, then to London, followed by Missouri, then back to California, then New York, on to Bahia for the second year in a row, and ended the year with seven stops in five weeks: Los Angeles, Denver, Florida's Delray Beach, Ireland, Baltimore, and two exhibitions in Minnesota and Winnipeg, Canada. It was a schedule that wasn't for the faint of heart, nor was it for the recently married. Lisa and I parted ways too. I would have given anything to have had her willpower and discipline when it came to food, but I just didn't. I was tired of sneaking out of the house, eating in my car, and lying to her about how well I'd been sticking to my diet. I couldn't keep it up and I wasn't losing weight. It was time for me to find another magical solution.

Before I had the chance to look for a new coach, I had a bigger problem to deal with. My right foot, which had been giving me problems on and off for the past two seasons, was flaring up big-time. My doctor gave me strict instructions to lay off it. I took that to mean stop working out and enjoy as many dinners with Benjamin as possible. I made a dozen trips to Boston to visit him and we ate our way through that city. I never once felt self-conscious with him: it was fantastic. I felt like he really liked me for me, not for how I looked on his arm. I thought being with him was freeing. But it wasn't. I started "shadow eating" with him. If he ordered dessert, then it was a bright green light for me to go ahead and order it too. If he ordered two fat-laden appetizers, then I certainly wasn't going to just order one. On and on I went, using his unhealthy actions to justify my own. It didn't take long before my size fourteens were holding a front-and-center position in my closet.

One weekend I flew up to Boston to see him. I hadn't met any of his friends and he was throwing a big dinner at his place so everyone could meet me. I filled a suitcase with my old waistless, flowy dresses and threw in some oversize sweaters to combat the northeastern cold. My physiotherapy sessions had been keeping me busy and I hadn't seen him in a few weeks. I couldn't wait to get there. The dinner was the night I arrived. A fire was crackling in the fireplace, great bottles of wine were opened, and the conversation was sparkling. We looked like an ad for the Brooks Brothers winter catalog. His friends were lovely and I was thinking how happy I was that I came up for the weekend. When I was in the middle of talking to his best friends about high-yield bonds—they were all very knowledgeable financial types—Benjamin came up behind me. I was sitting on an overstuffed ottoman and I slid over to make room for him. He sat down and put his arm around my waist. *Oh, how sweet,* I thought. *Minor PDA in front of his friends.* Then I felt his fingers curl around my side and he pinched a good chunk of my skin. *Ouch!*

"Whoa, honey, you better watch it. You're getting a little too pleasantly plump around there." He laughed and took a sip of wine as though he'd just said the wittiest thing. I felt like I'd just been slapped in the face.

All of his friends heard his comment and I could feel my face flushing red. I was shocked. Never once in four months had he ever mentioned my weight or made me feel like outward appearances mattered in the slightest. In fact, I thought he loved the fact that I could keep up with his gourmet habits. It was like I didn't even know him. Normally I would've laughed it off and meekly disappeared into another room. But his comment and whole demeanor had shocked me and my embarrassment turned into rip-roaring anger.

"Oh, really?" I challenged. "Have you looked in the mirror lately?" I gave his belly a swift smack and got up in a defiant huff.

"Whatever," he said dismissively. "You're a *chick*—it's different." Did he just call me a "chick"? He looked around at his friends as though waiting for their unanimous agreement. A few guys chuckled but the rest just busied themselves looking at their wineglasses. I was humiliated and furious. *That's it*, I thought. *I don't need him anymore. I am focusing 100 percent on getting back on the court.* We broke up later that night after everyone had gone home, and I caught the first flight back to Florida the next morning.

By the start of 2003, my foot had healed enough to play in the Asia/Australia swing. I'd also made a New Year's resolution to eat one boiled egg for breakfast every day until I weighed 140 pounds. Rational? Nope, not at all. These absolutes would just pop into my head and I'd convince myself that each one was the key to getting skinny. The egg obsession lasted eight days, hardly long enough to lose even one of the twenty-eight pounds clinging to my body like a stubborn barnacle on a rock.

My first stop of the year was an exhibition in Hong Kong, where the players were treated to tailor-made, exquisitely elegant dresses and an opening-day ceremony replete with fire-breathing dragons and enormous animal puppets dancing and singing. I was a little paranoid about how large my dress had to be cut, but the seamstress was a lovely woman who made me feel very comfortable. Four hours after she took my measurements, I had a stunning red gown delivered to my hotel room. Even Aunt Klara would have been impressed. I was coachless but brought Andreas, a hitting partner from Hamburg whose lighthearted, easy demeanor was what I needed as I contemplated my next step. Who was going to coach me? What diet should I go on? Did I need another food babysitter? How fast could I lose the weight?

My semifinal match was against a fifteen-year-old upstart with legs up to her ears. Her name? Maria Sharapova. I beat her 6–3, 6–0, but I could see the potential she had to shoot to the top. It didn't take her long: she won Wimbledon two years later. After our match, the conversation I had with Chris Evert all those years ago came flooding back to me. I finally understood with tremendous clarity what she'd been talking about. Someone younger and faster would come along to replace the seasoned veterans. The power hitters who emerged when I first came back in '95 were a new generation in terms of playing style, but Maria was taking things to another level still. After the match, the journalists were beside themselves.

"Monica, there is finally someone who is louder than you are! Maria grunts as loud as a small aircraft taking off!" Really? I had no idea. I hadn't noticed that she'd made a peep. I must have selective hearing when I'm playing, because I am completely oblivious to grunts.

I won in the final against Chanda Rubin and got ready to head Down Under for the Australian Open. The first match was easy as I cruised to a 6–0, 6–1 victory. I was all set for my next match against Klara Koukalova, a Czech player who was in insane shape. She ran down every ball, so it was impossible to get anything past her. I was going to have to bear down and get my legs moving. She hit a crosscourt zinger to my backhand, and as I was lunging to get it I twisted my ankle. I knew right away it was a sprain. *Crap!* I couldn't believe what had just happened. And on what had become like a home court to me. Melbourne's hard courts were unforgiving and notorious for being the cause of many an injured ankle during the tournament, but it had never, ever happened to me. I taped it up and did my best to make it through the rest of the match, but I ended up losing.

The medical staff in Melbourne is fantastic, so I stayed to get some treatment after being knocked out. For two weeks I put my ankle through a rigorous healing regimen and was in good enough playing shape to take on a chaotic four-week itinerary of Tokyo-Qatar-Dubai. In between packing, getting on planes, checking into hotels, unpacking, and finding restaurants willing to prepare chicken with no oil, I fit in as many hours of laser therapy on my ankle as possible. I held my own and made it to the finals twice, but the precarious state of my injury prevented me from doing any training off the court. My weight crept up and up. While the hotel room scales registered my weight at 168, I knew I was at least a few pounds heavier. One thing I learned over all the years of traveling was that hotel scales are never right. If they were, nobody would raid the minibar and order room service late at night!

Dubai was trying to promote the tournament, so they planned nonstop fun events for the players. I went four-wheel off-roading in the desert with Lindsay and Maria and taped up my ankle to play a promotional match on the roof of the only six-star hotel in the world. Everything in the hotel was gold, including the helicopter landing strip, which had been transformed into a temporary tennis court. While I took resting my foot very seriously when it came to off-court training, I wasn't about to let it interfere with doing cool things like that.

It wasn't a smart move. The stress from the ankle sprain woke up my dormant stress fracture. It came back stronger than ever, and by the time I got to Rome, I couldn't put an ounce of pressure on it. After years of refusing to take any painkillers or supplements, I gave in to the tournament doctors' advice and started taking Vioxx to get through the matches. It wasn't long before Vioxx became a staple in my diet. I knew precisely how much I needed to take and when to take it before I had to step onto the court. But not even Vioxx was strong enough to get me past the second round. I had to retire in the second set to Nadia Petrova, who beat me two weeks later in the first round of the French Open.

It was time to go home.

# Where Is the Panic Button?

"Your sesamoid bone has been shattered into pieces."

I was at my orthopedic surgeon's office in Denver. I'd seen a dozen doctors in Europe and had received just as many medical opinions and treatment options. I wanted to go to someone who'd successfully seen me through an injury before.

"What does that mean?"

"It means you have to take six months off." *Six months?* That would mean missing Wimbleton and the U.S. Open, too. That would mean missing the rest of the season. And by the time I could play again I'd almost be thirty. THIRTY. I saw that number spelled out in capital letters, just like that. In tennis, it was known as "dirty thirty." In terms of fitness, recovery time, endorsements—everything, really—it meant the end was near. This wasn't good. Maybe I didn't really need this bone. Maybe we could just pin it together in the interim, tape up my foot, throw a bottle of Vioxx down my throat, and get back on the tour.

"Okay, and how liberal is your definition of 'six months'?" I asked, making air quotes. The doctor raised his eyebrows. He meant business.

"My definition of 'six months' is six months. I'm not kidding: There's no wiggle room here. Your bone is destroyed and we'll have to put you in a cast for at least a few months. If you don't take care of this, it will keep getting worse until your tendons are so shot, you can't move your foot at all."

"What kind of therapy can I do to speed up the healing?" If it was a matter of hard work, I could take it on.

"There isn't any," he answered. "At least not yet. Other than icing and light massaging, the best thing you can do is to just leave it alone. It needs rest—nothing else."

*Well, that's that,* I thought. *Six months of not doing anything. Just wire my mouth shut right now. I'd be a blimp by the end of the year, guaranteed.* I held off on the cast and got some more opinions. I got through each day by getting cortisone shots and downing painkillers. But it didn't matter how many doctors I went to: each prognosis held varying degrees of disappointment. No matter how I sliced it, I was going to have to take a lot of time off. The same panic that struck me at the start of 2000 when I was laid up at home reading letters about how appealingly husky I'd become hit me again. But this time it was worse: I was older. Time was running out. Even if I came back at thirty, I'd only have one or two years—max— left in me. And I couldn't even think about my weight. To my dismay, the breakup with Benjamin had not plunged me into the "heartbreak diet." I was still wearing my size fourteens and I didn't have anything bigger in my closet. Surely if I weighed that much while I was working out, I'd inevitably pork up while I was sitting on my butt at home. I knew that wiring my jaw shut wasn't an option, so I started reading (again) every nutritional book on my shelf. How many calories should I consume daily? How many net carbs are acceptable? What is a net carb? Should I let my body fast for twelve full hours every night? How did normal people eat? What did they eat? When did they eat it? I was overwhelmed with the simple task of implementing a "normal" diet.

So I didn't. For the first time in my adult life, I didn't plan any meals. I didn't have a nutritionist or coach or trainer. I decided to wing it. It was scary, but I didn't know what else to do. I was tired and sore. I was sick of working hard and not seeing any results. I just needed to decompress for a while.

The first couple of months went by quickly. I hung out with my mom, cleaned the house, and read a lot of books. Of course, I had my share of freakouts. *Should I have this ice cream bar for dessert? I didn't expend a single calorie in any cardio activity: Do I deserve to have it?* Sometimes the answer was yes and sometimes it was no. But something groundbreaking was beginning to happen. If I did eat the ice cream bar, it wouldn't launch me into an all-out feeding frenzy. I'd eat it, then go in the other room and start doing something else. I didn't even notice the change until one night when I was out to dinner with my mom and the waitress came by to clear our plates.

"Can I get you ladies some dessert?" she asked. My mom ordered a scoop of ice cream and waited for me to order. The waitress stood there looking at me, ready to write down my dessert.

"Actually, I'm all set. I'm not having any, thank you." The waitress walked off but my mom was still looking at me.

"Really?" she asked. "You don't want anything?"

"No, I'm fine. Dinner was great and now I'm full."

"Are you on another diet?" she asked worriedly. After all, why else would I pass on dessert, my favorite meal of the day?

"No, Mom, really. I'm just not hungry." As the words came out of my mouth, I realized how rarely I'd ever said them and really meant them.

My anticipated freakout over the forced layoff had produced the opposite effect. Left to my own devices and free from the judging of my food babysitters, I felt calmer than I had in years. But there was another panic-inducing event just around the corner: the big THREE-OH birthday. When I was a little girl, thirty sounded so old. And so far away. Parents were thirty, and who among us ever thought we'd be that old? But thirty came racing up to hit me smack in the face. After the French Open loss in May, I'd stayed far away from the tennis world, spending most of my time at home or at the physiotherapist's office, getting massage and ice therapy. But in August I was stir-crazy and decided to run up to New York to check out the U.S. Open. I met up with Caitlin and Melissa, two friends I hadn't seen since the spring.

"Monica, did you lose weight?" Caitlin asked.

"Ha!" I laughed out loud. "No way. I haven't done a thing in two months. I feel like a whale."

"You've lost weight. You definitely look a little different," Melissa agreed. They started circling me like sharks, eyeing me up and down, convinced that I was keeping a secret from them.

"Honestly, I haven't. There's just no way."

They both shrugged their shoulders. "Okay then, but whatever you're 'not' doing, keep 'not' doing it. It's working for you," Caitlin said.

They looked skeptical. I'd made a point of not weighing myself during my time off but I knew what I weighed when I'd gotten back from France in June: 173. I had been terrified to step back on the scale since. But my friends were so emphatic that I looked different, I decided to weigh myself when I got back to Florida. *Don't freak out, don't freak out,* I thought as the red 00 digits blinked an interminable three times as they calculated my weight. The number 165 glowed up at me. *One hundred and sixty-five! How did that happen?* An eight-pound loss was what I used to shoot for during my two-week-starvation/seven-hour-workouts-a-day phases. If I could drop eight pounds at the end of one of those, I was rejoicing in the street over my success, and here I'd gone and done it without even trying. It didn't make any sense at all, but I wasn't about to start complaining.

Throughout the fall I did more of the same: reading, hanging out with my dog, and going to daily therapy sessions. But December 2, my birthday, was looming on the calendar like a dreaded final exam. I was also getting closer to the six-month mark but my foot wasn't healing as fast as the doctors had hoped. Surgery was an option, but the probability of it working was only 50 percent. I was still on a mission to get back on the tour, but more and more I was beginning to think about what I would do with my life after tennis. However, when these thoughts intruded, they weren't shrouded in depression and confusion as they had been after my stabbing.

Instead, I felt more intent on finding some real answers. A few days before my big birthday, I decided I wanted to spend it by myself. I found a room at a small eco-lodge in Costa Rica and booked a plane ticket.

❋

"How much longer did you say?" I ducked my head for the tenth time to avoid hitting the roof of the Jeep as we bounced over the rock-strewn dirt path. Actually, the "rocks" were more like boulders and the "road" was more like a rugged mountain bike trail. We'd been on the road for three hours.

"We are there soon!" the driver cheerily yelled over the noise of the diesel engine. "Soon" ended up being another hour, but as soon as I got my aching backside out of the Jeep, I knew the ride had been worth it. A handful of thatched cottages lined a beautiful white beach. Thick treetop canopies stretched back as far as I could see. When I checked in I was told there was no TV, phone, or electricity—basically no contact with the outside world—and would I be okay with that? *Okay? It sounded perfect!* I followed a trail through the trees and found my cottage. It had bamboo floors, a bed with pristine white sheets and a fluffy comforter at its foot, a reading chair, and a 180-degree view of blue water. The whole week was like a meditation. I rarely spotted other people and spent more time talking to the frogs and birds I saw on my hikes through the rain forest. Turtles were the only sign of life on the beach, so I tossed my sarong off, not caring whether the sea creatures thought my butt looked big. It was liberating. I walked along the shore during the incoming tide and felt, for a moment, a connection to my body I hadn't felt for years.

Without an agenda or a physical therapy appointment to get to, I settled into a natural rhythm of waking with the sun and going to sleep when it disappeared. Two days into my stay, I was walking along the beach at sunrise when I saw two women stretching on the hard-packed sand. I hadn't seen anyone in twenty-four hours so I was curious. I walked closer and one of them said, "Do you want to join us?" She had wild, curly hair thrown into a topknot and a warm smile. If they were getting ready to go for a run, I wasn't interested.

"What are you doing?" I needed to make sure I knew what I was getting into before I committed.

"Yoga. It's great to do when the sun is coming up."

I'd never done yoga in my life. Hamstring stretches were my arch nemesis: I used to drive my dad crazy when I complained about them during our track workouts. I never wanted to warm them up; I just wanted to jump right in and go at full speed. But this week was all about opening my mind, so—quite uncharacteristically for me—I said yes.

The woman with the topknot led us through sun salutations and all sorts of poses with names I couldn't pronounce. I spent a lot of time watching her to see what she was doing, and was amazed at how easy she made it look. My new yoga teacher was so graceful and peaceful as she flowed from one pose into the next. I was liking it more than I thought I would, and my foot felt fine. At the end of the impromptu class, we sat in the lotus position as she talked about peace, love, harmony, and all the other things I always assumed yogis were into. Then she said something that resonated with me.

"Feel the power that you just received from this morning's practice throughout your entire body." She breathed deeply. "Direct all of that energy into your core—who you are on the deepest of levels." I'd always thought my core was my abs and lower back. This was new information. "That is where the energy belongs. With a strong core, you will be like an old tree that is the tallest and strongest in the forest. Nothing will be able to shake you or throw you off of your path. With a strong core, you are you." That sounded appealing.

I spent most of my thirtieth birthday challenging myself to do something new: I was going to just relax. I threw myself into a hammock to read and nap. I wasn't going to feel guilty about relaxing. I was just going to be.

The first hour was trying. I got antsy and thought about going on a hike. Or a swim. *No, Monica, you are staying right here.* By the second hour

I had calmed down enough to read a few chapters of my book. By late morning I was digging the hammock life and realized I hadn't turned a page in half an hour. My mind started to drift off. The stress was evaporating. I had no timetable for getting back to tennis. If this fracture wasn't a career ender, then it was going to keep me out of the game for at least another couple of months. There was no point in freaking out about it: I couldn't speed up the healing process, so I just had to relax. I had no coaches, trainers, or nutritionists on the payroll and it was a relief. I felt like I was doing a major spring cleaning after letting fifteen years of clutter build up. That night I celebrated my birthday with a platter of fresh fruit and a sunset walk on the beach.

Being thirty wasn't so bad.

# – 42 –

## Worth a Thousand Words

Wait a minute, are you sure this thing weighs ten pounds?" The wetsuit was hindering my normal range of motion and I was struggling to fasten the heavy belt around my waist.

My friend Annabelle, a fitness buff, laughed. "Yes, I swear, it's ten pounds."

Annabelle and I were in the Bahamas for a girls' weekend. I'd barely finished unpacking from my Costa Rica trip when she'd called me with the idea. My first instinct was to say no. Two vacations in a row? I'd never done that before. In between tournaments and working out, I rarely had time to take even one vacation. Before Costa Rica, the last one I'd taken was when I'd gone to the Caribbean after Astro died. Seven years had gone by since then.

"Come on," Annabelle pleaded. "What else are you going to do—stare at your foot?"

She was right. I'd just finished another round of therapy and all I could do was wait for my injury to finish healing. This time the best thing I could do was to just do nothing. "Okay," I told her. "Why not?"

So there we were, standing on the platform of a dive boat as I was try-ing to attach a heavy weight belt around my midsection. "No way." I shook my head. "There is no way this is ten pounds." I turned to our dive master. "Are you sure this is ten pounds?"

"Yep, absolutely sure," he answered. "Ten pounds. And make sure it's on tight. If it falls off, you'll never sink beneath the water."

I was flabbergasted. I'd lugged ten- and twenty-pound dumbbells all over the gym for years, but I'd never taped one onto my stomach before. It was so burdensome, I was waddling around on the boat deck like an arthritic duck. Then a light went on in my head: this was how much I'd been carrying around for eight years, multiplied by three—and sometimes four. No wonder my feet hurt and my lateral movement had suffered so much! I knew I needed to lose weight, but this was a whole new perspective. I didn't need to lose it so I'd look good in a bikini; I needed to lose it to give my body a break.

When I got back to the hotel room, I made a decision. I was sick of lugging weight belts of fat around. I was going to drop them for good, but this time I'd do it differently. Nobody was going to take care of me and my problems. Nobody on the outside could fix what was going on inside of me. I was the only one who could and would do it.

When 2004 dawned, I made a resolution. My resolution was to not make a resolution. I'd been making weight-related declarations for years, and I'd always blow them before January was up. I wasn't falling into that trap again. My foot was still giving me problems and my doctor told me that if I wasn't going to have surgery, then my only option was the cast. Deep down I think some of my hesitation had to do with my fear of getting fatter. When I'd been doing therapy for the last six months I could at least be a little mobile, but in a cast I'd be in trouble. There'd be no hiking in rain forests or diving in the Bahamas. But if I wanted a chance at coming back again, I had to do it.

It was an adjustment. A big one. With the cast keeping me homebound, I was bored out of my mind sitting around all day, so I decided to put myself to good use. With the help of my crutches, I one-legged it to the storage closet in my garage. I sifted past boxes and boxes of things I didn't remember owning until I found what I was looking for: a neatly stacked pile of rectangular storage containers. They were all labeled the same: *Monica's Pictures*. It took six trips for me to bring them all into the living room, but I did it. Over the years my dad had taken thousands of photos of me and they'd been hibernating in the garage. I opened the boxes and started sifting through them. There were at least three thousand in there, and they weren't in any discernible order. I started taking them out, one by one, when I noticed some yellowed newspaper clippings lying on the bottom. The more I dug through the pictures, the more clippings I found. My dad had saved every article on me that he'd ever come across. They were cut along the margins with great care and, other than the discoloration, hadn't suffered the effects of passing years. I dumped everything on the floor and got to work.

It took me two weeks of sitting hunched over the boxes for eight hours a day, but I did it. In the end I filled twenty photo albums with a pictorial testament of my life. From the moment I joined the tour, I didn't have a spare second to reminisce about anything. I was too busy making travel arrangements and warming up for my next match. Leafing through the pages was like reliving my life. He'd saved every *Sports Illustrated* feature and Grand Slam final write-up. He'd even lugged along the clippings from my junior playing days when my parents left Novi Sad. I had a bad-hair flashback when I came across an article in *Vogue*. I was seventeen, I'd just cut my hair off, and I spent the better part of the morning's photo shoot painstakingly flat-ironing my two-inch locks. We were in Florida and the humidity was overpowering. I ended up looking like a Q-tip in the pictures.

And then there were my dad's photos . . . There I am, sitting in the top row at Roland Garros the first time I'd set foot in the stadium. Before he took the picture, he'd just spent twenty minutes telling me all the reasons I shouldn't be nervous. There we are at the fancy restaurant in Paris after winning my first Grand Slam, and I'm wearing the beloved vintage dress I'd bought in New Orleans. Every member of our family is smiling from ear to ear. There I am, standing on UCLA's legendary track with my hands on my hips, listening to my dad explain our next workout. There we are in the players' lounge after my comeback win in Australia, my parents looking more relieved than anything else. It had been a long road. There we are, making snowballs in the middle of a Minnesota winter when we thought his cancer had a good shot at going into remission. For two weeks I laughed and cried as I put my life in order in the pages of those albums. And somewhere, between the first album and the twentieth, I finally started to grieve for my dad.

# – 43 –

## The Little Black Dress

M y foot's second six-month prison term was almost up and I was in New York for two weeks of therapy. I'd graduated to a walking boot cast; it was as fashionable as it sounds but at least I could get around again. Kind of. Walking in Manhattan is a challenge even when both feet are in perfectly good working order; at my far slower, boot-impaired pace, I spent most of my time dodging important-looking people rushing along the sidewalk to get to their important meetings. In between a therapy session and a doctor's appointment, I had a couple of hours to waste, so I hopped on the subway and headed to my favorite store: Century 21. Just saying the name gets my competitive shopping juices flowing. Scoring good loot there is for the eagle-eyed, fleet-footed shopper; although my boot was going to hold me back a bit, it was worth a try.

Within the first five minutes of walking through the door I found it: a little black dress. Actually, it wasn't *a* little black dress; it was *the* little black dress. The simple, classic dress that looks appropriate in any venue. The dress that exudes a casual elegance that would make Audrey Hepburn smile with approval. The kind of dress that every woman dreams of finding. And it was on sale. Oh, how I love Century 21. Just one problem, though: it was a size four. I'd lost some more weight (I weighed 159 the last time I'd checked), but I wasn't anywhere near a size four. In fact, I hadn't been a size four since I was nineteen. I was about to put the dress back on the rack when a simple thought stopped me. *Why not?* I'd been asking that question more and more lately. Why shouldn't I buy it? I was already down two dress sizes. What was to stop me from going down some more? I didn't have a deadline set, so who cared if I never fit into it? At least it would be hanging in the closet in case I ever did. I headed back uptown for my therapy session with my new purchase in hand.

A few weeks later my boot cast finally came off, but things weren't going as well as I'd wanted. I tried playing on it, but dagger-sharp pain kept shooting through my big toe, and my Vioxx consumption was back in full force. Around this time the news about the possible negative side effects of the drug was starting to surface. I panicked. If I couldn't take it anymore, what chance did I have of playing? The pain had transformed me from someone who viewed Gatorade as an extreme supplement to someone who couldn't set foot on a practice court without a shot of cortisone and a mouthful of painkillers. It was beginning to dawn on me that, like masking my emotional issues with food, I was again engaging in self-sabotage by masking the physical pain with drugs. What was I doing? At what cost was I going to stay in tennis? Was it really worth it? The mental strength that had been my ally in close-fought matches was beginning to work against me. My body was saying no more, but my head was refusing to end my career. Some days I'd hit for hours and my foot would feel fine, while other days I could barely walk on it. But my dad's mantra that I should have a good life after tennis kept echoing through my head. What was I risking my health for, anyway?

There was one thing that kept depression at bay. My little black dress was hanging in my closet, but unlike the other small sizes that had been hanging untouched in the back of my closet for years, it didn't taunt me or make me feel discouraged. Every time I caught a glimpse of it while reaching for a flowy dress, I felt a little spark of inspiration. I was beginning to realize I had a say in whether I was happy or not, whether I was feeling strong or hopeless. I had the power to control what I put into my mouth and over the thoughts I chose to obsess upon. I didn't have a coach or a nutritionist or a boyfriend giving me the answers. But somehow that little black dress was becoming a symbol of reclaiming the real me—my true core.

By the end of the year I was down to 153. I'd lost twenty pounds in a year without trying. Well, that's not entirely true. I did try, but my efforts were so different from those I'd made before that it didn't feel like I was "trying." There were a few big changes I'd made in my thinking, which then affected some deep-seated behaviors I'd struggled with for years. First, I refused to say I was on a diet. Being "on" a diet implies that I would one day go "off" it. I also banished the absolutes. Instead, I lived in the liberating and calming gray area of moderation.

I stopped classifying foods as "allowed" or "forbidden." After all, what's more tempting than something forbidden? If I wanted a piece of cake, I'd ask whoever I was with if they wanted to share it. If they didn't and I really still wanted it, I'd order it and eat a quarter of it and wait ten minutes. If I still wanted more, I'd eat another quarter and wait again. Very rarely did I end up devouring the whole thing. It wasn't easy—I had to work at slowing down during my meals—but it was empowering to begin to eat consciously. Taking the time to taste my food was nothing short of revelatory, and the more I did it, the easier it became. The first time I tried implementing conscious eating was at a pizza parlor in Florida. *Okay, here we go,* I thought as the heavenly smelling pie was placed in front of me. In the past I'd get anxious and start eating like I was a contestant in a Coney Island eating contest. This time I approached the pizza like an athlete perfecting a new technique. I took a couple of deep breaths and, with my full attention focused on my food, took a bite. Chewing each piece calmly, I savored my food. In between bites I talked to my friends and sipped my drink. *This is not a race. This is not the last pizza I will ever see for the rest of my life. I don't have to inhale the whole thing tonight.* By the time I finished my slice, I wasn't hungry anymore. I'd just experienced firsthand the meaning of quality over quantity.

Another change in my thought process was that more isn't necessarily better. I was learning to question the value I placed on excess. In professional athletics, more is better, faster is better, stronger is better: more, more, more. But in everyday life, especially in American grocery stores, we're constantly battling against the soldiers of excess. Extra-large bottles of soda, two packages of cookies for the price of one, three boxes of sugar cereal for the price of two . . . more, more, more. But what if I didn't want more?

I'd lived my life in such extremes—seven-hour workouts followed by five-thousand-calorie binges—that I wanted a change. I wanted less. Just the word "less" sounds soothing when it rolls off the tongue. I started carrying the concept with me everywhere, viewing the word "less" as connected to the word "lesson." Every time I made a choice that emphasized the "Less is more" theory, I gave myself a little symbolic pat on the back. I was learning how to live my life more fully by choosing *less*. At the grocery store I filled my cart with less. I passed over the fat-free items for whole-grain options. Anything that advertised itself as being "free" of something didn't go into my cart. Fat-free, carb-free, sugar-free? No, thanks. I wanted to stay as far away from processed foods as possible. A piece of multigrain bread with almond butter kept me fuller for longer than an entire bag of pretzels. The "less" theory affected my workouts too. Even on days when my foot felt good, I didn't go to the gym or hit the beach for a run. Instead, I walked—not at a furious pace or with the intention of getting somewhere, but just to walk. It felt good to move my body without feeling like I was inflicting a punishment on it. Henry David Thoreau once said that the moment his legs began to move, his thoughts began to flow. That is exactly what happened to me during my year of walks.

Poring over my dad's photos was the key to opening up the long-locked door to my grief; lacing up my shoes every evening empowered me to walk through that door without fearing what was on the other side. It was the most powerful therapy I ever had. In the past I used exercise to outrun my demons, to exhaust myself beyond the point of rational thinking. Walking was a gentle salve that gave me the time and space to sort through the layers and layers of thoughts and worries that had built up over the years.

Step by step—literally—I was getting stronger and closer to knowing who I was and what I wanted. On these walks I slowly and sadly came to terms with my life. I lost my dad way too early and it was agonizingly awful. I missed him so much and I hated knowing that I could never again pick up the phone to tell him about my day. We'd never again hit a ball back and forth as we argued over whether I was bending my knees enough; I used to dread those arguments, but now I would've given anything to have one. I hated knowing that I'd never see his hand busily hovering over a dinner napkin as he dashed off another cartoon for me. A part of my heart would always be broken, and the frustration over what "could have been" if I'd never been stabbed was still in my head; but as I wrestled with these emotions, something was growing deep within me.

In my very core I finally knew that I would be okay on my own. I would be okay if I never won another Grand Slam. I would be okay if justice was never served. I would be okay if I never played another professional match. I would be okay if I had to find a new purpose, find a new reason to get up every morning. As an athlete, the "No pain, no gain" credo was deeply ingrained into my psyche. But something totally unexpected happened during those evening walks in my neighborhood. My walks helped heal the rift between my mind and my body. These soothing walks did more to quiet the demons in my head than any of the punishing workouts I'd endured. The weight loss I achieved that year felt almost effortless.

# – 44 –

## *Just Jump*

Y ou're doing *what?*" Martina Navratilova looked stunned.

"I'm going skydiving," I answered.

"No way, I don't believe it." She was shaking her head and laughing as she packed up her tennis bag.

"I swear, I am. I really am!" I insisted.

"We'll see," she replied. That was all I needed to get me going. A challenge issued by one of the greatest athletes of all time. I'd show her. We'd just finished the second of our two exhibition matches in New Zealand. At the beginning of 2005 my foot felt good, so I decided to give it a test run to see if I still had a chance to get back on the tour. It was a once-in-a-lifetime trip and I brought my mom along for the ride. My body was feeling strong and healthy, and I was going full speed ahead with my desire to get as much as I could out of my travels. After our matches in Auckland and Christchurch, I decided I wanted to shake things up a little. My foot hadn't held up as well as I'd hoped and I needed to do something fun. When I asked the locals for a must-see recommendation, I got the same answer over and over: "You have to go to Queenstown!"

For an adrenaline junkie, it was *the* place to go. At that moment it sounded perfect. As soon as I saw it, I knew I'd found the right place. The town is nestled on pristine Lake Wakatipu and sheltered by soaring mountains. I wanted to go skipping through town, doing an impersonation of Maria from *The Sound of Music*. Everyone looked like they were headed for the X Games. Jet boating, river surfing, canyon swinging, whitewater rafting, paragliding . . . I had my pick of hardcore adventures. Did I want to terrify myself by land, water, or air? I'd always been terrified of heights—anytime I stayed in a hotel room on the tenth floor or higher, I refused to look out the window—so I decided that jumping out of a plane would be a surefire way to conquer my fear. However, I chose to ease myself into it by warming up with a bungee jump.

Since Bahia, I'd been taking small leaps at life that shook me out of the fog I'd been living in for so many years. I'd spent too long living in my tennis bubble and being worried about injuries. I was bursting to make up for lost time. Now I was ready to take a big leap of faith right off a bridge.

My legs shook as I stood at the top of the bridge, stealing quick glances at the water hundreds of feet below. My mom stood next to me ready to make a fast getaway as soon as her crazy daughter came to her senses and decided not to jump. I came close to bailing out when the very ruggedly handsome "bungee expert" (I don't know what technically qualified him as an expert, but I prayed he knew enough to get me down safely) was adjusting my harness.

"How much do you weigh?" Wow, he just got right to it. I barely knew the guy and he was already asking me the most personal of personal questions. I caught my mom's bemused look. *Well, this should be interesting* was written all over her face. *Hmm, this is a tough one,* I thought. I had two choices:

Number one: slide back into my old insecurities and shave fifteen pounds off my real weight, even though I'd be risking death or serious bodily injury strapped into a harness that might break under the pressure of weight it was not prepared to handle.

Number two: get real, get honest, and get over myself by putting my real weight out on the table. Who cares? At least I'd survive the jump.

"One hundred and fifty-two," I said in a clear voice. He didn't flinch at all. I survived the bungee, miraculously didn't break my back, and gradu-ated to the plane the following day.

I met up with Mel Jones, a friend of mine from New Zealand who never says no to a new adventure. I wasn't sure I could make the jump without the support of a friendly face nearby and Mel was a willing volunteer. Dur-ing our ascent in the tiny plane, he tried to calm my nerves.

"There's nothing to it," he insisted. "You'll love it!" I glanced down at the landscape that was rapidly growing smaller and smaller beneath us. It didn't seem like nothing to me! After watching him gleefully leap out of the plane, I was as ready as I was ever going to be. Strapped to an instruc-tor who was another "expert"—this time I really did hope he knew what he was doing—I didn't have to do much. My only responsibility was to take the first step out of the plane. It had to be my choice. I stood on the edge for twenty seconds with clouds whipping by beneath me.

Ten thousand feet is really, really high. I could barely make out the land below. I adjusted and readjusted my goggles at least six times. Finally, I took a deep breath and jumped. To be completely honest, it was more like a hesitant shuffle forward aided by a helpful nudge from my instruc-tor's knees. Good thing he took that initiative, because I would have stood at that threshold messing around with my goggles all day. The first five seconds were a blur of screaming and wishing my feet were still on solid ground, but the initial shock quickly disappeared and I settled in for the most amazing flight of my life. I don't think I stopped laughing and smiling until we hit the ground. Much like dating an Italian, it is a life ex-perience that everyone should try once.

When I got back to Florida, there was an e-mail from Martina. It was one line: *Did you do it?*

I wrote back one word: *Yes.*

My in-box immediately beeped with a reply: *You go, girl!*

# – 45 –

# A Certain
# Je ne sais quoi

I'd been to Paris a dozen times but I'd never seen much of it beyond the borders of Roland Garros. That fall I did something about it. I was determined to see the City of Light the way it is meant to be seen. My good friend Nicole lived there and I decided to pay her a long-overdue visit. While she worked during the day, I spent hours rambling along the streets of the different arrondissements, each with its own distinct personality. Crisscrossing the Seine, I explored every inch of the Left and Right Banks. I browsed the funky boutiques in the Marais district; stood in wonderment before the architectural feat of the bizarre Centre Georges-Pompidou with its exposed skeleton of tubes snaking around its outside; finally checked out the Place des Vosges, the oldest square in Paris (the girls in Madrid were right—I could definitely see the resemblance) strolled around the opulent Opera Quarter; hiked up an endless set of stairs and navigated winding cobblestone streets to get to the top of Montmartre for a stunning view of Paris; and indulged my inner foodie at the outdoor market along the Rue de Buci.

I loved walking to the market in the late morning, where I'd do my daily round: picking up a small baguette, a wedge of soft cheese, and an apple. Then I'd stroll the city before taking my little picnic to the Luxembourg Gardens, where I'd find a sunny spot and bask in the beauty of early autumn in Paris. Biting into the crisp red apple, I remembered how good fresh produce tasted. Growing up in Novi Sad, my mom went to the market every day. Produce never lasted longer than twenty-four hours in our kitchen, and eating a banana or an orange was a delicacy. Who needed added sugar when the sweetness of fresh fruit filled your mouth?

In the ten bites it took me to finish my apple—which was much smaller than the ones I'd grown accustomed to seeing in my supermarket in Florida—I realized that the further I ate away from food in its most natural state, the further away I was from building my core. One year, right before I left for the Australian Open, I left a pear and an apple in my fridge. Usually I clean out the fridge before a long trip, but I'd been in a hurry and totally forgot. Two months later, when I returned home, there they sat in the fridge, like perfect plastic replicas of real fruit, looking exactly the same as they had the day I bought them. And you wonder if your food is filled with preservatives? That apple in my fridge was nothing like the apple I ate in Paris. It was like they were two completely different foods.

"You are what you eat" isn't just a worn-out cliché. What I was putting into my body had a direct effect on my mood and my well-being. Nourishing myself with food that was free from preservatives and that had as little packaging as possible was an integral step in rebuilding my core. After I had the time and space to grieve for my father and contemplate my life without tennis, I started to see that some of my weight issues were due to focusing on what I was eating instead of looking inward to see what was eating me.

I knew I used food to cope with emotions, but just knowing it wasn't enough to completely stop it. That's why I created the twenty-second rule: Before letting myself rip into a bag of junk food, I forced myself to sit down and count to twenty. Slowly. During those twenty seconds I made myself answer a very simple question: What was really bothering me? Almost every single time, I came up with the answer before the twenty seconds were up. The next question was: What can I do right this minute to help fix it? Do I need to call someone to sort out a misunderstanding? Do

I need to get paperwork done? Do I need to run overdue errands? Do I need to sort out an account with the cable company that sent me an inaccurate bill? Do I need to make a decision about whether to participate in a fund-raiser? Do I need to decide whether my foot is feeling strong enough to play in an upcoming exhibition?

By the time I came up with something that I could do right at that moment—even if it was a tiny action—my urge to eat had subsided and I was tackling the underlying problem. Soon the twenty-second rule became a habit and it became easier every single time I used it. My dad had drilled into me over and over that I had only one life to live, so I'd better live it the best I could. Every time I sat down to a meal, I could make a decision. Was I going to treat myself with love and respect, or was I going to sabotage my own happiness and health for a short-term rush? When I approached my meals from a place of empowerment, the decision was an easy one: I chose nourishment over destruction every time.

Sitting in the middle of a Parisian royal garden, enjoying bites of cheese that I would have tortured myself over two years earlier, was the best nourishment I could have wished for. Eating wholesome food left me satiated much more quickly than mounds of fat-free processed fake food ever did. In Paris I ate anything I wanted, but it was always fresh and of the highest quality, and I walked after every meal. Allowing myself to enjoy some Brie left me feeling satisfied after three bites. *Reasonable portions*— that was another new concept for me.

When Nicole and I enjoyed our morning cappuccinos at her local café, I was struck by the size of the cups. Our frothy concoctions were easily half the size of what I was used to in the States. My eyes had grown so accustomed to the supersize portions in American restaurants that it took some conscientious mental retraining to know that I didn't need a soup bowl full of coffee to get my morning started. The same went for food. The flaky croissants looked like petite distant cousins of the bloated American pastries. At first I was worried I wouldn't be satisfied with such a meager breakfast. There was a time when I could have downed four croissants, no problem, my hunger was so insatiable. But this time, over breakfast with one of the good friends I was finally getting a chance to catch up with, that cappuccino and that croissant were plenty for me.

One afternoon my exploring took me to the ritzy 16th Arrondissement, the neighborhood my dad and I had walked through on our very first visit to Roland Garros. I took pictures of the stunning Art Nouveau architecture and spotted the tops of the Bois de Boulogne trees I'd been so enthralled with at fifteen. I headed east toward the Champs-Élysées, the high-end shopping avenue that was the only sight I ever saw apart from Roland Garros during my playing days. In 2002 I'd popped into one of the intimidatingly chic boutiques before my quarterfinal match against Venus. I was stressed about playing well and I thought an hourlong jaunt down the coolest shopping street in the world would take my mind away from the court. As soon as I walked in, I knew I'd made a mistake. I was twice as big as any of the clothes on display, and the saleswomen (there were three of them and I was the only one in the store) refused to look at me. I made my way over to a table of cashmere sweaters and picked up a vanilla-colored one that was deliciously soft. It was stunning but it looked like it could fit a six-year-old. I looked over to the saleswomen chatting by the register and asked if they had any other sizes. Finally one of them lifted her head up from their conversation and said simply, "No, we do not have clothes in your size."

"Oh, okay, thanks." I quickly put the sweater back and tried to will away the humiliated blush that was spreading over my cheeks. The three of them were silent as I hurried toward the exit. That was the last time I tried shopping for clothes in Paris. The only things I ever let myself look at were shoes and bags, the great weight equalizers in fashion. And here I was three years later, walking past Chanel, Prada, Armani, and Louis Vuitton, when I caught a glimpse of my reflection in a store window. My fitted shirt, long trousers, and cute flats gave me a lean silhouette and I was having a great-hair day. More than anything, though, I looked content. My brow wasn't furrowed and I wasn't rushing to get somewhere. It was just me looking strong, healthy, and just plain good. Paris was agreeing with me this time around. I thought about paying a visit to that boutique again with my arms loaded down with bags from the most expensive stores, finding that saleswoman, and pulling a *Pretty Woman*—"You work on commission, right? Big mistake. Big. Huge."—and then sashaying back out the door. But really, why did I have to prove my worth to her? I'd already proven it to myself.

On one of my last mornings in Paris, I took a walk along the Seine. I was leisurely browsing a used-book stand and chatting with the older gentleman who was working there in my rudimentary French.

"*Bonjour, Mademoiselle.*" He tipped his tweed cap toward me.

"*Bonjour, Monsieur.*"

"*Ça va?*" He didn't smile—not many French people do—but his eyes kindly crinkled up in the corners.

"*Oui, ça va bien, merci. Et vous?*" I was feeling proud of my Français 101. During my time off due to yet another foot injury, I'd been taking language lessons at the community college in Sarasota. I wasn't a natural by any stretch of the imagination, but if the vendor kept it simple, I'd be good for another few exchanges of pleasantries.

"*Avec une belle journée comme aujourd'hui, ça va très bien!*" He gestured emphatically to the sky. He was right, it was an incredible day. Paris is infamous for its gray, gloomy weather so when you luck out with a blue sky and a shining sun it seems exceptionally glorious. I took my time leafing through the dusty pages of books whose previous owners had tired of them and wished my linguistic skills were good enough to buy the works of French writers in their original language. I was a long way off from that, so I found the tiny English section and settled on a copy of John Grisham's latest legal thriller. It wasn't exactly Proust but I wasn't complaining. I knew it'd be a page-turner.

The gentleman wrapped my book in brown butcher paper and expertly tied a piece of twine around it. The result was simple and elegant. It was so French. Even a used-book transaction carried with it a flash of unexpected beauty. I strolled across Pont Neuf, the bridge that connects the Left Bank to the Right Bank, and stopped midway. I leaned against a tall, elegant lamppost and took in the view. A few fluffy clouds dotted the blue sky and a breeze ran over the Seine, leaving subtle ripples behind. Some bohemian-cool students were sitting by the water, playing guitar and passing around a bottle of wine. An elegant, middle-aged woman wearing a sundress and high heels rode by them on an ancient-looking bike. *So this is Paris.* I didn't have to be anywhere, do anything, or meet anyone. I wasn't playing tennis, but life was still going on all around me. And then I realized with a bit of a jolt that, even without tennis, *my* life was still going on.

Tennis had taken me all over the world and exposed me to so many different ways to appreciate life. Those lessons were finally starting to sink in.

# – 46 –

## *Embrace the Fear*

"Do one thing every day that scares you."
—Eleanor Roosevelt

That was my motto for 2006. I was feeling healthy enough to play a handful of exhibitions, and my new weight of 141 pounds(!) was doing wonders for keeping my foot in good shape. But it wasn't yet strong enough to hold up to the rigorous demands of the tour, so I had a lot of free time on my hands. I decided to use it. I threw myself into reading photography, art, and design books and accepted a three-month internship in one of Chicago's top architecture firms. After the first day I knew I didn't have a future in the profession—there was too much math—but it was a fun few months anyway.

In the fall I was presented with an incredible opportunity. After my forced break in 2003, I started to work with the Laureus Foundation, an organization that promotes the use of sports as a tool for social change. My dad's artwork had always been based on the power of sports to transcend politics and bring people together, so the Laureus mission was right up my alley. I'd acted as an ambassador for them on trips to disadvantaged areas in the States and had found it to be one of the most fulfilling things I'd ever done. When they asked me to join a group of athletes heading to South Africa in the fall, I jumped at the chance. Along with Edwin Moses, the chairman and incomparable track legend (my dad would have loved to meet him!), former European Footballer of the Year Bobby Charlton, cricket legend Kapil Dev, Olympic gold medalist runner Kip Keino, former world number one tennis player Ilie Nastase, Olympic gold medalist alpine ski racer Franz Klammer, Olympic gold medalist decathlete Daley Thompson, rugby star Morné du Plessis, English football star Lucas Radebe, and Martina Navratilova, I headed to South Africa. Being given the chance to travel with such a distinguished and accomplished group of people from all over the world—each one with the intent of doing some good—was a thrill. I was so honored to have been included.

We took a bus from Johannesburg to Soweto, a city that had been developed as a township for black people under the apartheid system. The city's outskirts looked like ruins, with makeshift shacks filling every inch of space. We got out of the van to walk around. Immediately, Lucas, the footballer, was mobbed by kids screaming his name. We quickly found out he had grown up there and used his football skills to get out—all the way to the Premier League in England. It was like walking down a street in Memphis with Elvis, but better. The next day we visited two orphanages, one for boys and one for girls. The buildings were immaculate and the kids were dressed in spotless uniforms. We got them dirty pretty fast. Loaded down with chocolates—the international icebreaker—and the sports equipment we brought for them, we were welcomed onto the grass field with high-pitched squeals and open arms. Hours went by and we all worked up a good sweat teaching the kids the basics of each of our sports. The kids had no idea who we were—except for Lucas, of course—but they were thrilled with their new friends and didn't take a minute's break from playing all day long.

I remembered how ecstatic I'd been when I was seven years old and Yannick Noah, the most famous tennis player at the time, came to my town to play in the Davis Cup. My dad took my brother and me to see him. After the match I was leaning over the railing with the rest of the crowd when he reached up and placed his broken racket and sweaty wristbands right into my hands. I was beside myself with happiness. Everyone oohed and aahed over my loot as I made my way out of the stadium and through the parking lot to our car. It was a very powerful feeling of *Hey, I'm something special.* Even though the racket had broken strings, I didn't let it out of my sight for months. I even slept with it next to me with its head on my pillow. I never forgot that kindness, and that one small gesture fueled my passion to practice against the brick wall even harder every morning. I'd always loved kids and made time in my schedule for charity events, but this trip reinforced the powerful connection between kids and sports that I'd always believed in. I was going to work harder to make a difference.

After the orphanage, we drove into Johannesburg to meet Nelson Mandela. As we walked into his office I was struck by the light and energy that came from him before he even uttered a word. I was almost speechless. Before the trip I'd read as much about him as I could, and I was awed by his courage, strength, and determination. During the apartheid era he was unjustly imprisoned for twenty-seven years. Almost three decades of his life were stolen from him. Most people would have been destroyed. After his release he continued his tireless work for equality. Instead of being angry and bitter, he pursued peaceful and empowering strategies like reconciliation and negotiation. It worked. He was the first fully democratically elected president of South Africa and was a recipient of the Nobel Peace Prize. Meeting him was one of the highlights of my life. We talked about kids and sports: he told me he'd followed my career in the early nineties and had loved watching me play. *Me? Nelson Mandela knew who I was?* I couldn't believe it.

I left his office feeling hopeful. He has a magical way of doing that to people. Throughout my trip, I'd been carrying around a piece of paper with one of his quotes written on it: "There is no passion to be found playing small—in settling for a life that is less than the one you are capable of living." He lived that philosophy every single day. I wanted to live it, too.

The Laureus trip was a life-changing experience, and I promised myself that I was going to carry that inspiration home with me and put it to good use. But I wasn't ready to head back to Florida yet. I had some more living to do. My mom and I headed to Kruger National Park so I could fulfill one of my life's dreams: to go on a safari. We stayed in a treetop lodge and had a brilliant guide who met us at 5 a.m. every morning. After hours and hours of hiking, we came across a lioness and her cub, a leopard, a herd of buffalo, a giraffe, and a family of rhinos. I had to pinch myself. When you are trying to find animals in their own habitat, you have to be patient and quiet. You have to be in the moment. For me, being in the presence of animals is calming and humbling. I truly believe that there is a primal connection between the human soul and the animal soul that gets lost in our busy day-to-day life. But when you get a glimpse of it, you are almost knocked over by its power.

One afternoon I was taking a nap up in our tree house. Our hike had been particularly grueling and I was exhausted. After about an hour, I felt something tugging on my leg.

"Mom, just give me fifteen more minutes," I said from underneath my pillow. The tapping on my leg continued. "Come on, just fifteen minutes, please!" I begged. The tapping got harder. "Fine, I'll get up." I threw the pillow off my face, sat up in bed, and found myself face-to-face with a baboon. I don't know which of us was more shocked. My eyes grew wider and so did his. I started screaming, then he started screaming. I jumped out of my bed, then he jumped out of my bed, ran to the open window, turned around, and gave me one more confused look before scampering off into the trees. It took an hour for my heart rate to return to normal.

When I told my mom what had happened, she couldn't stop laughing. "Well, you said you wanted an up-close experience with the animals!" I got more than I bargained for, that's for sure. On that trip I decided that no matter what had happened to me in the past and no matter what fears were trying to hold me back, I was not going to lead a small life.

I'd heard about a shark-diving trip near Cape Town so, after our safari week came to a close, it was our next stop. My mom thought I was even crazier than when I jumped out of the plane. Voluntarily coming face-to-face with a great white shark was not her idea of fun. It wasn't mine, either, but I had to do it. On the day of the dive, I put on a wetsuit and oxygen tank, took a few deep breaths, and got into the protective steel cage. It was slowly lowered down into the water. My heart was pounding as they dropped the bloody bait into the water above my head. The ninety seconds I'd been in the cage felt like an hour, when suddenly I saw a flash of white out of the corner of my eye. I whipped my head around and saw an enormous shark heading right toward me. *Go for the fish, the fish!* I kept thinking. When it was about two feet away, it jerked its entire body up with one big thrust and the impact pushed me to the back of my cage.

No sooner had I regained my balance than another shark came charging in my direction. It stopped a few feet in front of me and began to glide back and forth. It angled its head toward me and I got a full frontal of its jagged teeth. If I reached my hand out, I could have touched it—and lost my arm in the process. If the cage door opened, I was dead. All I could hear was the sound of my respirator, and all I could see was this terrifying and beautiful animal that could end my life in two seconds if it wanted to. *This is life*, I thought. *Right now, and now, and now . . . I am living right this very second.* The entire dive wasn't longer than thirty minutes, but when I resurfaced I felt like I'd taken an extended trip to another universe. For the rest of the day I felt as if a gentle buzz of energy surrounded me. I wasn't just living life—I was feeling it. The sun seemed brighter, the ocean smelled stronger, and every noise was amplified. It was like life as I knew it had been a two and it was now cranked up to an eight. Everything seemed more real and I wanted to experience all of it. The life I was creating for myself was turning out to be anything but small.

# Life 101

Go to a late-night movie.
Learn to make risotto.
Have a glass of wine without guilt.
Master my digital camera.

My planner was filled with a checklist of "normal" things I wanted to do, and I was marking them off one by one. I was embracing my new life at home and filling my days with things other than tennis. There was one thing that I never thought would go on a checklist, but in 2007 I added it:

*Go to the gym.*

My weight was holding steady in the mid-140s but I hadn't lost sight of my target weight of 136, the weight that had remained elusive for four-teen years. I'd made tremendous progress—I'd lost thirty pounds already—but I knew I could reclaim my old body if I set my mind to it. And without going crazy. I just wanted to feel like I was in the body I was meant to be in. Of course, I could easily have lived with those extra ten pounds, but I didn't want to. They were more than just a little extra weight: they were a symbol of all the bad things I'd been through since I was nineteen years old. Those pounds reminded me of my old self-sabotaging state of mind.

Now I had a new mind-set and I wanted my body to reflect it. Thirty pounds had been lost by dealing with the built-up emotional wreckage in my head and by incorporating the "Less is more" theory into my life, but I needed one last kick to get to my target weight. I had to step it up if I wanted to reach my goal.

I called Gyll, a trainer at my local gym who had worked with me several years earlier. She was in incredible shape and ran a notoriously difficult boot-camp class. I'd never taken it—it always looked too intimidating— but I thought it would help shake up my new life. I told her I wanted to try her class.

"Have you been working out lately?" she asked.

"I've been walking a lot, but I don't remember the last time I lifted an ounce."

"Monica, don't worry. Just increase your walking, start lifting a little to build up your confidence, and observe the class a couple more times so you get comfortable with what we are doing. The last thing I want is for you to join us, get discouraged, and never come back again."

The irony of being a professional athlete but not being able to jump right into the class was funny. But I did just what she told me: I walked every morning and every evening, went to the gym for two weeks to do lightweight circuits, and watched her class. Her students were on a mission: for an hour and fifteen minutes they pushed themselves and pushed each other. I'd never done a group class before—during my playing days it was the last thing I had the energy or desire to do—but there was a strong vibe coming out of that room that, even as an outsider, I could feel. Still, I hesitated.

I didn't know if I was ready to go back to gym life, no matter how different it seemed from my old tennis workouts. I'd spent four years off the tour and away from trainers, coaches, and nutritionists. The quiet was something I'd desperately needed in my life. It gave me the space I craved to finally hear myself and to discern what my own needs were. Being on my own had calmed me down, and my trip to South Africa had challenged me to jump into the life I was capable of living. For the past year

I'd been keeping my weight steady and spending my time presenting fitness and confidence-building programs for kids in local schools and fostering abused and neglected dogs. Even without tennis as a full-time job, I was still managing to fill up my life. The more full my life felt, the less need I had to turn to food for temporary comfort. My inside was healing and my outside was following close behind.

But I still had a fear. I was anxious that returning to the gym would catapult me back into my old mind-set: *I'm not good enough, I'm too fat, I hate this, I am miserable on this treadmill, I have to lose more weight, I have to push myself more, etc*. I thought about it for another week and I came to a conclusion: *I had the control*. There were things—*a lot* of things—that I didn't have control over. Being stabbed, my dad's cancer, an unjust court ruling, losing my number one ranking, losing endorsements, losing two and a half years of my career, losing the peak of my playing days, my dad dying, the critical and hurtful comments people made—these were all things that I couldn't control. They were out of my hands, but for years I'd wanted to believe I could control them. If I just tried hard enough, I thought I could bend them to my will. Unfortunately, that set me up for an avalanche of negativity, because the moment another bad thing happened, I'd be even more angry, frustrated, and upset because I had failed to control it. What I should have been doing was just letting it go. And the one thing I did have control over—the way I treated my body and myself—was the one thing that got more out of control than everything else. I'd had it backwards the entire time.

Once I let go of the things I couldn't control, an enormous amount of space opened up in my mind and the things I could control suddenly became clear. How I chose to move my body, what I chose to put into my mouth, how I chose to view myself, and what I chose to do with the rest of my life were the things I *did* have control over. Going back to a gym wasn't going to take that power away from me: It was part of me now. It was in my core. It was time to lose those last pounds. I wasn't going to the gym because I had to: I was going to the gym because I *wanted* to.

Sometimes it took more than a little self-motivation to get me there, but working out in a group made me accountable. If I missed a day, at least three people would ask me where I was. When I was playing tennis, I had to show up for workouts because it was my job. When I showed up for Gyll's class, it was my choice. I started going to her class twice a week. On the other days I went for walks. It was the perfect balance. I was careful not to get caught up in unrealistic expectations. Gyll has the body of a fitness model: toned, lean, and strong. The kind of body that looks great running along the beach in a bikini. During our first workout I could feel myself starting to engage in the damaging comparison game. I put an end to it immediately and I got real with myself. Gyll's body looks like that because she has tremendous discipline and she works extremely hard. My body was not meant to be a size two. It just wasn't. If I wanted to be a size two—and there were more than a few in the class—I'd have to go to the gym six times a week and supplement that with hours and hours of extra cardio. I'd also have to go back to the days of calorie counting, food-journal keeping, and cheese shunning. Even then, being that tiny was unlikely and I knew I'd be miserable. Extreme approaches like that didn't work for me; in fact, they had the opposite effect. I had to find what I was comfortable with and compare myself to my own expectations, not to anyone else's.

I focused on my own journey. At the start I couldn't do fifty sit-ups in a row, let alone the three hundred everyone else was churning out. But I didn't let it bother me. *Focus on your own mission*, I told myself. *Stop focusing on the big numbers. All or nothing never works.* Baby steps taken consistently achieve great feats. After six weeks I could keep up with the whole class like a veteran. By the time I reached the four-year mark of my early exit from the French Open, I was at my goal weight of 136 pounds. And I hadn't dieted once.

# – 48 –

## *Home*

When 2008 began, I knew it was time to say good-bye to tennis. Do I wish I'd learned how to treat myself with compassion and forgiveness earlier? Yes. Would that have given me a better shot at regaining my old game? Probably. Do I regret not winning a tenth Grand Slam? Sometimes. But when it comes down to it, one more Grand Slam doesn't really mean anything. It's just another line in my obituary. It doesn't define me as the person I am today. And if I had to make the choice between winning another Grand Slam or attaining this peace I have with my body now, I'd pick the latter without a flicker of hesitation. It has been a long, painful, and challenging journey, but I love where I am today. I wouldn't give any of it back. It's made me who I am.

Shortly after I got back to Florida after *Dancing with the Stars*, I got the most unexpected call of my life. There was an inquiry from *Playboy:* they wanted to know if I would be interested in doing a shoot for them. *Playboy?* As in the ultimate men's magazine with the most stunning women in the world? They wanted to see me naked? Me? It had to be a joke. No, it wasn't a joke, I was assured. I got a satisfied giggle out of the offer but declined it. I didn't need to prove how good I looked and felt to anyone.

Proving it to myself was more than enough. But it was nice to be asked just the same.

I'd been away from home for over a month and spent the first few days catching up with texts, e-mails, and voice messages. Despite my early ejection, my friends had been overwhelmingly supportive and encouraging of my attempt to find the dancer in me. (I still didn't know where she was, but I hadn't given up all hope: I was still determined to nail the mambo one day.) I called a few of my girlfriends up and told them to meet me for dinner at my favorite local Italian spot. I hadn't had a good plate of pasta in a long time. I opened up my closet, which was still a disaster from my trip to L.A., and searched for something clean to wear. My laundry was about two months behind. I was rifling through a pile of T-shirts when I saw it peeking out from behind a blazer: the little black dress I'd bought at Century 21 four years earlier. The tags were still hanging off of it. I hadn't ever tried it on. I slipped it off the hanger and stepped into it. *If it doesn't fit,* I promised myself, *I won't stress out about it. After all, I did indulge in a few too many Hungarian pastries in L.A.* It slid right past my hips and I zipped up the side without a moment's hesitation. It fit like it was made for me. I twirled in front of the mirror a few times and couldn't wipe the smile off my face.

It felt good to be home.

# Index